is th...
South Ba...
International...
comedy industry aw...ds,
and 2015. She was also no...
Award (2014) and a British Comed...
Television Comic (2014). Her 2013 sh...
became the top-selling comedy show at the Soho...
She was named *Red* magazine's creative woman of the...
2015, and a 2015 *Marie Claire* woman at the Top.

Bridget can also load and fire a 17th century musket (though
not while under pressure or any time constraints), scuba dive
and drive a tractor. She lives in north London with her family
and cat.

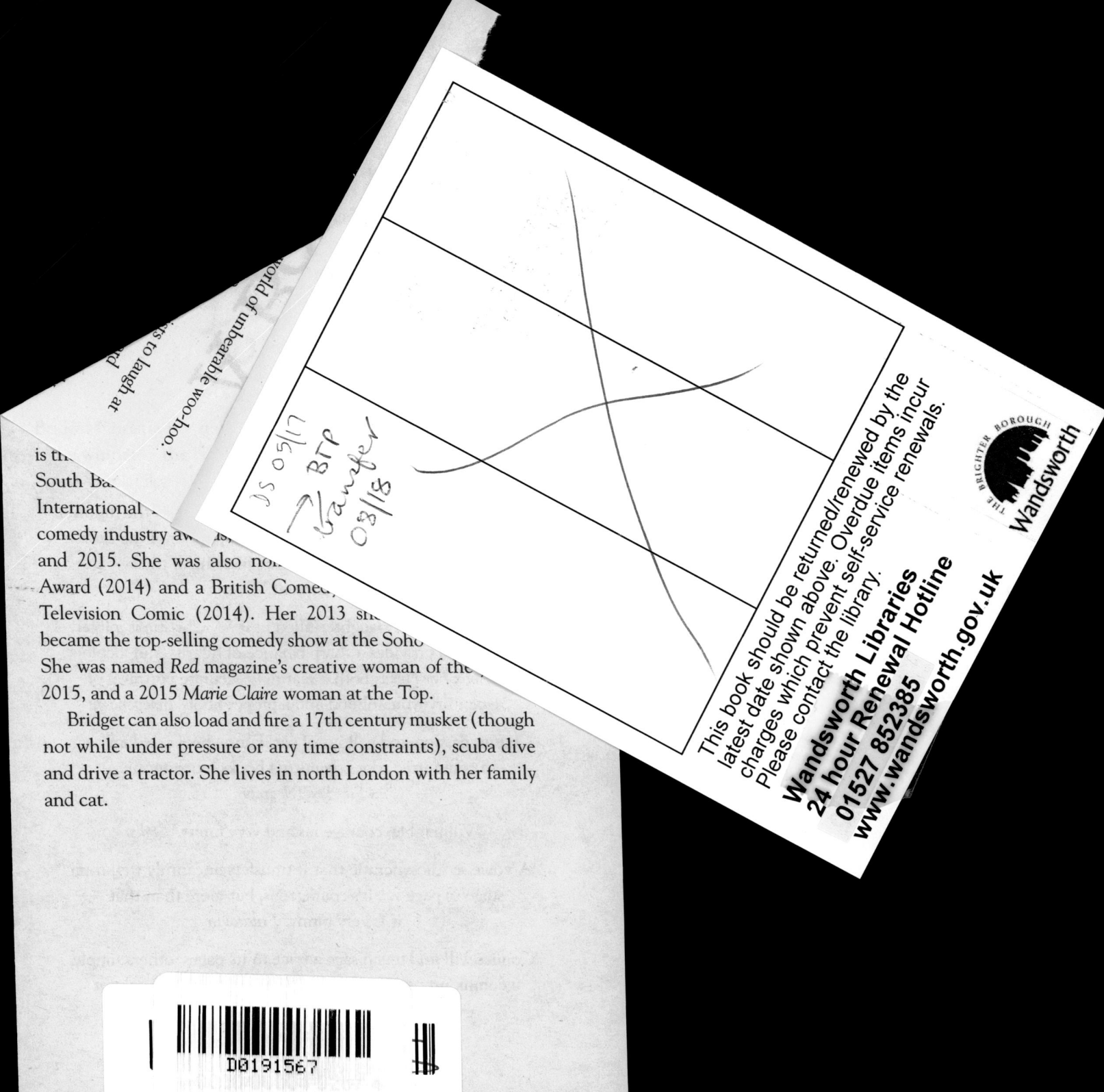

Bridget Christie

A Book
For Her

arrow books

1 3 5 7 9 10 8 6 4 2

Arrow Books
20 Vauxhall Bridge Road
London SW1V 2SA

Arrow Books is part of the Penguin Random House group of companies
whose addresses can be found at global.penguinrandomhouse.com.

Penguin
Random House
UK

Copyright © Bridget Christie 2015

Bridget Christie has asserted her right to be identified as the author of this
Work in accordance with the Copyright, Designs and Patents Act 1988.

First published in Great Britain by Century in 2015

www.randomhouse.co.uk

A CIP catalogue record for this book
is available from the British Library.

ISBN 9780099590842

Printed and bound in Great Britain by Clays Ltd, St Ives Plc

'We always need more feminist memoirs, when they're funny and insightful and clever and honest. Bridget Christie's A Book for Her is all of those things.' *Stylist*

'[Christie] made me laugh loudly on the tube like a loud, shameless, lipstick-covered walrus . . . funny and passionate and inspiring, all at the same time.' *Huffington Post*

'[Christie's] humility sucks you in and makes you laugh . . . funny in all the right places.' *Irish Times*

'It reads very much like a stand-up routine, from the running gags and callbacks. Whatever the seriousness of the subject she's discussing, however passionately she's laying into her pet notes, Christie never forgets also to make herself an object of mirth, and she does so with charm and brio to spare.' *Telegraph Best Books of the Year*

'Part memoir, part rant, Christie brilliantly and hilariously points out the utter absurdity and nonsensical cruelty of sexism, it left me smiling but furious.' *WH Smith blog*

For all the women in my family and ALL WOMEN.
Whether they want it or not.

INTRODUCTION

'It was the best of farts, it was the worst of farts.'

I didn't want to talk about farts in this book. If anything, I tried to avoid them altogether.

I said to myself, 'Bridget Christie, try to stay away from farts for your debut book. You've been doing really well since the summer of 2013. You've inadvertently become a critically acclaimed and financially viable stand-up act by talking about feminism after eleven years doing stand-up about nothing at a personal monetary loss to massive public and critical indifference. Don't throw it all away by talking about something as alienating and divisive as farts.'

But my editor at Random House (who also publish the long-standing best-seller *Mein Kampf* by A. Hitler[1]), insisted upon farts. She (my editor) does have a point. This book wouldn't even exist if it weren't for a particular fart that came

---

[1] My publisher asked me to point out that their edition of *Mein Kampf* is a critical annotated academic publication. All proceeds are donated in confidence to charities and academic institutions. None of the proceeds go towards funding Mel Brooks musicals.

out of an unhelpful man's ass at 17.20 Greenwich Mean Time on 30 April 2012.

The unhelpful man wasn't Hitler, by the way. He was long gone by then. He's got nothing to do with it. Forget about Hitler now. The only link between A. Hitler and myself is that we have the same publisher. That's it. So don't go looking up my genealogy or clips of my early stand-up, because you won't find anything incriminating there.

God, I wish I hadn't brought up Hitler now, but someone from Random House's art department mentioned in passing that they also published *Mein Kampf* by A. Hitler at the photo shoot for the book, which was the first I knew about it, so I thought I'd better mention it straight away or people would think I'd wilfully chosen to ignore it, and I didn't want a genocidal maniac to be the elephant in the book.

Just to be clear, the man from the art department wasn't boasting about publishing Hitler's tome. He didn't say, 'We've got a brilliantly eclectic list here at Random House, Bridget, so you're in good company. We've got Harper Lee, Katie Price, Hitler, you. So I thought, for the front cover, we could have you sitting on planet Venus, looking over at planet Mars with a sort of confused look on your face, like on all those other books by women now. We just need to let the readers know that this book is a funny, light-hearted look at feminism, and how you approach feminism and violations of human rights in your stand-up, Bridget. We need to reassure them it's not going to be full of photographs of men being horrifically tortured and suffocated with their own cocks while loads of feminists stand around laughing, drinking yards of ale, welding metals and thermoplastics and playing darts with the donated embalmed penes of dead male feminists. Many of our readers won't want to read a book like that. We are a commercial publishing house.'

The Hitler thing was just presented as fact. Then he took some grapes from a bowl and ate them. So I conceded that yes, okay, the fart should be included somewhere in the book because it was such a pivotal one, but suggested it might be introduced somewhere after page 11, once I'd established myself properly as not being like Hitler, and gained the trust of the reader; once I'd proved to them that I could write about things other than farts. It's the same with stand-up, I told my female editor. First gain the audience's trust, then you can do whatever you like.

'Even fart?' she said.

'Yes. Even fart,' I said.

'I see,' she said.

'The reader,' I explained to my editor (who is a woman), 'doesn't know who I am yet. I haven't introduced myself properly. They don't know anything about me. I don't want them thinking, Who the hell is this fart-obsessed idiot? Oh no, this book isn't going to be all about farts, is it? I hate farts at the best of times. I hope it's not going to be like a book version of the musical *Cats*,[2] without the cats and music but with farts and pages instead.

'I don't want them thinking I'm a one-fart pony. Or a one-trick fart. Or one pony's fart trick,' I said. 'Also, what if the Head of Women, Jimmy Somerville from Bronski Beat, hears

---

[2] I hated *Cats* the musical. First of all a cat came out and sang a song, and then another cat came out and did a dance, and then two more cats came out and sang a duet. After about half an hour I thought, Oh no, it's not all about cats, is it? I suspected that one of them might even be a human in a cat costume, Bonnie Langford I think its name was, but it was only when it sang, and sprayed all over the first five rows, that I was completely convinced of it. It was, indeed, a real cat.

on the feminist-practice-and-post-structuralist-theory-lecture grapevine that this book is supposed to be about feminism and becomes so infuriated and confused by all this early fart discourse that he only reads the Introduction and then writes a horrible review of it for the *Spectator* with the headline "BRIDGET CHRISTIE IS NOT A FEMINIST. SHE'S A FLATULIST IN FEMINIST CLOTHING"?

'What if his horrible review is always the first thing that comes up if you search for my name? It happens all the time. Then your family thinks you're deluded and lying about your career, because they only see the terrible things people say about you. My auntie is a nun in California. My brother, who lives in the States, has told her I'm doing really well. What if she looks me up on the convent computer with some other nuns and they all see the Head of Women Jimmy Somerville from Bronski Beat's horrible review? I'll just have to hope and pray that my auntie's convent doesn't have internet access. I'm Irish. My Catholic priest follows my career as well. What if he sees the horrible review and thinks I just write about farts? That is a conversation I do not want to have. I've already got to try to find a way of broaching the thorny issue of abortion with him. Farts might just be a step too far. I'll be *persona non grata* on the feminist panel/talk/debate circuit *and* at the altar. This book is turning into a bit of a nightmare for me,' I told my editor.

'Don't worry about the Head of Women, Jimmy Somerville from Bronski Beat,' my editor said. 'You have to make it clear, right from the beginning of the book, that you're not going to be answering any questions in this book. Or even asking any. This book is going to be in the Humour section in book-shops, not in the Critical Thinking section. No one's going to be thinking as they read this book, let alone critically, and if they are, you've written it wrong. No one's expecting you to be the next de Beauvoir or Friedan or Hildegard of Bingen. It just needs to not be shit, and to not have loads of photos of you in school plays in it.' This made me feel slightly better but I was still worried.

I'd been burned by farts before. This was a review for my 2012 Edinburgh Fringe show, *War Donkey*:

> If you think a tape of fart sound effects is
> the last word in quality stand-up, then you
> may enjoy this show. For everyone else, it's
> probably best avoided. And the farts are
> the best jokes…in a world where female
> comics are treated seriously, they will still
> sometimes get a bad review; but it won't be
> because of their gender. I really wanted to
> like this show, but don't let Christie take
> your money and give you nothing but farts
> in return.
>
> *The List*

So yes, I have to talk about farts, I'm afraid, because in April 2012, one of them changed the course of my life for ever. Not a private fart. This was a very public fart. It is the reason I have been commissioned to write this book. My views on everything from yoghurts and cave paintings to the economy and terrorism to Jeremy Clarkson and patterns on toilet paper can be traced back to this one apocalyptic expulsion of intestinal gas. This effluvium is at the heart of everything I now think, do and say. I will bring my children up with the values and ideologies I hold as a result of this sphincter disturbance. This anal reflex was my gateway into the very bowels of feminism itself. I was catapulted from a position of utter uneducated ignorance of even the tiniest aspect of feminism right into the epicentre of modern British feminist discourse by this single smelly smell.

I would not have received a Chortle Award from Christopher Biggins without this fart. Ed Miliband would not have watched my 2013 show, A Bic for Her, at the Stand Comedy Club in Edinburgh standing up by a pillar because there weren't any available seats for him to sit down on, without this fart. Dr Helen Pankhurst, activist and great-granddaughter of pioneering suffragette Emmeline Pankhurst, would not have invited me to speak on a panel with her and Radio 4's Woman's Hour's Jane Garvey, music's Annie Lennox, Radio 1 DJ and feminist Gemma Cairney, founder of worldwide phenomenon the Everyday Sexism Project Laura Bates and Sri Lankan equal rights campaigner Jayanthi Kuru-Utumpala on International Women's Day 2015 without this fart. I would not have been invited to perform in New York, LA, Melbourne, Montreal or Russia, or at Hugh Grant's birthday party, without this fart. Naomi Wolf, former political consultant, best-selling author of The Beauty Myth, democracy activist and leading spokeswoman for third wave feminism, would not have mistaken me for Sandi Toksvig's wife without this singular and significant fart.

In fact, let me just tell you about that before I really get into the fart bit. At the start of the Women of the World Festival in March 2013 I was asked to take part in a photo shoot to launch the weekend, along with (amongst others) the Pulitzer Prize-winning novelist and activist Alice Walker, Wolf (who I've just mentioned above, remember?), writer, presenter, comedian, actress and producer Sandi Toksvig, the human rights campaigner Shami Chakrabarti, writer, comedian, actress, interviewer, producer and campaigner Ruby Wax and the psychotherapist, psychoanalyst, writer and social critic Susie Orbach. I was out of my depth. Before we went up on to the roof, for the photos, where we were all asked to hold red umbrellas up above our heads, some of us had met up inside while we waited for everyone to arrive. I was sitting on a sofa with Naomi Wolf, Sandi Toksvig and Sandi's wife, Debbie. Wolf, who was there to promote women (like us all) and her latest book, *Vagina*, asked me why I was there. Not in an accusatory way – she didn't emphasise the 'you' in the question, as in 'What the fuck are *you* doing here?' Rather, she just wanted to know what everyone did.

I managed to splutter out something vaguely coherent about not knowing why I was there, that I thought there had clearly been a terrible mistake, and that I didn't want to be in the photos anyway as I would look like the Where's Wally of Feminism; then I told her I wrote jokes about feminism. Then she very kindly added that I wouldn't have been asked by Jude Kelly – artistic director of the South Bank Centre and founder of the WOW Festival – if I didn't have something to bring to the table, so they must be good jokes. Little did she know that what I was bringing to the Women of the World Festival 2013 was a man's fart. And my own shame.

Shami Chakrabarti, CBE, director of Liberty, the British civil liberties advocacy organisation, overheard me telling Naomi Wolf I was a stand-up and said she thought I seemed funny and that she might come to a gig, but she had a very neutral expression on her face when she said it so I don't know if she was being sarcastic or not. Anyway, Naomi Wolf then mistook me for Sandi Toksvig's wife, probably because I was sat next to Sandi's wife, Debbie, at the time. I don't know how it happened, to be honest, but it was an easy mistake to make. Debbie – Sandi's actual wife – and Sandi – Sandi's actual self – and I didn't feel like we needed to immediately correct Naomi Wolf because it didn't really matter if she thought I was Sandi's wife, did it? Also, I was flattered and delighted that Wolf considered me smart enough to be Sandi Toksvig's wife so I thought I'd enjoy pretending to be clever for as long as I could. In the end we had to come clean and tell Naomi Wolf that not only was I not gay, but I wasn't even a feminist either. I was an imposter. I was Bridget Christie: the Borat of the Women of the World Festival.

* * *

Before I tell you about my smelly Damascene moment, first I'd like to explore quickly the complexities and nuances of farts and farting. It's important that you know this in order for you to understand how a fart came to be the key protagonist in my story. Farts can tell us as much about a person, if not more, as their voting or online purchasing habits.

By the way, if you think you've read enough about farts for one book, I haven't even scratched the surface of them yet. Need I remind you that I have to live every single day of my life in the shadow of this man's fart and there's no escape for me. Every time my cat makes a smell, I am transported back to 30 April 2012, back to the Women's Studies section, back to the unhelpful man's ass, back to sexism and the oppression of women, and I have to live through it all over again. The very least you can do is read a few pages about it. So. A 'public' fart, one that is emitted out and about amongst strangers, is a statement. The public farter (PF) has consciously made a decision to ignore the comfort and well-being of those in close proximity and is therefore establishing themselves as superior. They are saying that their comfort is more important than yours.

The PF's default position is to claim freedom of expression, to proclaim that his (*or her*) rights to make a smell are being eroded by the United Nations' overly zealous radical left-wing agenda: 'It's just methane-based banter!' 'You wouldn't accuse a Muslim of farting!' For them, forcing strangers to smell your farts is just the same as Jeremy Clarkson tweeting a picture of himself asleep, next to a sign saying 'Gay Cunt', with his *Top Gear* co-presenter James May laughing in the background. For them, farts, full English breakfasts and 'Gay Cunt' signs put the 'Great' into 'Great Britain'.

The PF is beyond complying with the generally accepted social norm that farting in public is antisocial and splits communities. The PF is saying, 'I am better than you and have higher status. I do not recognise your PC lefty liberal laws. Sniff this, losers. It came out of my ass and made a funny noise. Legislate your way out of that.'

Only the disenfranchised are exempt. They have sphincter carte blanche. You can hardly complain when a homeless person farts. They *are* home. We have not provided for them. Why should they comply with our fart bureaucracy? Society has failed them. Why should they abide by society's rules? It would be interesting to find out if Scandinavia, with its hugely superior and efficient state systems, has a problem with incongruous smells.

To many people the fart experience would have been just an unpleasant moment, but it ended up being my political awakening. A chemical composition of nitrogen, hydrogen, carbon dioxide, oxygen and methane introduced me to Simone de Beauvoir. To me, this total disregard for the well-being of others was just one more damning indictment of current Prime Minister David Cameron's failed Big Society. This man's fart, emitted in a public space, displayed a total lack of empathy for any feminists that might be lurking there. Or for anyone else that might be lurking there, just to get out of the rain; like a homeless war veteran for example, forced out of a south London doorway by the installation of 'anti-homeless studs' by a property developer to deter him from sleeping there. Or a pigeon. Or maybe a teenager who has nowhere else to their homework because their home is too cramped and noisy, and whose local library has been closed down and turned into a pawnbroker's. Or a dying bee.

A fart is not only a political statement; it is also a weapon. I have often commandeered farts for private use during arguments. As a retort, the fart can be more powerful than any single word in the English language. As a slight, it is more effective than a raised eyebrow, a tut or a yawn. It can have multiple interpretations, depending on the timing and circumstances in which it is expelled. A fart can be joyous, illuminating, insulting, confusing, helpful, unhelpful, disarming, liberating, puerile or the height of sophistication. If deployed with integrity and impeccable timing, a fart can be up there with the best of Wilde, Johnson, Swift, Beckett, Chaucer, Shakespeare or McGuinness (Paddy, not Martin)[3].

---

[3] Between October 1988 and September 1994, when voices and farts of representatives from Sinn Féin and several Irish republican and Loyalist parliamentary groups were banned by the British government from being broadcast on television and radio, in the United Kingdom, Martin McGuinness' farts were dubbed with those of an actor; they weren't his own actual farts.

All of the above only applies to men's farts, of course. If you're a woman, no context will ever exist that is suitable for you to fart into. Unless you live in Sweden, which has one of the best equal rights records in the world. I'm sure Sweden women release gas from their *analöppning* whenever they like, and good luck to them!

So I hope that's cleared up farts for you. Perhaps now you will understand how, on 30 April 2012, one came to change my life. The epiphanic public fart that altered me for ever was not only unbelievably smelly, but was also clearly a potent critique on feminist literature and the state of modern feminism today: a powerful metaphor for how an entire ideology is viewed.

I'd gone into a bookshop to buy three feminist books: the Bible, the Quran and the Torah. But they were all sold out, so instead I thought I'd get Mary Wollstonecraft's *A Vindication of the Rights of Woman*, Virginia Woolf's *A Room of One's Own*, and *She-Wolves* by the historian Dr Helen Castor,[4] whose brilliant TV series about England's early queens (who used to dress up as wolves so that they'd be taken more seriously) I'd just watched and loved.

Now before I go any further, I need to put this fart into context, as all good farts should be: 30 April 2012 hadn't been a good day. In the morning I'd received an email from a producer at Amnesty International telling me that the

---

[4] *She-Wolves* isn't an explicitly feminist book, but it is about four excellent women who ruled medieval England before Elizabeth who no one really knows about. I can't even recall any of their names now, to be honest. I remember watching it, thinking, I must remember all these brilliant women's names, so that I can list them during arguments with people who say Margaret bloody Thatcher is the only powerful woman Britain's ever had. But then instantly forgot all of their names.

comedy film they'd commissioned me to write about infant mortality and maternal health in developing countries wasn't going to be made after all. Their reasons were completely reasonable and justified. It was just a bit disappointing. I was inspired to research the subject by my daughter's NHS health visitor, a brilliant woman from Sierra Leone called Lucy Sandi, who I dubbed 'the Baby Whisperer'. Lucy could make a baby daughter instantly stop crying by talking quietly to her about how vulnerable she was, and telling her that it was in her best interests to keep on the right side of me because I was breastfeeding and the one that changed her nappy, and that a good way of doing this was not to cry all the time.[5]

Anyway, Lucy would meet me for a coffee and tell me all about the conditions women in Sierra Leone give birth under, especially women from rural communities. Sierra Leone has one of the highest infant mortality rates in the world. It's one of the worst places in the world to give birth in. According to the World Health Organization, as of March 2015 every day 1,500 women die due to complications in pregnancy or childbirth.

I live in Stoke Newington in north London. Stoke Newington parents take their children very seriously (Stoke Newington parents apply for nursery places so far in advance that the deposit paid for a child to attend a Stoke Newington nursery in 2015 was paid for in pre-decimal coins), but taking our children seriously is the last thing we should be doing, isn't it? They're children. Being taken seriously is the last thing they need. Children should be taken with a pinch of salt.

If you wander around Stoke Newington on a weekend

---

[5] Not really. I don't know how she makes them stop crying. She just does.

you'd be forgiven for thinking that there weren't any other children left in the world, and that these Stoke Newington children were the last children on earth. The atmosphere of the playground in Clissold Park is like a smug version of P. D. James's novel *The Children of Men*, in which two decades of human infertility have left society on the brink of collapse, except for in Stoke Newington, where humans have managed to survive by being cocooned inside limited-edition Bugaboo prams.

Here's the pitch and script I sent to Amnesty TV in 2011:

AMNESTY TV – MATERNAL HEALTH IN DEVELOPING COUNTRIES

A NORTH LONDON ANTENATAL CLASS

There are various expectant mums in attendance, all of whom are accompanied by at least one birthing partner. Some are husbands/boyfriends, friends, grandparents, some are hired doulas. They should all look middle class and comfortable. They are sat on yoga mats and passing around baby stuff (brochures/catalogues/nappies/babygros with stupid witty slogans on them/slings/pram accessories etc.) that they are discussing. There is even a birthing chair set up in the room that one of them is trying out. One of the women is demonstrating how to use a sling using a baby (that keeps being dropped on the floor).

The midwife is sitting on a table, where someone has laid out leaflets/baby booklets ('Emma's diary' type things)/printed information sheets. No overacting or winks to the camera.

Think *Police Squad* with Leslie Nielsen, but in an antenatal class.

MIDWIFE

Morning, ladies, I'm Lucy. Jackie, who normally takes the class, is away so I'll be taking her place for you today. I hope I don't scare you off! It's a bit late to back out now anyway!
(laughs)

MUM 1

Scare us? I don't think so.
We're all *One Born Every Minute* and *Call the Midwife* addicts. There's not much you can tell us that we don't know already.

MIDWIFE

I must just say how nice it is to see some dads here today. Because of course, you will be bringing up baby on your own when mum dies during childbirth. That is, of course, if the baby survives.

(the group all look horrified)

DAD 1

What?
(whispering to his partner, MUM 6)
I thought you said it was all breathing techniques and birthing pools at these things?

MIDWIFE

It's impossible to say at the moment which
ones of you will survive, but realistically I'd
say that two or three of you might make it. If
you're lucky.

MUM 2

Will yoga help? It's just that I've spent
a fortune on getting the right breathing
technique.

MIDWIFE

Not if you're lying on a dirt track needing an
emergency caesarean it won't, my dear.
By the time you've walked to
the main road, which could
be miles away, waited for
someone to stop and give you
a lift to the hospital, you'll
be long dead, I'm afraid.
So you won't be breathing at
all. Let alone properly.

MUM 3

Only two or three of us?

MIDWIFE

Yes. The rest of you will just suffer serious illness
or permanent disability.

DAD 1

Is there anything we can do to prevent it?
Because I'd really like Jenny and the baby to
survive.

MIDWIFE

I'm afraid not. You will all die of completely
unnecessary complications. I'm sorry, but it's
just the way it is. If you were born somewhere
else maybe you could have the basic human
rights most of us take for granted, but you
weren't. So sorry, but your wife and baby will
probably die. You'll just have to suck it up.

MUM 1

But surely any complications will be spotted in
our check-ups? When we're examined?

MIDWIFE

No. There are no check-ups.
You can't afford the consultant's fees. And he
or she (probably a he) won't examine you until
you've paid. So you'll just do without check-
ups and hope for the best.

MUM 3

Why didn't my mum tell me it was going to be
like this?

MIDWIFE

Because she died giving birth to you.

MUM 1

What do you think is the best type of nappy to use? Because the *Guardian* says that terries are better than disposables because they produce less waste.

MUM 2

Well, it's not as simple as that actually. Terries don't produce as much waste, but they have a bigger carbon footprint because you use up so much water and electricity washing them all the time.

MIDWIFE

If your baby is born healthy and you survive, you will tear pieces of your own clothing off into squares, wrap that around your baby, and then put plastic bags over the top of that to prevent baby's mess from going everywhere.

MUM 2

Can't we just buy some? It's much easier.

MIDWIFE

No, you can't. Because disposable nappies cost three pounds each. And that is more than you or your husband earns in a month.

MUM 4

My husband will be taking two weeks' paternity leave when the baby arrives to help out. Will it be okay for him to do some of the night feeds?

MIDWIFE

If your husband misses two weeks' collecting plastic bottles from the tip to sell on, all the other dads will find them and you will be even poorer than you were before. So I would let him go to the tip if I were you, and do the night feeds yourself.

MUM 2

Do all midwives have a little case like in *Call the Midwife* with all their sterilised equipment in?

MIDWIFE

Not quite like that, no. They might have a razor blade to cut the cord, and some black thread and a needle to stitch you up if you tear. They only have one colour though, black.

MUM 3

If I'd known all this I'd have made him wear a condom!

(they all laugh, uncomfortably)

MIDWIFE

No, you wouldn't have. The Pope doesn't want you to. Although he has just changed his mind. But let's save that conversation for next week.

DAD 1

Thank you very much, Lucy. I didn't realise
there was quite so much to it. I look forward to
next week. Will you be here or is Jackie back
next week?

MIDWIFE

Jackie died.

DAD 2

Oh! She was due, wasn't she? Did the baby
make it?

MIDWIFE

No. Neither of them made it.
The consultant wouldn't help until he had her
credit card.
And she forgot her wallet, what with being in
labour and everything, so they both died.

DAD 2

(to MUM 1)
You do that all the time, don't you, darling?
Forget your wallet, especially when you want
some new shoes. I'd better make sure I have
mine with me, otherwise...
(makes a cut-throat gesture and stupid 'dead'
faces)

MUM 1

Shut up, Roger. You really are a prick sometimes.

MIDWIFE

Okay, see you next week. Hopefully.

I did a read-through of the script with some mates at the Camden Head in Camden in front of an audience and it went down pretty well, so that was a relief. Although this may have been down to the skill and talent of the performers[6], rather than the script itself. Sometimes you're not sure if you've horribly misjudged something, so it's always worth having a read-through of scripts in front of a live audience. Whether it's for radio, TV or for a live show, it's never a waste of time and it always tells you something. Most importantly, Lucy thought it was a great idea. She just wanted to raise awareness for what was happening in Sierra Leone. Anyway, it didn't happen. So that was the first thing.

Another thing that happened on 30 April was that I stumbled across a legitimate, published review of myself that included the sentence 'Anyone watching Christie would wonder who you had to fuck to get on in this business.' He didn't even asterisk the word 'fuck', which I thought was just really impolite.

Ironically, I was nowhere in my career at that point. I'd been doing stand-up for about eight years and I hadn't really made any progress. I still wasn't really being paid for gigs, my shows weren't generating any other work for me on TV or radio, and none of the scripts or ideas I'd submitted to radio or TV had gone anywhere. At this point, I didn't even have an agent. Also, the night the critic was in, he was one of about fourteen people in the audience. So I'm obviously not very

6 Danielle Ward, Dave Reed, John Luke Roberts, Nadia Kamil, Sara Pascoe.

good at the sex, am I, if, after all those years of having sex with people to get on in the business, I was still only playing to fourteen people?

The review made me feel depressed and angry. I thought about how upset my dad would be if he saw it. My dad's known me for literally all my life. He knows how passionate and serious I've always been about comedy, since I was four, when we used to watch *Laurel and Hardy* together and I said that I wanted to do that, and how I'd never risk sullying my love for comedy with something as precarious as sex. He saw the comedy sketches I wrote at school, he saw the local amateur dramatics productions I did, he was there when I got the letter from Gloucestershire County Council telling me I'd won the only grant in the County for Drama that year (who paid for most of the fees), and when I subsequently won a part-scholarship from the school to make up the shortfall. He knew I worked in offices from the ages of fifteen to thirty-six doing jobs I hated. He knew how many times I was rejected. He was there on the day of my graduation. And my dad watched me doing all this, without my having sex with any of the people involved. There were no orgies at the Gloucester Operatic and Dramatic Society, Gloucestershire County Council, or at the Academy of Live and Recorded Arts. None that I was invited to anyway. I couldn't stop staring at this sentence. 'Anyone watching Christie would wonder who you had to fuck to get on in this business.' I thought about all the awful gigs I'd had; all the feelings of shame and humiliation and self-loathing and failure I felt until I did my next gig and it went OK and everything reset to zero again; the years of circuit gigs; the seven Edinburgh shows I'd written and performed. I thought about all the sex I hadn't had during that time, and wasn't having. But worst of all, I felt disgusted with myself for being so angry about it. It was just a stupid twat's sexist comment, nothing I hadn't read about myself countless of times before. I checked my privilege and slapped myself across my First World-problemmed face. The information pack Amnesty gave me about maternal health and infant mortality rates was lying open next to my computer on my desk, burning my corneas like an electric arc, reminding me of all the women in Bo, who would probably give their right arm to read a stupid twat's sexist review of themselves, rather than being needlessly dead. I knew all this, I knew how weak and pathetic I was being, but I couldn't help it. He'd reduced a life's worth of dreams and ambitions and work to nothing, in one sentence. The implication being that everything I'd ever achieved, up until this point (which wasn't much, admittedly), had been down to sexual favours. I thought about how the achievements of women were continually demeaned or doubted or reclassified as achievements 'for women' rather than 'for humanity'; that I'd never seen a male comedian reviewed like this; I thought about the bigger picture – that his comments didn't exist in a vacuum, that thousands of women probably had to deal with comments like this, all the time, whether they were said in published reviews, or whispered in boardrooms, or shouted into female earlobes in cockpits or in science laboratories; I thought about the cumulative effect of reading or listening to comments like this about yourself year after year, and that many women probably decide that, on balance, it's not really worth it in the end, and they give up. Not all women have the same levels of tolerance and confidence, and I thought that if he'd said it about a newer, less experienced female comic, she might have thought twice about carrying on.

So that's why I was upset, not because it was a bad review. I'm used to those. I love them! In fact, bad reviews often really cheer me up, like the fart sound-effects review I already mentioned. But I was also baffled by the idea that you could get on in comedy by having sex with people. There isn't a casting couch in stand-up comedy. There isn't even a couch. That's why we're always standing up. Most of the time there isn't even a backstage toilet. We have to use the same toilets as our audiences, which can be really awkward if you've had a bad gig, or a bad stomach, or need to fuck someone in a cubicle to try and get on in this business.

How stand-up comedy works is this. You write some jokes and then get up on a stage in a room above a pub and tell them to strangers. If the audience thinks you're funny, they will laugh. If they don't think you're funny, they won't. Then you do hundreds and hundreds of gigs to improve your jokes and your delivery. If you're one of the lucky ones, you can earn a decent living from circuit gigs and might even be able to tour in your own right. You can't really 'get on in this business' by having sex with people. It just doesn't work like that.

Unless you're Dara Ó Briain. He's slept with everyone he works for and that's how he got all his work. He's slept with scientist Brian Cox and the comedian Robin Ince, to name but two. And those blokes in that boat – Griff Rhys Jones and Rory McGrath. And all the gag writers from *Mock the Week* in a simultaneous no-holes-barred orgy. God knows how many others there are. He had sex with Ed Byrne as well, so that Ed Byrne would do that travel programme with him, *Dara and Ed's Great Big Adventure*. And he had sex with that bloke who jumped off the rocks into the sea in it as well, just to keep his options open. He's even had sex with an actual television, just in case.

So that was another thing: a stupid twat's sexist review. It made me think about how female stand-ups are written about, and how, if this is how women are talked about or written about in comedy, it is probably how women in other professions are being talked about as well, except for perhaps in the world of the high-class escort, where it is a given that you can sleep your way to the top.

Then, at about 3 p.m. that day, I saw five minutes of *The Only Way is Essex* on TV. In those short few minutes, two young girls decided to have Botox injections before they went out to a quiz night. The conversation went like this:

'Are you going to the quiz night?'

'Yes. Let's go together. We can get our Botox done, then head down there after.'

I was a bit confused. Why would they have their faces filled with botulinum toxin for a quiz night? I could see their logic if they were playing poker. But a quiz night? You don't need a poker face for a quiz night, do you? You just write the answers down on a piece of paper. Have things changed this much in twenty years? When I was eighteen, I would get ready for a quiz night by swotting up on my general knowledge.

It was the casual way in which the girls talked about having intrusive surgery, and at such a young age. It made me feel so out of touch. I felt upset, alienated and depressed. I worried about my own tiny daughter. How will she be getting ready for a karaoke night in fifteen years' time? By having a labia minora reduction party? (Which is also on the increase, by the way, and not in some far-off place either. NHS figures for 2010 show a five-fold rise since 2001 and one London-based surgeon has seen an 80 per cent rise in labiaplasty procedures between 2013 and 2014.)

Just in case there's anyone reading this who doesn't know what labia minora reduction surgery is, it's the surgical trimming, by choice, by a cosmetic surgeon, who you've paid, of your ladies' bits so that they look like porn stars' bits, which don't look like normal women's bits. Porn is also why young teenage girls are shaving off all their pubic hair. Teenage boys see so much internet porn now, they're traumatised when they see a normal vagina with all the usual vagina stuff on it.

I find it very difficult to talk about this sort of thing, by the way. It's not something I ever thought I would talk about. Most parents say to their children, 'Don't look directly at the sun or you'll go blind.' Well, my Irish Catholic parents said that to us, but about our genitals. We weren't even allowed to look at them during a full solar eclipse when it went dark. I had to make a pinhole camera out of a massive cardboard box and put my back to the mirror and view mine as shadows through a colander. One year I was taken to Regent's Park in London to try and see it through enormous telescopes provided by the Royal Astronomical Society, which I found to be incredibly intimidating.

I don't even like modern vaginas, to be honest. Or modern houses. They are both bad examples of streamlined interior design. I go into other people's houses and the female changing areas at my local pool and I think, Where's all your stuff? Where are all your books and CDs and labia minora? You've decluttered your vaginas.

What's going to happen when this trimmed, clean-lined look isn't in any more, when they want all their original fixtures and natural character put back in? There aren't going to be reclamation yards full of discarded labia that you can pick up for a fiver and just get a man to weld back on.

When I explained all this surgical trimming and shaving business to my fictional husband, he said, 'Oh! So that's why all the vaginas you see nowadays aren't like the ones in the 1970s.'

I said, 'What do you mean, "nowadays"? What vaginas are you looking at "nowadays"?'

He said, 'You know, just the ones that are about.'

'"About"?' I said. '"Just the ones that are about"? Around where? You only go to the post office, the supermarket and pre-historic burial chambers. Where are all these random, modern vaginas that are about?'

Anyway, that was our son's birthday party ruined. And the people on the table next to us at the Pirates Playhouse asked to be moved. Still, that's pirates for you. Vagina-hating, parrot-wearing, rum-drinking, one-eyed, wooden-legged twats. As my seven-year-old said to them.

So what with terrible maternal health and infant mortality rates in Sierra Leone, a twat's sexist review, Botoxed Essex faces and modern vaginas, I had to get out of the house. I strapped my little girl into her pram and went to collect my son from school. Then I went to buy three books about women by women, which I thought might cheer me up. I don't really know why. Perhaps recent events had conspired together to send me out to seek answers, and the day's Amnesty script turn-down and Botox TV conversation had spurred me into some kind of action. But I couldn't find any of the books, so I went up to the counter and asked the man to check if they were in stock.

What followed was a drawn-out, surreal, hostile exchange with a man whose heart was clearly not in the job. It was the kind of exchange that is only made tolerable by the possibility of writing a routine about it at some point in the future. I honestly don't know how people who are not journalists or writers or comedians or artists or musicians cope without the possibility of this deferred creative revenge on the tedious admin of life.

I ended up having to spell out, many times, all the titles of the books, and all the authors' names, as the bored man typed them into his internal database system. He kept getting thrown out of the page he needed to be on and spelling the authors' names wrong, while my two children asked for every single item that was piled up high on shelves around the counter. In all this time, the man didn't make eye contact with me once, and the queue behind me got longer and longer.

The conversation, as I eventually recounted it in my 2012 show *War Donkey*, went like this:

ME: So, the first one is *A Vindication of the Rights of Woman*, please. By Mary Wollstonecraft.

MAN: What?

ME: *A VINDICATION OF THE RIGHTS OF WOMAN*.

MAN: How do you spell it?

ME: How do you spell what? A? Well, A. A for algorithm.

MAN: Nothing under A. I'll check under the author's name. Who wrote it?

ME: Wollstonecraft. Mary Wollstonecraft.

MAN: What? (*Sighs.*)

ME: Wollstonecraft. W.O.L.L.S.T.O.N.E.C.R.A.F.T. Wollstonecraft. (*Then quietly under my breath*) The inventor of modern feminism, that's all, Lord of the Sighs.

MAN: Nothing in the database for this Wollstonecraft.

ME: Oh, okay, I'll have a look online. Don't worry.

MAN: I'm not worried.

ME: Good.

MAN: What were the other books? (*Another death sigh.*)

ME: A *Room of One's Own* by Virginia Woolf.

MAN: How do you spell it?

ME: How do I spell what? A *Room of One's Own*? Or Woolf?

MAN: (*Silence.*)

ME: Well, A, as in A *Room of One's Own*. A.

MAN: Nothing under that. What's the author again?

ME: Woolf.

MAN: How do you spell it?

ME: How do you spell what? Woolf? Are you joking?

MAN: No.

ME: Woolf. W.O.O.L.F. Woolf. As in wolf, like a wolf, that howls at the moon (*then I howled like a wolf and the kids laughed*) but with two Os. Double O.

MAN: Nothing under Woolf in the database.

ME: You have nothing in your database for Virginia Woolf? Is this a bookshop or have I walked into a fishmonger's by mistake?

MAN: I hate fish.

ME: What?

MAN: The look of it, and the smell...awful.

ME: I don't care if you like fish or not. Are you sure you don't have anything under Woolf?

MAN: There's nothing in the database.

ME: Well, I don't believe that. Have you got *She-Wolves* by Dr Helen Castor?

MAN: What's it called?

ME: Oh, God. Kids, pack it in!!!! SHE. NEW WORD. WOLVES. SHE, AS IN FEMALE. S.H.E. WOMAN. HER. SO, SHE, YEAH? THEN WOLVES. LIKE WOLF, BUT PLURAL. THE PLURAL OF WOLF. I.E. MORE OF THEM. WOLVES. SHE – WOLVES. SHE. S.H.E. – NEW WORD – WOLVES. W.O.L.V.E.S.

MAN: Nothing under She.

But I knew that they did have *She-Wolves* because there was a huge display of them in the window.

ME: Right, well, thanks for all your help. I'll have a look myself and see what you do have. Where's the Women's Studies section, please?

MAN: The what?

ME: THE WOMEN'S STUDIES SECTION.

MAN: Upstairs. There is a lift for the pram.

ME: Thank you.

The lift was out of order so I carried the pram upstairs. There was no Women's Studies section upstairs. It was all Hitler and cookery up there. Luckily there was a fish tank upstairs in the Children's section so I pushed the pram in front of that and quietly and menacingly threatened the kids to be quiet, a bit like how I imagine a murderer might.

Anyway, the kids looked at some fish and I went off for a bit to find my three books. Then a female shop assistant told me the Women's section was downstairs. 'Downstairs?!' I said to her. 'That tall, moody bloke told me it was up here. He hadn't heard of Virginia Woolf. Does he hate women writers or something? He was very blunt.'

She said, 'He's just a bit of an illiterate. I know that doesn't sound like much of an insult, but in bookshop circles, that's pretty much the worst thing you can say about someone.'

Anyway. On my way downstairs I saw the guy standing in

the Women's Studies section and when he saw me he looked really sheepish, like a dog that's just lapped up a tray of congealed fat, boiled water and washing-up liquid. And enjoyed it. Then he looked at his watch and pretended to be late for something and sped off to Non-Fiction. When I got to the Women's Studies section it was heavily cloaked in the familiar yet objectionable odour of sulphur. Yes. What I mean is, it absolutely stunk of farts.

I was confused at first, but then the penny dropped. This man, who'd seemed so reluctant to sell me any feminist literature, and so keen to be rid of me, had obviously decided that the Women's Studies section was the least-populated area of the bookshop and that this was the safest place for him to expel his daily flatus.

And to be fair to him, this guy needed some personal space. For his effluvium won all the prizes. It was apocalyptic. I truly expected to leave the bookshop to find that civilisation had collapsed and crowds of zombies were roaming the streets. I could hardly breathe. The flatus had almost become matter. With the slightest change in local air pressure, this man's gas could've become a solid.

And as I stood there, in the Women's Studies section, choking, my nostrils and lungs filled with an obstructive sexist's gas, while I tried to locate Wollstonecraft's feminist manifesto, I had an epiphany.

This is where feminism is today (or was on 30 April 2012). This is what people think of the fight for equality. It's irrelevant, redundant and pointless. Something to be farted at. No one goes to the Women's Studies section any more, not now. There's no need for it! That's all done now, isn't it? Women can vote and vajazzle and vomit at weekends now, can't they?

They are free to do anything they like. I'll be safe here, the man thought, in the Women's Studies section, where I will do all my day's farts, without fear of any feminists turning up. Whatever they are.

And it was then, in that moment, that smelly moment, that everything fell into place. My life was given clarity that it hadn't had before. I felt as if I'd been given a feminist Ordnance Survey map with which I could now negotiate my way through life. I felt that all the things I'd ever been annoyed about, all the times I'd been made to feel stupid, or paranoid, or weak, or frightened, or a prude, or frigid; all the times I'd been called feisty or spunky or gobby or bossy or fierce or weird; all the times I'd thought something was my fault when it wasn't; all the stupid things everyone had ever said to me simply because I was a girl. I understood all the violence and all the oppression happening around the world to women and girls every minute of every day; all these things had been given a provenance. But most importantly, I thought that this man's fart was also funny, and it made me realise that terrible things can also be funny things. And that if I could make a terrible thing funny, I might be on to something.

This man's fart didn't just give me the light from which I would now see the world; it also handed me the keys to a career.

And for that I am for ever in his debt.

CHAPTER ONE

'People think feminists are all a load of butch hairy lesbians, stomping around academia using impenetrable language, calling all men rapists and drawing trousers on ladies toilet signs. But that's not all feminists. That's just me, working alone.'

Hello. I'm Bridget Christie. You've just met me in the Introduction, although you still might not know who I am. As of writing, I've been a stand-up comedian for eleven years. I used to dress up as dead kings and insects and plagues and fire and things like that. Not very many people came to see me and I didn't earn any money. Then, in 2013, I did a show about how, in terms of gender equality, women are still getting the shitty end of the phallic-looking stick.

The show didn't say anything new because it's pretty impossible to say anything new about feminism. Most of it's been said before and said brilliantly by our foremothers. I only said what other women have already said and continued to say. I just put some jokes in and pulled faces. And did it in comedy clubs instead of university lecture theatres.

There is a reading list of some of these brilliant women's works at the end of this book that you can tear out, bring into a bookshop and shove into the face of an obstinate, unhelpful smelly man. So the show was popular with audiences and awards panels. It won the Foster's Edinburgh Comedy Award for Best Show, the 2014 South Bank Sky Arts Award for Best Comedy, and Best Show at the 2014 Chortle Awards. It also won a 2014 Hospital Club 100 Award for Theatre and Performance and a 2015 Chortle Award for Best Tour. I'm not saying that winning all those awards means it was the best show in any of those categories in that year. It was just the one that – finally – got me noticed.

I was described as an 'unfunnywoman' (all one word) by the *Sun* columnist Ally Ross, received an email from icon of British motorsport Sir Stirling Moss, congratulating me on all of my success, and became the top-selling comedy show ever at the Soho Theatre. (Although admittedly the room I was in has only 145 seats. I'm not competing with the stadium set and it could all be over tomorrow.)

The fact remains: I've profited from women's pain and misery as surely as the pimps that work on my road. I need to get myself a white suit, a panama hat, a solid-gold cane and a multicoloured fur coat. Making money from the oppression of women was never my objective. It was a completely unexpected by-product.

I genuinely didn't expect a show about feminism to do well. I thought it would go down badly and that I could then give up and be financially supported by my fictional husband. The whole thing's been a complete disaster. I've only had about ten nights off in a year and a half.

I mean, what's the point of being a liberated free woman if I'm too busy and knackered to enjoy it? Just because I believe in employment equality laws, doesn't mean that I personally want to work. Feminism may have improved the quality of many women's lives, but it's completely ruined mine.

We didn't think about that, did we, ladies, in the fight, that we'd have to actually do something with all of our freedom? I had hoped to spend 2014 lying on a chaise longue, eating grapes and pretending to be delicate and coquettish. But oh no, I've had to think again. I don't know how the men do it. I take my hat off to them, I really do.

Anyway, after I did my show on feminism, everyone then started calling me 'Bridget Christie the feminist comedian'. I was asked to write a book about feminism, which was a very good idea of my publishers, especially after Mary Wollstonecraft, Virginia Woolf, Susan B. Anthony, Simone de Beauvoir, Betty Friedan, Gloria Steinem, Germaine Greer, Naomi Wolf, Kat Banyard, Doris Lessing, Margaret Atwood, Natasha Walter, Caroline Criado-Perez, Laura Bates, Susan Faludi, Ariel Levy, bell hooks, Alice Walker, Elizabeth Cady Stanton, Kate Austin, Dora Montefiore, Kate Millett, Shulamith Firestone, Adrienne Rich, Susie Orbach, Eve Ensler and Millie Tant all made such a mess of it.

I thought I'd better look up feminism in case I was interviewed on *Newsnight* about it by the Head of Women, Jimmy Somerville from Bronski Beat. So I'll just quickly explain to you what I found out feminism means, and then I'll get on with all the more interesting stuff about cheese and ants.

I'm a feminist. All this means is that I am extremely hairy and hate all men, both as individuals and collectively, with no exceptions. Nope. Not even Laurence Llewelyn-Bowen/ Paul Hollywood/Ronnie Corbett/Trevor McDonald/David Attenborough or John Nettles circa *Bergerac* are good enough for me.

Oh…it could've been you, John. Oh, John. Those blue eyes, those blue jeans, that burgundy car…Oh, John. You could've been the thinking feminist's crumpet, John. But Jersey has no gender equality laws, John. Oh, John, what a wasted opportunity.

I even hate Ban Ki-moon. It's one thing to try to eradicate female genital mutilation (FGM) and forced marriage, but Mrs Ban Ki-moon told me she can't remember the last time her husband put the hoover round. Or sprayed his own soiled pants with pre-wash Vanish. Feminism begins at home, Mr Ban, not at the UN. Huh! Ban Ki-hypocrite, more like.

I also learnt that us feminists hate being complimented, praised or having our lives improved or enhanced in any way by a man. A feminist would rather be dead than have her life saved by a man.

Feminists don't like humour, except slapstick. Charlie Chaplin, Harold Lloyd, Laurel and Hardy and *Bottom* are all very popular at feminist comedy nights. Anything that involves men being physically harmed always goes down very well with feminists. They also enjoy watching *Tom and Jerry*, Road Runner cartoons and war documentaries.

Feminists never have sex and hate men opening doors for them, even into other dimensions.

Christmas is banned in the 'feminist community', along with birthdays, wallpaper, nuance, giving people the benefit of the doubt and all music. Feminists only ever listen to one song, on a loop: k.d. lang's 'Constant Craving'.

Feminists hate all visual and conceptual art except for Jamie McCartney's *Great Wall of Vagina*, a nine-metre long polyptych consisting of 400 plaster casts of vulvas. Apparently you can see it from space.

All feminists are lesbians. There is not a single heterosexual woman in the world who believes that women should have equal rights. Not one. If a feminist says she is heterosexual or bisexual or asexual, she is lying. They are all lesbians.

Every feminist became a feminist because they were so fat and ugly that they couldn't get a man, even the most repulsive man in the world. We've all tried to get him, and he just doesn't want to know. I personally tried everything. I sent him boxes of pork scratchings, I dressed up like a sexy pork scratching and poured salt all over myself, and I even polished his tool kit. And that's not a metaphor.

I did everything. I was a cook in the kitchen, a cook in the bedroom and a cook in the living room. I think that's what annoyed him, actually – all the cooking. And peelings everywhere.

I'm not going to reveal the identity of the most repulsive man in the world. But here's a drawing I did of him:

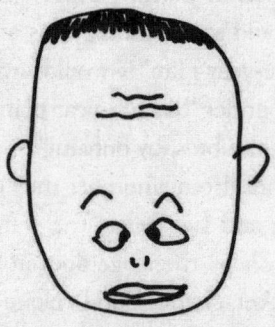

Feminism is the sole cause of the recession, global warming, terrorism, pandemics, cancelled flights, volcanos, delayed trains and overly pedantic health and safety regulations. You can't have hot drinks at work now because of feminism, or climb up small stepladders in libraries. You can't eat a lobster without safety goggles now because of feminists. You can't even open a door now because of all the feminists. You have to hurl yourself through plate-glass windows to get in and out of buildings now because of the feminists. All doors have been bricked up now because of feminists. It's like the window tax of 1696 all over again, but with doors.

All feminists are from the 1960s. There are no feminists from any other decade.

All feminists wear glasses and look like Velma from *Scooby-Doo* circa 1969, Olive from *On the Buses* or Elton John from the gay community. And Princess Di's funeral.

All feminists do all day is burn bras. Twenty-four hours a day, seven days a week, without eating, sleeping or taking toilet breaks. A feminist would rather wet herself than leave a bra unburned. If you read the CV of a feminist, under 'Occupation' it would say: 'Bra-burner'. And under 'Skills' it would say: 'Very good at burning bras'. And under 'Hobbies and interests' it would say: 'Finding bras and burning them'. And under 'My five-year plan' it would say: 'To have burned loads of bras'. And under 'My ten-year plan' it would say: 'To have eliminated all the bras, by burning'.

Feminists steal bras from wherever they can. From lingerie departments, barns and hay bales, the wardrobe department for *The Benny Hill Show*, the stage floor at a Tom Jones concert, milkmen's pockets, James Bond's glove compartment and *Carry On Camping* star Kenneth Williams's face.

Then they burn the brassieres in braziers, singing their politically correct nursery rhyme, which goes:

> Bra, bra, black sheep,
> Have you any bras?

Yes, sir, yes, sir,
Three bras full.
One for the master,
And one for the dame,
And a tiny double-A one for the
little girl who lives down the lane,
who doesn't need one yet,
and won't do for years to come,
but who wants one because she
saw an American Apparel advert,
before it was banned by the
Advertising Standards Authority,
for using gratuitous sexual imagery,
involving underage-looking models
on its website.[7]

Feminists also despise waterslides, clichéd romantic gestures, hundreds and thousands, glacé cherries, balloons, mime artists, candy floss, optimism, surprises, musicals, marshmallows, gondoliers and Russell Grant.

Feminists never wear hair accessories, dresses, skirts, feathers, bracelets, coats or jackets that aren't fully waterproof,

---

[7] That's the end of the bra burning bit now. Oh, did I mention? Feminists never actually burned bras 'as a means of protest'. In 1968 and 1969 protestors demonstrated at the annual Miss America Beauty pageant held in Atlantic City, NJ. The New York Radical Women were one of the earliest women's lib groups in the country. They threw items they viewed as oppressive to women (high heels, girdles, women's magazines, tweezers, bras, etc) into a 'freedom trash can'. They applied for but didn't get a permit from the Police allowing them to burn the items, because of 'health and safety gone mad' regulations (the protest was held on a wooden boardwalk), so they just binned everything instead. Nothing was ever burned. But the media said they burned everything and have been saying it ever since, and now twats and anti-feminists use the term 'bra burners' as a way of trivialising the movement. Just thought I'd clear that one up.

humorous socks and ties, bras, glitter, false eyelashes, foundation, sunblock, mosquito repellent, lace, stockings, small pants, skinny jeans, stilettos, boleros, ermine cloaks, Genghis Khan costumes, perfume, deodorant.

Feminists never brush their teeth, clip their toenails or remove stubborn ear wax from their ears. They leave the wax there and use it as a sexist twat sound barrier.

The American actress Zooey Deschanel is not a feminist, even though she says she is and believes in equal rights for women, because she is very pretty, wears dresses and has a nice voice. The quality of being female is not allowed in the feminist community. You cannot be a feminist until you realise this. Feminism is not about a woman's personal ideologies or life choices, it's about the way in which she wears material and presents herself to the media.

Michelle Obama is not a feminist because she has good upper arms.

Laura Bates, the pioneering founder of the Everyday Sexism Project, is not a feminist because when we were on a panel together, she was wearing lipstick and also had a very slight heel on her boots. Not too high, but just high enough to make me doubt her feminist credentials. How can she be a feminist if she has deliberately tried to make herself half an inch taller and therefore more attractive to men? She's also not a feminist because she mentioned once or twice (out of all the hundreds of interviews she's given) that the fight for equality cannot be won by women alone, and that men needed to be involved too. She is clearly only interested in men and her entire project is obviously just an attempt to get their attention.

Us feminists – or 'feminazis', as we are affectionately called by certain members of the right-wing press and other informed

social commentators and stand-up comedians who are trying
to drive traffic to their websites, blogs, Facebook pages and
Twitter feeds – only ever wear clothes designed by Hugo Boss,
who also made clothes for the Nazi Party. We also often dress
up as Robert Mugabe, Idi Amin and Ratko Mladić. In fact, the
feminist and human rights activist Gloria Steinem often wears
a Benito Mussolini outfit for her lectures.[8]

In the entire history of feminism, no female feminist has ever
been funny. In fact, Germaine Greer, the female feminist, said
in a national newspaper that female feminists weren't as funny
as male feminists because they couldn't remember punchlines.
Luckily, in the entire history of feminism, no feminist has ever
told a joke. Not even a joke about feminist sociological theory.
At a feminist sociological theory conference.

I am a feminist. This means I think that all men are rapists,
without exception. Even paralysed men, who can only move
one eyeball. All rapists. Even my seven-year-old son is a rapist,
and that is how I introduce him to people. 'Have you met my
son? He's seven. Rapist.' That's what I think, because I am a
feminist.

Even dead men are rapists. A bit of soil and science doesn't
stop them. Mud and physics is just more bureaucratic nonsense
for them to negotiate their way around, like CCTV cameras
and sentencing.

Even half the French language are rapists, all those mascu-
line words, raping all the feminine ones. That's what I think,
because I am a feminist.

---

[8] I don't mind being called a hairy, humourless lesbian, because that is what I aspire to
be, but I do mind being called a 'feminazi', because it doesn't make any sense. It's an
oxymoron.

Feminists never laugh at anything. They didn't even laugh at that YouTube clip of babies in car seats going through tunnels that went viral.[9] Or at that clip where someone called St Sanders has made Mick Jagger make funny noises. Even when Germaine Greer told her now-legendary joke on feminist practice and post-structuralist theory, to a lecture hall filled with feminists, not a single feminist laughed. She even distorted her voice with helium and wore a funny Marx Brothers mask to encourage the feminists, but she got nothing at all. Mind you, she did mess up the punchline by forgetting it. And she got her Marxes mixed up. They were all probably trying to work out why Germaine Greer was doing a Joe Pasquale impression and was wearing a mask of a German revolutionary socialist.

If a feminist is made to pull a cracker at Christmas, she quickly eats the joke so that she doesn't have to tell it. Feminists only ever eat paper. Paper. And carpets.

If a feminist is found to love her husband, enjoy cooking, having a facial or interacting with her own children, she is publicly flogged and thrown out of feminism by Julie Bindel and Julie Burchill, who go out undercover, posing as eyebrow-threaders, sugar daddies and John Nettles to try to trick us.

So that's feminism. I hope I've cleared that up for you.

While I'm at it, I think I'd better explain what a woman is as well, in case you didn't listen to my radio series, see any of my shows or have access to a dictionary or the internet or don't know what a woman is. There is a very high chance

---

[9] You've got to watch this. It's one of the funniest things I've ever seen. Take some time out and treat yourself. Just search for 'babies going through tunnels looking scared'.

that you might not have come into contact with any women. Even if you are a woman. By the way, I'm not judging you if you don't know what a woman is. Or if you are a woman. I only found out what one was recently when I had to write this book. It turns out that some women are born women and others become women. But they are all women; it's just a timing thing, really. It's not that these women then fancied a change, like going over to skimmed milk. They were always women, but were given the wrong body (i.e. their assigned sex at birth didn't match up with their gender identity). These women are called trans women.

Anyway, there's a little bit of a disagreement happening in the 'feminist community' about what all the different types of women should be calling themselves and who is privileged and who isn't.

I'm not saying this is not a valid debate; what I am saying is that while radical feminists and trans women are having it, men men, who are men, and who identify as men, are not all arguing about whether they are men or not, but are getting down to the serious business of raping and killing all the different types of women that there are.

So. I am a woman. I sound like one, and I look like one. Look at me on the front of the book. That's me. I didn't always look like this. I used to look like a baby. Whether you are born a woman, or have become a woman, the way a woman looks is very important. A woman's looks are more important than anything she could ever think, say, do or achieve. In fact, a woman's looks are so important that women are often asked to give people a 'twirl', so that they can be approved in 3D.

But us women don't just turn around in circles all day long, looking hopeful and getting dizzy; we do lots of other things as well. For example, when Christine Lagarde isn't turning around in a circle, she's the head of the International Monetary Fund. Angela Merkel fills her time between turns by being the German Chancellor. Jayne Torvill...is not a good example to use here. In fact, in the entire history of revolving women, the only woman who wasn't very good at turning was Margaret Thatcher.

She wasn't. She admitted it herself, and she even wrote a speech about it. 'I am a lady but I'm not going to be doing any of that silly twirling around so that you can see what I look like from behind and the side as well,' or something like that...

Women were invented ages ago, before the 1960s, because God realised very quickly that Adam needed an audience for his jokes. Anyway, 'his' plan went badly wrong, because Eve was much funnier than Adam. This annoyed God very much. He went all red in the face, his feet swelled up and he popped a couple of buttons on his shirt and so as a punishment, all female comedians have had to endure the pain of being edited out of TV comedy panel shows ever since.

If you're still unsure about what a woman is, a woman is often contextualised in social situations to make it easier for you to understand what the point of her is. For example, she will often be introduced to you as being the wife, mother, daughter, sister, auntie, grandmother, niece, nanny, cleaner or secretary of one of the men in the room. She might also be introduced as his boss, or as the president or monarch of the country that you are currently in. If the woman is introduced to you as being the gentleman's boss, or as the monarch or prime minister, or the man's physical trainer, or his pilot or doctor or bank manager, you mustn't be confused, threatened or angered by this. Just say, 'Oh? How lovely to meet you, [insert name here].' Don't say, 'Well, *good for you*,' in a passive-aggressive manner. Then quickly bring the conversation back round to the man again, wherever possible. Don't leave a pause, or try to ask her something about herself that doesn't involve the man in the room, only to find yourself trailing off at the end and looking around the place. That's even worse than not acknowledging her existence, because it's dishonest. Just remember that a mixed-gender social gathering is not the place to be celebrating or championing women. The phenomenon (which I experience all the time) of only being able to imagine or comprehend women within the context of males is not a new one. It was mentioned by Virginia Woolf in Chapter 5 of her 1929 essay *A Room of One's Own*:

> All these relationships between women, I thought, rapidly recalling the splendid gallery of fictitious women, are too simple ... And I tried to remember any case in the course of my reading where two women are represented as friends ... They are now and then mothers and daughters. But almost without exception they are shown in their relation to men. It was strange to think that all the great women of fiction were, until Jane Austen's day, not only seen by the other sex, but seen only in relation to the other sex. And how small a part of a woman's life is that.

Then in 1985 American cartoonist Alison Bechdel developed the Bechdel test, which asks if a work of fiction features at least two women who talk to each other about something other than a man. In 2013, four Swedish cinemas and the Scandinavian cable television channel Viasat Film incorporated the Bechdel test into some of their ratings, a move supported by the Swedish Film Institute. Obviously, it doesn't work for films like *12 Angry Men* or *The Shawshank Redemption* or *Three Men and a Baby*, but it's interesting to see the numbers – look them up yourself! By the way, if you're thinking this book has failed because the main protagonist was a man's fart, then you're wrong. This book is non-fiction, so the Bechdel test doesn't apply.

So that's women. I hope I've cleared them up for you.

I won't explain what a book is. Oh, go on then. A book is lots of words on pieces of paper, bound together. The pages are often numbered. Sometimes books have photos in them as well. If you're still not sure, the object that you are holding in your hands is defined as a book. But I'll let you be the judge of that!

In this book I will be exploring all different types of fun and girly things, like misogyny, female oppression, why women treat each other like shit sometimes, the hypersexualisation of our culture, female genital mutilation, the current state of feminism, feminist infighting, gratitude within feminism, role models, anti-rape pants, gendered language, the objectification of women's bodies, ladies' pens and why clever women – who should know better – fancy Boris Johnson.

Oh God, I can hear you thinking, not *another* funny feminist book! (And that's just the feminists.) We've already had *one* funny book about feminism in the entire history of feminism – Caitlin Moran's *How to Be a Woman* – we don't need *another* one, surely? At least not for another fifty or a hundred years, anyway. There's only room for one! Although one was a journalist and author and the other a stand-up, we DON'T BLOODY NEED IT!

Jesus, you're thinking. These feminists will need their own bloody bookshops soon – to fit all these two books in. What about all the men's books? Where are they going to go now? Out in the bloody street, I suppose, piled up in boxes without even a thought to what genre they are. The genre of 'Men' I suppose!

You're thinking, Good grief, there's just no room for these two books. We'll have to expand out into other galaxies to fit all these two bloody funny books about feminism into. We'll have to ask Brian Cox and Richard Branson and Dara Ó Briain and Robin Ince if they can build a bookshop in another solar system to fit all these two bloody funny feminist books into. Perhaps they can ask Jesus to knock some shelves up for them...

Incidentally, there is every possibility that you won't agree with the things I say in this book. This might be because we're not the same person. We've had different experiences and come from different backgrounds. You may not be the same race as me, the same class or have the same-sized feet. (I'm size 6, by the way, wide-fitting to accommodate my bunions and mutant Irish webbed toes.)

You might be fat or thin, young or old, single, married, divorced, cohabiting, dating or widowed. You might be glamorous, wear high heels and low-cut tops, or you might wear dungarees, Dr Martens boots and have short hair.

You might be well educated, or not educated at all. You might be Christian, Muslim, Buddhist, Sikh, Jewish, atheist, agnostic, Scientologist, Unitarian, humanist or something else. You might be straight or gay or rich or poor.

You may come from a culture or community that oppresses and abuses women and girls within the law, or outside of the law, but we are connected by our shared experiences of being female. I could make a joke about doing the washing-up or blow jobs or being sacked from being a milkmaid – which I was – to a Maasai woman, and I'm pretty sure we'd make a connection. But being a feminist doesn't mean agreeing with other feminists on everything. That would be really boring and weird. We need to accept our different approaches and different ideas and fight on for our common goals. Don't worry about what your sister's rules are. They're hers and yours are yours. Forget about it. Unless she's being a total dick, in which case, tell her she's wrong and cut all contact.

If women didn't exist, neither would sexism. But I don't think the answer is to eradicate women. Yes, yes, that does work with bovine spongiform encephalopathy, but we can't just apply DEFRA's vicious scorched earth policy to women as well as mad cows. We're not an infected herd.[10] Being a woman isn't a treatable disease.

Even if you come from a country with one of the best equal rights records in the world, like Finland, you will still have experienced some form of sexual discrimination, however obvious or subtle. You may not even have noticed. One of the first things the former Finnish President Tarja Halonen did when she was elected was to ban prostitution. She said, 'I suppose men will just have to get used to the fact that women are not for sale.' So now all Finnish women have to have sex

---

[10] I am not saying farmers are sexists, though I was sacked by one in Frampton on Severn in 1986, who just laughed at me out of his kitchen window all day. In fact, I think he had his kitchen built facing that way so he could laugh at all the farm girls. Anyway, I fed the cows gravel and crashed his tractor.

with Finnish men for free. And she calls herself a feminist! Absolutely unbelievable.

I have nothing else to bring to the feminist table. I am not an academic, I left school at fourteen, I have no formal qualifications, no practical skills, and I cry all the time.

There are many brilliant feminist books you can read written by some of the finest minds in literature; books that sparked off each new wave of feminism; books that have inspired generation after generation of women to pick up the spangly baton of change and bash the patriarchy in the nuts with it; books that you will learn from; and books that you will cry into. This isn't one of those books. And luckily for me, it's not meant to be.

I came to feminist literature pretty late in life. Four years ago I'd never heard of Mary Wollstonecraft and I thought Simone de Beauvoir was a villain in *Poirot*. I'm not ashamed of this. Four years ago I didn't have one feminist book. Not one! Now I have a modest library of them, most of them unread, admittedly.

If you need to know exactly how many, I have more than Waterstones and fewer than Foyles, who have a pant-wettingly exciting well-stocked Women's Studies section. After Chessington World of Adventures, the Women's Studies section in Foyles is my favourite place to be.

All my feminist books are on a lovely bookshelf next to my bed. It's called 'Woman's Corner' and no one's allowed to go near it until they've washed their hands, and bums. I don't want a child's excrement on my rare copies of *Spare Rib*.

Anyway, you don't need to have read all about feminism to be a feminist. You just need to know what it means and agree with its basic tenets.

The four main tenets of feminism[11] are:

Number One: Sense of Humour Rights

A woman's right to choose what she finds funny, without being called a militant lesbian. Or frigid. Or German. This includes being able to walk down a street, on her own, with a neutral facial expression, without fear of having a strange man shout at her in an aggressive way to cheer up. If a man does this, it should carry a minimum sentence of three years in prison, and he should also have points on his licence and a restraining order. And to be made to work as a children's clown at four-year-olds' birthday parties for ever.

It should also be pointed out to the man that if the woman in question were, indeed, walking along the street, on her own, openly laughing at nothing, as he suggested she do, he would not have approached her in the first place. He would've avoided her like the plague. He would've looked at the floor.

This new bill should also include guidelines on how much and when women are allowed to laugh. It seems to me that if a woman wants to laugh while in the company of men, or when she is alone, or when she is with other women, there is a strict set of rules to adhere to.

In my experience I am either laughing too much and am therefore hysterical, I've 'clearly had too much wine' (which all women know is impossible), or I'm an evil hag. Why am I a cackling witch for laughing too much and a frigid harridan for not laughing? What's the balance? Is there some midway point between laughing too much and not laughing at all that is acceptable to men?

---

[11] There's only one.

I'm too busy to commit to feminism in any worthwhile capacity at the moment. I only really have time to write silly jokes about it. I am to Simone de Beauvoir what *Horrible Histories* is to Simon Schama. My feminist book won't be full of alienating terminology or references like feminist post-structuralist discourse analysis, gynocentric essentialism, feminist revisionist mythology, feminist anthropology, hegemonic masculinity, intersectionality, feminist empiricism or separatist feminism, mainly because I barely understand any of them and nor does hardly anyone I know.

You won't need a degree in gender studies to read it. You won't need a degree in anything. Or a gender. Or a study. You'll just need to be exactly like me in every single way, with the same sense of humour, the same opinions, the same level of education, economic background, superstitions, webbed toes and ideologies.

I won't be explaining all the various waves of feminism, what the different feminists fought for, or what they were wearing. You can find that out in lots of other places – see your handy pull-out at the back of the book. I also won't be telling you how liberal feminism, socialist feminism, radical feminism, ecofeminism and post-feminism differ. I must say, though, that post-feminism is shit and stupid and ruined everything. How can you have a 'post' version of something that hasn't finished yet? Well, you can, but I'm saying you can't do that with feminism, and if you disagree then you're wrong. There is no room to manoeuvre within my feminism. You either agree with me on absolutely everything I say, and also the style with which I say it, or you are wrong and an idiot.

Why 'choose' to objectify yourself anyway? Why make yourself an object at all? Why not just not objectify yourself?

You can if you want to, because women fought for your right to be able to choose to objectify yourself. Well, they didn't actually, they fought for you to have sexual freedom and reproductive rights, which isn't necessarily the same thing as the right to objectify yourself, I don't think.

But don't listen to me; I haven't read enough about it to be able to give you an informed opinion, and I'm not going to pretend that I have. But like I said earlier, feminism is instinctive to me, a sixth sense. It's formed by the real world and how I react and respond to it. So I don't know academia's position on whether women should be objectifying themselves or not. All I know is that when I watch most music videos these days, by female artists, with my seven-year-old boy and my four-year-old girl, the women in them don't look like they are trying to communicate their ideas to me, or to my children, or to most people. They don't look like they're trying to drive a narrative along. They just look like their main objective is to make loads of men come in their pants.

But this book isn't about all that. It's mainly just about how I discovered feminism for myself and how I then wrote stand-up about it, after a decade of not really knowing exactly what I was writing about at all.

CHAPTER TWO

'The world has Tina Fey and Sharon Horgan in it, and yet the "are women funny?" debate continues to drag itself along, like a rectal prolapse on a tortoise.'

When I was growing up I was socially aware, I suppose. But I didn't really engage with politics myself. I was the youngest of nine kids, and we were all very opinionated. Being surrounded by older people all the time meant that I was emotionally mature at a young age, though I have, thankfully, discovered immaturity late in life, as you will see. Academically I always struggled, and left school early with nothing to show for it, but I was advanced socially. My dad told me recently he never worried about me when I was away from home and that all of us kids were capable, independent and streetwise. Good job, really, as a lot of us left home quite young. I like to think my siblings leaving home as soon as it was legally allowed wasn't just to get away from me.

I supported Greenpeace, CND and voted Green. I was vegetarian – not because I thought eating animals was cruel and disgusting, but because I just didn't like the idea of meat. Later I thought: I'll just say it's cruel as well. The only march

I ever went on was for the Motorcycle Action Group, during my 'biker' period, which ran from 1987 to 1996. I can't even remember what it said on my placard. Probably something like: 'Hey, car drivers. Stop running us down. Cheers then.'

My mum, who died in 1997, was an auxiliary nurse, and she was a spokesperson for the National Union of People's Employees and had a letter of thanks from striking Welsh miners. She was really active in the community and took in various temporary waifs and strays from the local Catholic community. How she found time to do all of this as well as bringing up nine children and keeping down a job is beyond me. I struggle with just two kids.

Mum and Dad met in London as teenage Irish immigrants and would go to Speakers' Corner, around the time of the Hungarian Revolution in 1956, where they used to enjoy watching other people shouting at each other. Dad said that Mum was quite outspoken, and would sometimes join in. My parents were lifelong Irish Catholics and lifelong Labour Party supporters and lifelong Tory-haters, but they didn't really talk about politics with us kids very much. So for me, politics and feminism wasn't something I grew up with particularly. I remember Mum really encouraging me from an early age to have a career. She always told me that not all women were destined for marriage and children. She was fiercely feminist in practice, but she'd never have identified as one. I wish she was still around. I could've told her about the fart. And the children, obviously.

Anyway, around October 2009 I read some reviews of female comedians and noticed they were full of irrelevant information about their looks and clothes, cooking skills, how well they could throw a ball, their fertility capabilities, how many previous boyfriends they'd had, their ability to sew hems well, how well they could use a stream iron and how badly they ran on to the stage, with their arms all flailing about. There wasn't too much about their actual material. It really annoyed me, so I started talking about it onstage.

I also started talking about some of the annoyances female comedians have to endure, such as being forced to use smelly, dirty, manly black or grey microphones after the men comedians have just dribbled patriarchal spittle all over them. Is it too much to ask for compères to switch them to scented pink ones whenever a lady comic comes on?! I'm not sure about female quotas for TV panel shows, or being paid more than the blokes, but at least give us our own microphones, for goodness' sake. I can't believe no one's sorted this out yet. Oh, and just to be clear, yes I am speaking on behalf of *all* female comedians on this issue. Every single one of them. From Josie Long and Shazia Mirza to Tig Notaro and Hannah Gadsby. We all want pink microphones. It's all we ever talk about when we meet up. Pink microphones and men's cocks. If the Bechdel test were applied to female comedians' get-togethers, we'd always fail.

Another routine I had was about how people would often lump all of us female comics in together, as if we were a genre of comedy, like musical acts or double acts or flatulists. There was also lots of blather about how female comedians only ever did whimsy or relationship stuff, but it just wasn't the case. There are loads of female comics, all doing different things. The first time I saw the stand-up and clown Holly Burn, for example, she was lying on the floor with a makeshift hooking device (I think it was a coat hanger, unbent), and was trying to get things off a sort of washing line above her head, in silence. It didn't strike me as a particularly gender-specific routine. Unless of course it was a satire about voiceless women, trapped by domesticity. Of course none of us would be allowed onstage at all, had the previous generation of female comics not paved the way for us. Women like Jo Brand, Jenny Eclair, Hattie Hayridge, Donna McPhail, Rhona Cameron and Dame Edna Everage.

I also noticed how rubbish female parts in sitcoms were, so I started to pitch all-female TV ideas to flood the market with women like a big XX tide in any way that I could, so that people stopped noticing we were women. Unfortunately in my early days, as I was writing so much stand-up about historical figures, it was difficult to shoehorn in a female character just for the sake of it (like they do on panel shows) because there weren't any women in history.

This is a pitch I made to BBC Radio 4 in 2008, at the request of a producer called Colin Anderson, called *Bridget Christie: A Simple View*. It was going to involve me giving a lecture each week on a different historical subject to a women's group. This episode about the Vikings didn't have any women in it at all, apart from me and a small Irish man. Women are already out-numbered 2:1 in my cast list and production team, even in a pitch specifically written to get more women into comedy. I chose to cast myself for all the female parts when I could have given seven different women their big break.

BRIDGET COMES OUT AND BLOWS A COW'S HORN, OR A HORN

That's a Viking horn, I'll explain why I blew that later. Or maybe I won't.

Now we're all used to listening to excellent documentaries on

Radio 4 by experts in their field. Well, I'm not an expert. In any field. I've been in a field, but I wouldn't be able to tell you what type of field it was, how long it had been there, what it was used for, or even who invented it. You'd have to ask a farmer; they know about fields. Then you could run up to him and say, 'Hey, farmer, you are literally an expert in your field.' And he would say, 'Please. I haven't got time for this. Climate change has been enough for me to deal with lately, without you pestering me as well. I've just lost my entire wheat crop because of all these flash floods. I'm not in the mood for your stupid jokes about field experts. Go and look at those rabbits over there, before they all explode.'

Talking about exploding rabbits, let's get back to the Vikings. Here are three Viking-based jokes:

1 What do you call a Norse god with third degree burns and a speech impediment? You call him Thor.
2 How do you get a hundred Vikings into a phone box? You get them in there by putting something of value inside it.
3 What do you call a deaf Viking with one leg? You'd better not call him anything. He can lip-read and will slaughter you. You know what those Vikings are like.

Never mind, let's get our first and only guest on. He's a bit of a loose cannon this one, but I've been assured he'll be entertaining. All the way from Asgard, it's Thor!

THUNDER AND LIGHTNING

Greetings. I'm Thor. The one-eyed, red-haired and bearded Norse god of thunder and my default emotional setting is angry. Anyhoo, I don't go in much for killing and godness these days,

I got myself a day job. I'm the guy on those low-rate international calling cards. Listen. 'Greetings, mortals. To access your low-rate calling charge, please enter the twelve-digit number on the card, followed by the telephone number you wish to be connected to, followed by the hash key. You will be charged one pence per minute.

Ah well, it was seven years ago. Radio 4 weren't keen. It didn't even get past the script-development stage. Although I repitched it to them recently after my radio series *Bridget Christie Minds the Gap* won two Chortle Awards and a Rose d'Or International Broadcasting Award for Best Radio Comedy and was nominated for a Sony, and they're now saying it has 'potential'. Although they did also put loads of dots after the word 'potential', which made it look as if they were being sarcastic, or that the person writing the note had just been murdered in the act of finishing their sentence.

Attitudes towards female stand-ups are much better now because there are loads more of us. People are used to seeing us now, like recycling bins. Remember when recycling was introduced? We didn't trust it at all. Now *we love recycling bins*! We get the recycling bins to look after our kids, drive us home from the pub and lock up when they go to bed. Also, there are loads of *great* female comics. I'm not going to name them because chances are I'll miss someone out and then they'll all miss me out of their lists. And I'm never in them anyway since I started doing well and they can't all patronise me. Bitches.

If you were to read the online comments section under any article about female comedians, you'd think there had only ever been three funny women in the world, ever. Lucille Ball,

Lucille Ball and Lucille Ball. All those women are funny, of course, but they are not the only ones.

Audience expectations of female stand-ups were once so low that a female comic began her set in debt, and spent the rest of it trying to pay it off in instalments, joke by joke. I was introduced so badly in Glasgow once that I walked onstage to silence. The compère's build-up went something like this:

> Ladies and gentleman, are you ready for
> the next act? I want you to go wild, go
> crazy, start stamping your feet...She's a
> WOMAN, but don't let that put you off.
> I certainly didn't the other night. Whoops!
> Don't tell the wife...no, no, seriously,
> I have not had sex with the following
> act...as far as I know...and even if I have,
> that is NOT how she got the gig. Come
> on now, let's get her on, shall we? She's
> LOVELY, so go easy on her. Not that I
> need to say that because she's VERY funny,
> and I know you're going to love her to
> bits...Okay, everybody, settle down. If you
> wouldn't mind just waiting until the next
> act, who is a WOMAN, has done her set,
> we'll have an interval and you can get a
> drink and go to the toilet then. Ladies and
> gentlemen, would you please give a very
> warm welcome to the very pretty and very
> nice – Bridget Christie!

Compères. You never have to flag up the fact that the next act is a woman. She is not a strobe light. No one is going to have an epileptic fit when a woman comes out. Unless the gig is in Saudi Arabia. And she comes on driving a clown car.

It's not only female stand-ups who have to deal with this kind of prejudice, though. Women in all different professions get it. We see this type of reaction all the time, in boardrooms and garages and vasectomy clinics. A lot of men are uncomfortable about leaving their sense of humour, engines or vasa deferentia in the hands of a woman. Especially if the woman is also drunk and is laughing. Or not laughing, which in many ways is even worse.

Men don't have this problem. They're not immediately judged in the same way. I watched a young male comedian, who was on before me at a gig recently, not get a laugh for eight minutes and he wasn't bottled off at all; in fact, he got a few rounds of applause for just stating facts. I didn't get a laugh for eight minutes once, while I ate a whole stick of celery. No one clapped me. The fact is, on the whole, we just trust men more,

Before I did my 'successful' feminist character, I did loads of other 'unsuccessful' characters, mainly men from the seventeenth century. I did two shows about Charles II called *The Court of King Charles II* and *The Court of King Charles II – The Second*, where I pretended to be men from that period who'd come to the modern day to have a bit of a look around. One was Guy Fawkes. I dressed up like a guy that kids push round in a pram on Bonfire Night, not like Guy Fawkes himself, in an old tracksuit, with plastic carrier bags on my hands, covered in bin liners and rubbish. To this day I still can't fathom why my earlier work didn't have mass appeal. For me personally, I'd much rather watch someone sat in a pram pretending to be a seventeenth-century terrorist than listen to an embarrassing middle-aged woman shouting about the rise of gender capitalism. Here's an example of what I used to do, while speaking and swaggering like Liam Gallagher from Oasis.

Hiya. I'm Guido Fawkes. It's all going off!
Some say I was a revolutionary, fighting in
the name of freedom. Others say I was the
first British terrorist. But generally, I am
best known as a dummy made of plastic
carrier bags, being pushed around in a
supermarket trolley by children shouting,
'Penny for the Guy! Penny for the Guy!'

A penny? Fook me, is that all I'm worth?
I'm the most famous terrorist we've ever
had. I'm a proper terrorist. I'm bigger than
bin Laden, I am. You don't see American
kids pushing a dummy of him around,
on 9/11, with a towel wrapped round
its head, shouting, 'A dime for the Bin!
A dime for the Bin!' They've got more
respect for their terrorists, the Americans.
Admittedly, his plot succeeded whereas
mine failed, but that's not the point.
Terrorism isn't all about winning, it's the
taking part that counts.

It's funnier if you try to imagine me walking around like Liam and sitting in a pram. I did all my costume changes in front of the audience, which would take ages. Remember, I was doing a character of Charles II, who was introducing all these other characters, so Charles II's costume was underneath all these other costumes. But there were also parts of the show where I was myself, Bridget Christie, and so underneath Charles II's costume I had my own clothes on as well. Looking back, my costume changes must've taken up about half the show.

Now I am just a feminist in my own clothes it feels a bit one-dimensional. Maybe I should start performing as a feminist from a long time ago, who has come to the future to see how things have worked out and introduce notable feminists of today.

Anyway, it was in the *Charles II* show that I ate a whole stick of celery. I was doing a character of Samuel Pepys, who'd come to the future to read some modern-day blogs, which he found boring, and so to illustrate how boring they were, he would make the audience watch him eat an entire stick of celery. When I say 'him', I mean me doing a character of Charles II doing a character of Samuel Pepys. Eating the celery took much longer than I thought, because I forgot that celery's really stringy and I didn't have a drink of water onstage with me. I nearly choked to death one day. The audience didn't laugh at that either.

What I was getting at, before I got distracted by Guy Fawkes and celery, is that eating celery is not the point. I could eat celery for ages onstage as a historical man, but not as a present-day me. It's not about celery. It's about authority, and the occupation of space, which men are much better at doing than us, whether it's a space in a comedy club, a space on a train or a space in space in a space rocket. Audiences are more likely to trust a male comedian who is eating a stick of celery than they are a female comedian eating a stick of celery, because the audience will assume that the man has made a creative decision to eat the celery, whereas if a woman eats celery onstage, she's gone mad.

There's a feminist movement in Sweden called Macho i kollektivtrafiken (which translates as 'Macho in Public Transport'), which encourages women to take photographs of men sprawled out on buses and trains. There's one particularly funny picture of a man lying across two seats, with one of his legs halfway up the window. Naked. With Abba lyrics written all over his body. The website looks like a funny spoof at first, but Macho in Public Transport makes a very interesting point.[12] The blog's founder, My Vingren, thinks that men taking up more space than they need are practising an 'invisible and unconscious expression of power in an everyday, public space'. It could be that, or it could just be that they have sweaty testicles. But even if that's true, and men just want to be comfortable, I can't imagine a woman spreading herself out like that. No matter how sweaty her testicles were.[13]

Clammy scrotums aside, it's a fact that men do own space better than women. They use their arms, they stretch out their legs. Russell Brand is the maestro of dominating space. Watch him on any chat show, or on *Newsnight*, or *Question Time*, or live onstage, and he takes up as much space as is humanly possible. He spreads himself out like some sort of a pirate octopus. I don't know if Russell is even aware of what he's doing, but whether he is or he isn't, he is consciously or subconsciously 'dominating space'.

---

[12] Awful name, though.

[13] That's not a transphobic joke about women in transition. It's just a joke about sweaty testicles

Men live in positions of influence, in life and in the comedy clubs. The difficulties women comics face are nothing to do with women being funny or not. The audience have already decided that what we have to say is irrelevant. You haven't got the right to express your opinion. Where does your authority come from? Why should we listen to you or care about what you have to say? You are a woman. And also, you're not funny.

Girls are told, from an early age, to be quiet. Don't make a fuss. Be nice. Don't put your hand up. Don't have an opinion. Don't pull faces. Don't get muddy. Stop being silly. Put that pigeon down. Don't get your hair wet. Stop being so noisy. Get off that dog. We're not encouraged to speak up.

I was so bored of the question 'So, Bridget Christie, you're a stand-up 'comedienne', (which would always be said in a sarcastic way) writer and comedy actress – let me ask you, can women be funny?' Journalists and presenters, please stop asking us this. It makes us want to die. Why would you ask someone whose JOB IT WAS TO BE FUNNY, WHO WAS FUNNY FOR MONEY, whether they thought their biological sex interfered with their ability to provoke laugher or provide amusement? Asking a female comic if women are funny or not is like saying to weather forecaster Michael Fish, 'So, Michael, you work in weather. Can men feel the weather?'

According to Christopher Hitchens, who is now conveniently dead, and so was unavailable to comment, women aren't funny because we don't need to be funny in order to get laid. We don't *need* to develop that skill. Women are not going to die out if they can't tell a good joke, whereas men will, according to Christopher Hitchens who tried to prove his theory by not putting any jokes into his essay and dying.

Us women can use our beauty to get sex instead, he said. But what if you're a beautiful, funny woman who would rather be funny instead of having sex all over the place? What if you're not beautiful? Are you allowed to be funny to get men to have sex with you then? What if you're an unfunny man? What if you don't like sex or jokes and aren't a man or a woman? Where does that leave you? Out of Christopher Hitchens' stupid essay, that's where.

He then went on to say that the only funny women were Jews or dykes or butch. Or some kind of combination of the three. When challenged on this, Hitchens conceded that there were some female stand-ups coming through now who weren't Jews or dykes or butch, but that these female stand-ups 'played by the men's rules'. He didn't go on to explain what these rules were. Presumably because he didn't know. *Because there aren't any*. To say that the only reason some female stand-ups were doing well was because they played by the men's rules is idiotic. He is saying comedy is a man's domain and if the girls want some of the action they must first become honorary men, but the most successful and best stand-ups have simply worked out the best way of communicating their ideas (whether male or female) to an audience. Gender doesn't come into it. I'm going to start saying that male comedians 'who are coming through now' are only doing so because they've started 'playing by the women's rules'.

If Christopher Hitchens was right about this, and men are funnier than women because they need to be in order to have sex, then why do so many men have to pay for sex so often? There must be a shitload of unfunny men out there, because sex work is going really well. Always has done. Unless men who pay for sex are actually just paying for women to laugh at their jokes?

If that's true, then we might be able to end the illegal sex trade and the 'Are women funny?' debate in one fell swoop.

We should impose by law, stand-up comedy courses that every human being on earth has to attend for two years, so it would be a bit like national service, but with jokes. That way, all men will learn how to be properly funny, thereby removing the need for them to pay for sex, and also everyone will finally realise that women are funnier than men.

Anyway, it's not as simple as that, and of course I don't believe that women are funnier than men. I believe that some men are funny and some aren't and some women are funny and some aren't. God didn't divvy it all up: Right, I'll give men physical strength, vulnerable genitals and humour, and women can have beauty, childbirth and *Schadenfreude*.

Women cannot live on beauty alone. Even the Miss World Competition knows the importance of a GSOH. 'The thing is, Miss Venezuela, everyone on the panel agrees that while your bottom is unprecedented, your timing stinks. And Miss Venezuela, the Rule of Three does not mean that you simply repeat the same joke three times. In different accents.'

Another theory for why female comics aren't funny is that women are risk-averse. We don't like humiliating ourselves, so our routines aren't as dynamic or original as men's. That's not true. Women take risks all the time. The coitus interruptus withdrawal method is used by women and it is both risky and – when you tell the man you are pregnant with his unwanted child – funny. I am not risk-averse. I take many risks, all the time. For example, I put my slippers on the other day without first checking to see if my cat had put another dead mouse in them or not. He got me again, the cat bastard.

When people say 'women aren't funny', they haven't

thought it through properly. They don't mean that women can't be funny, because we all know that they can be, from Nell Gwynn and Marie Lloyd to Joyce Grenfell and oh no, I've just listed some when I said I wouldn't. Best stop there. What they mean is that female stand-ups aren't funny. They're saying that women's ideas and opinions and the way we express them aren't funny. What's in our heads isn't funny. And our opinions are not valid, so why should we listen to you? And also, you're not funny.

The prejudice is that women comics will do body image, periods, cake, boyfriends and dieting. There are women who do that, and many who do it very well, because subject material doesn't define whether an act is funny or not, as anyone who has ever tried to write one knows. And there are many women comics who don't talk about any of those things. But because there are fewer female stand-ups, we remember the ones who fit our prejudices more. If the same prejudice was applied to male comics every man who got onstage would get 'Oh no, not more masturbation jokes, rape routines and complex-relationship-with-their-father stuff again.'

Even women don't think women are funny. My harshest critics, from professional reviewers to the public and internet trolls, have all been women. You'll remember from the previous chapter that Germaine Greer, the female feminist, said in a national newspaper that women weren't as funny as men because they couldn't remember punchlines. I've never heard anything so ridiculous in all my life. That's like saying men aren't good at sewing because...no, hang on, not sewing, is it, oh, what's this one again? Auntie Jackie said it at Bob's funeral, do you remember? It really lifted the mood. Not sewing – quilting, is it? No, not quilting. Tapestry maybe. Oh never mind, I'll come back to that one later.

Whenever the question comes up of whether or not women are funny, I always think about a story I read. A Western female journalist had travelled to Afghanistan to talk to the women there about their lives. She noticed that all the women were trailing behind their husbands, so she asked one of the women why, after years of fighting and struggling to try to change the old regimes, was she now happy to go back to the old customs and walk ten paces behind her husband again. And the Afghan woman said, 'Landmines.' See? Even the most oppressed women in the world are funny. And yet the 'are women funny?' debate drags itself along, like a rectal prolapse on a tortoise.

When I started doing stand-up eleven years ago, attitudes towards female comedians were much worse than they are now. It's much better now as there are more of us, but sometimes, back then, the disappointment caused by the arrival of my point of view and X chromosomes onstage was palpable. How I got around that was by presenting myself as non-human matter. Some of my earlier stand-up characters were weeds, viruses and types of wood, all achieved with tawdry home-made costumes. Any preconceived notions of what a female stand-up talks about are soon eliminated by the arrival onstage of a person-shaped clump of Japanese knotweed.[14]

---

[14] When I performed as Japanese knotweed at sparsely attended new-material nights, I also wore a Comic Relief red nose, just to reassure the audience that my intention was to entertain them. If you look hard enough, you'll probably find a photo on the internet of me like it. This decision made no discernible difference. Most people just looked visibly threatened and uncomfortable. Sometimes I'd shout 'I've been on Comic Relief doing this, you idiots!' But that just made matters worse, because it looked like I'd made a joke about starving children.

Sometimes I wouldn't even let them see me until I'd got my first laugh. For the wood routine, I'd wheel myself onstage in a wooden laundry basket and hold up other things made of wood, like clogs, pencils, toilet paper and spoons, until I'd beaten them into submission. I was the Trojan Horse of female stand-up. It didn't work for me as well as it did for the Greeks. People hated it. Especially Turkish men.

Anyway, I wondered if there was any way I could start talking about attitudes towards women, which can be extremely alienating for a lot of people, onstage, without alienating an already-alienated audience. I wondered if I could sneak the subject in without them knowing. I genuinely did think that an audience would be less alienated by a woman dressed up as Japanese knotweed than by a woman dressed up as herself. But people try to eradicate Japanese knotweed from their gardens and, as it turns out, from Jongleurs Camden as well. So that didn't work out.

I actually think that people didn't buy into my Japanese knotweed character because they saw its internal flaws. It was too far-fetched: Japanese knotweed can't speak. So then I thought my next character needed to be more realistic. If I was going to talk about attitudes towards women, the conduit I used to facilitate me doing so needed to make more sense.

I remembered how clever ants were and thought that if I dressed up as an ant, and talked about what it was like being an 'ant' comedian, audiences might be more willing to buy into it. Everyone knows how intelligent ants are. I mean, they've been communicating with David Attenborough for years. It's just a shame he still hasn't learnt ant for 'Fuck off, mate, we're really busy here', which is what they've been saying to him since the 1960s.

An ant talking about being an ant comedian would be far less alienating to a comedy audience than a woman talking about being a woman comedian. I'd just make it about ant comedians rather than female comedians. I'd come on to 'Ant Music' by Adam and the Ants and make a joke about that. So, in the winter of 2010–11, I made an ant costume out of swimming goggles, cardboard tubing and a balaclava and said the following, which was the point at which I started to understand what I could do with stand-up:

> What's this? 'Ant Music'? By Adam Ant?
> Why has the technician played that?
> What, because I'm an ant? Unbelievable.
> If I was the black and blind comic on the
> bill, they wouldn't have played Stevie
> Wonder for me, would they? Or 'Kung Fu
> Fighting' for the Chinese one? Of course not.
> Because that would be politically incorrect.
>
> Let's play 'Ant Music' for the ant comic.
> It won't mind: it's only got 250,000 brain
> cells, surely not enough to process the
> concept of offence. Well, I am offended.
> I am a professional comedian. This is
> my job. Look at me. I've put a tie on.
> It has taken us ants years to be taken
> seriously on the comedy circuit, and a
> little stunt like this can put us right back
> to 1983. You probably hadn't even noticed
> I was an ant until Nick Griffin on the
> sound there pointed it out.

It's hard for us, okay? Even before an ant has got to the microphone, you've already made assumptions. I saw you two looking at each other when I came out: 'Oh no, not another ant, talking about jam and the division of labour.' We don't do that stuff any more. We've moved on.

I'm sick of the 'Are ants funny?' debate. It's so tedious. Some of us are funny, and some of us aren't. It's as simple as that. Critics complain that ants only ever do whimsy or relationship stuff, but that's just not true. There's loads of us ants on the circuit now, doing all types of comedy. Some do whimsy, yes, and some talk about everyday stuff like leaves and sugar, shocking stuff like having sex with the queen, but other ants do political or surreal stuff. We're all different. No one ever talks about bee comics like this. The fact that they're bees isn't even ever mentioned.

It's all different now. In the eighties you'd be lucky to get one ant on a bill, let alone three or four. I did Jongleurs Birmingham at the weekend. There were only ants on, apart from the compère, who was a wasp. He wasn't very good, actually. He just did loads of material about being a wasp. Who's interested in that? He obviously only got the gig because he was the token wasp.

I'm a political comic. That's what I do. I'm
an expert on Islam. But people don't want
it. They don't trust an ant to make the
Quran funny. That is ridiculous. Anyone
can make the Quran funny, yes, even an
ant. This is the problem in comedy today.
They just want ants to do stuff about ants.
I take my comedy very seriously. I even did
one of those stand-up comedy courses.
Not to learn how to do comedy, because,
as you all know, us ants are naturally funny,
but to learn how to stand up. So, here we
go. Because it's what you want. Because
it's what you expect from me, the ant
comic. Ant jokes by A Ant.

Then I'd read out lots of ant jokes from a small red notebook, which were rubbish and just a play on the word 'ant'. This bit often went down much better than the actual routine, especially with audiences who hadn't quite understood the metaphor, which is perfectly understandable.

'What do you call an ant that is nice? A pleas-ant. What do you call an ant that wears feathers and hats? A flamboy-ant. What do you call an ant that cheers you up? An anti-depress-ant.' And so on. Audiences normally really perked up at this point, and wholeheartedly joined in. One night a man shouted out, 'Have I gone mad or have all these jokes got the word "ant" in them?'

My ant act went well if I did it in a proper venue with a decent-sized audience, in front of a comedy-savvy crowd, for example at the Soho Theatre for one of Alexei Sayle's curated gigs, or as part of a really good bill, but it always bombed at new-material or open mic nights.

Comedy is all about the context. It's about who is saying what, and why. What is their position in the world? Who is the person onstage? Are they high or low status? Are they a victim or a perpetrator? What is their 'clown', i.e. the unique thing about them that makes them funny? Are they even aware of what their clown is? What are they wearing? Are they a support act or a headline act? Where are you seeing them? In a basement, with five other people, or in a sold-out stadium? What do we know about the stand-up's personal life? Do they have a high profile or are they completely unknown?

These are the elements that shape and inform our perception of the person talking onstage. Just one of these things can alter the way we interpret a comedian's material. It can turn it from being acceptable to unacceptable, funny to unfunny, bad awkward to good awkward, or a surreal flight of fancy to just shit. Is it okay for a fat stand-up to make fat jokes? Yes, of course. Is it okay for a thin person to tell fat jokes? Yes, of course. Comics are allowed to do material about whatever they want, but if their material has the potential to offend, upset or traumatise an audience member, or to incite hatred or to even break hate laws, then I think they have a responsibility to try to find the funniest way of doing that.

I can laugh at something I don't necessarily agree with. For example, I'm much more likely to laugh at material that is considered sexist if the character of the comedian is pitiful, powerless and pathetic . . . if he genuinely has nothing, and if his contempt for women is outmatched by his own self-loathing; if the comedian has made it clear to us that he himself is beneath contempt, and that his opinions are extreme and ridiculous; if his jokes say more about himself, than the supposed failures of women; or if the comedian has taken a position in which he is obviously satirising misogynist belief systems. I could also imagine laughing if he is indiscriminately bigoted, and appears to hate everyone equally, due to some incident in his past that is alluded to early in his set, that gives us 'permission to laugh'.[15] I think I'd struggle to laugh at sexist material if it was being said by a famous, successful comedian who didn't seem to have any good reason for hating women, and who was known for not treating women very well in his private life. Then, we are not being invited to laugh at bigots or sexists, we are being invited to join them, and by laughing along with them, whether out of nervousness or peer pressure, we are complicit in it. Freedom of speech is the political right to communicate one's opinions and ideas. It doesn't mean you have carte blanche to be a twat, and to encourage others to be twats as well. My point is that I don't have to agree with someone's politics in order to find them funny and I don't believe in censorship of certain words or certain subjects. It's all about context.

If it looked like I'd been endorsed by a reputable venue, act and/or promoter, the audience trusted A Ant. If they saw it in a sparsely attended small room at the back of a pub, for free, they pretty much thought I was just a madwoman dressed as an ant. And that's all there is to it, which is why I find it difficult to attach any objective value to critical acclaim and its trailing handmaiden, success. I doubt lots of the people that like me now would have liked me if they'd seen me doing the same stuff in the attic of a pub in Tooting as they have in a sold-out four-month run in the cabaret room at the Soho Theatre.

---

[15] Jerry Sadowitz does this very well.

In an empty room, for example, people were just a bit embarrassed by the ant. But actually it didn't matter to me whether it went well or badly, because either response could be incorporated into the act. The ant was angry, and didn't want to be there, and was as happy to do its act to indifference as to approval. If the act went to silence, the ant could accuse them of antism, and A Ant would have proved its point. And if it went well, it went well. It was a win–win act. The ant was always triumph-ant.

So the ant was the start of me talking about 'the annoying things women have to put up with'. Then, in 2012, a man farted in the Women's Studies section of a bookshop (you'll know all about that from the Introduction) and I dropped the ant facade. And became myself. Not A Ant. But A Woman.

CHAPTER THREE

'Many of my friends, feminist activists, writers and campaigners, are subjected to an extraordinary amount of online sexist abuse. And that's just from me. Using a series of pseudonyms.'

The 30 April 2012 bookshop fart turned me into an activist. Of sorts. I don't go on marches, or do any fund-raising or anything like that.[16] I don't even give any of my own time up to it. What I do is I go to men's areas and I fart. I wade out into the middle of rivers, where they're all fly fishing, and I fart. It doesn't achieve anything except confuse them, and I nearly drowned once but I see that as a badge of honour. Farting in a river might not sound as dangerous as throwing yourself under a horse, but as any paramedic will tell you, it's not only dangerous, it is also silly. As I said to the

---

[16] Though I did go on a London Feminist Network protest march once with loads of other women but the route went right across Oxford Street where there were loads of sales on. The whole thing had dissipated within five minutes. What? Feminist protestors need clothes as well you know! Apart from FEMEN, the controversial Ukrainian feminist group who protest topless. But apart from the topless feminist protestors, all the other feminist protestors need clothes. Especially feminists who live in cold climates.

ambulance driver, 'It might sound silly to you, but women's rights are worth farting for.'

So, remember the Introduction? The Amnesty film, the *Only Way is Essex* episode and the offensive review all happened on 30 April 2012, and I wanted to write about them, about that strange day. I also wanted to talk about a weird phenomenon I kept reading about in the papers: Tory feminism. And I thought the fart could be the perfect framing device for all the heavier topics. Who doesn't like a fart story?

It sounds like it might jar, but I began my 2012 Edinburgh show, *War Donkey*, dressed as a donkey and performed as a donkey, with all that that might entail, for about ten minutes. This was the show that people started coming to, after seven consecutive years at the Fringe, so even though it wasn't a *great* show, I was gaining in confidence all the time and starting to talk about things that mattered to me, in my own voice. I didn't take the donkey costume off to talk about feminism. I thought, at the time, that if I was going to write about labia minora reduction surgery it might be better if I just remained disguised as a mule.

At the time, Louise Mensch, the former Tory MP for Corby and self-styled Tory feminist, was getting a lot of media coverage. There were lots of articles about 'Tory feminism' and 'the new Tory feminists'. Theresa May wore a 'This is what a feminist looks like' T-shirt while at the same time making decisions that negatively impacted on women. I will never not love her shoes, though.

I'm not entirely sure about women wearing a 'This is what a feminist looks like' T-shirt. Or men, for that matter. It's overstating the case a bit, isn't it? It's like wearing a T-shirt with 'I am not a racist' on it. It makes me suspicious. I assume that most people's default setting is feminist, until they do or say something that makes me think otherwise. If I went bowling with a friend, for example, and they took their coat off to reveal an 'I am not a racist' T-shirt underneath, I don't think I'd feel relieved at all. On the contrary, it would make me very on edge. I'd spend the whole night worried I was bowling with an ironic racist.

Of course, wearing a T-shirt saying you're a feminist doesn't mean you are one. I'm sure lots of women would've preferred Nick Clegg to tell Lib Dem peer Lord Rennard to take an enforced leave of absence from the party until the results of the various investigations into his conduct were made known, and for Ed Miliband to have let his brother David – who is significantly easier on the eyes and ears – win the Labour leadership. Resulting in a shoo-in for Labour. But oh no, he had to settle some childhood score...and let UKIP take hold.

Still, it's nice that they pretended to care about women's rights in the run-up to the 2015 general election. It's almost as if they remembered women make up half the population and are allowed to vote now. As of April 2015, the UK had fewer female MPs than Afghanistan. This means that more women go into politics in a country that has the Taliban in it, who, in case you'd forgotten, hate women. Especially ones that speak in public. I must remember to cancel that Jongleurs Kabul gig. Or, at the very least, keep tabs on the guest list.

Since the first female MP to take her seat – Nancy Astor in 1919[17] – the *total* number of women MPs is smaller than the number of men sitting today, which just goes to show how rude

[17] Countess Constance Markievicz actually beat her in 1918 but never took her seat.

A BOOK FOR HER

British male MPs are. If they had any manners at all or were proper gentlemen, they'd have offered their seats to the ladies long ago. Quotas or no quotas.

We obviously need more women in British politics. Not only because a huge proportion of the public is under-represented, but also because if there were more women at Prime Minister's Questions there'd be less jeering, braying and heckling and more funny jokes! Male-dominated, testosterone-driven environments aren't that appealing to women. Also, female politicians often have to deal with online abuse and ridiculous, demeaning media attention. And that's just from their husbands. On the day of Cameron's Cabinet reshuffle, when Ester McVey was appointed Employment Minister, the *Daily Mail* wrote, 'She sashayed into Downing Street…her blonde mane was thrown backwards as in a shampoo advert.'

The *Daily Mail* mentioned the men, too:

> And here comes the man Philip
> Hammond, the new male Foreign
> Secretary, walking normally into work,
> with his man's legs. His man's hair isn't
> moving very much at all. The man Philip
> Hammond, the male politician, doesn't
> look like he's in a shampoo advert at all.
> Luckily for the man Philip Hammond,
> having moving hair is not an integral
> part of being the male Secretary of
> State for Foreign and Commonwealth
> Affairs. Having hair that moves is only a
> prerequisite if you are the female Minister
> for Employment.

Male MPs are also subjected to a high level of media scrutiny, of course, as they should be, but not in the same way. A male politician has to do something really stupid, like send a photo of himself wearing pyjamas with his willy out to an undercover journalist, or call a policeman a pleb, or defect to UKIP, to be a target. But even after he's done all that, he's very rarely threatened with rape. By the way, it wasn't the same politician doing those three things. It was three different ones. Mind you, they were all Tory MPs, so it might as well have been.

It's not just female politicians, though. Many of my friends, feminist activists and campaigners, are subjected to an extraordinary amount of online abuse. And that's just from me. Using a series of pseudonyms.

Seriously, though, I'm just a comedian. I have no power or influence. I'm not solving anything, or pretending to. I just write jokes. That's my only input. If a campaign wants me to mention them I will. But I don't want to take any credit where it's really not due. The criticism I've had is nothing compared with my friends. I've had the odd slightly misjudged violent and threatening rape threat, and been torn to pieces by other feminists, and accused of profiting from other women's pain: nothing too serious. Just light-hearted banter, really. It tends to just be a bit libellous or silly or sarcastic; nothing too upsetting.

Anyway, at the time, because Tory feminists were in the papers, talking about Tory feminism, it made me think about what Tory feminism was, which fed into the stand-up in *War Donkey* in Edinburgh in the summer of 2012.

> I've been trying to work out what a
> Tory feminist is, because I keep seeing

photographs of female Tory MPs in the
newspapers, wearing T-shirts with 'This is
what a feminist looks like' on them. What,
like a T-shirt? How can a T-shirt look like
a feminist? A T-shirt looks like a T-shirt,
doesn't it? It should say, 'This is what a
T-shirt with "This is what a feminist looks
like" written on it looks like.'

That's what it says on the front, anyway,
of the Tory feminists' T-shirts that they're
all wearing now. And on the back it says,
'Not really, I'm a Tory, you gullible dick.'
Then underneath that it says, 'I axed the
Health in Pregnancy Grant. I closed Sure
Start Centres.' That one's got a smiley
face next to it. 'I cut Child Benefit and
slashed tax credits. I shut down shelters
for battered wives and children. I cut rape
counselling and Legal Aid.' Winking face.
'I cut funding for CCTV cameras and
street lighting, making women much more
vulnerable. I closed down all twenty-three
Specialist Domestic Violence Courts. I cut
benefits for disabled children.' Sad face
with sunglasses on. 'I tried to amend the
Abortion Act so that women receive one-
to-one abortion counselling from the Pope
before they go ahead with it.' Winking face
with tongue out. The back is much longer

than the front, by the way. It's a tailcoat,
basically. They're wearing tailcoats.

Tory feminism, from what I can gather, is free market
feminism. Privatise women, creating competition in the
humanity marketplace, and the strongest will survive,
eliminating female oppression in the process. Just say no, yeah,
ladies? Tory feminism is 'I've done well so why can't everyone
else; oh yes, and also, I'm pulling the ladder up behind me.'

It's a survival of the fittest. The best will rise to the top. The
others do not deserve to be at the top. The top 1 per cent of
the 51 per cent will procreate and produce the next generation
of strong, beautiful, independent, wealthy white women just
like them, and then all the other women, the weak ones, the
ones who aren't rich and white, will hopefully, gradually die
out, and then there will be no need for all this boring feminism
and intersectionality and other shit like that. Evolution will
take care of the 'Women Problem'.

* * *

My 2012 Edinburgh Fringe show *War Donkey* had covered donkeys, maternal health in developing countries, labia minora
reduction surgery, Tory feminism and the fart-in-the-bookshop
story, which ended up being a call to arms, a call for all women
to stand up for their rights, and fart in men's areas. At the end
of the show I would invite a male audience member up on to
the stage and make him stand facing the back, where I'd hung
a sign that I'd made to look like a bookshelf in a shop, with
'Wollstonecraft', 'Woolf' and 'Dr Helen Castor' written on it.

With the man's back to the audience, my technician then

played a sound effect of three different farts, on a loop, as the rest of the audience walked out in silence. The man would always stand there happily, with his back to the audience, to the sound of a fart, until the last audience member had left the room. On tour, it was funnier in large rooms because it would take a long time for everyone to get out. It was never awkward and the farting man got a set of badges, free.

On the whole, the reviews weren't that great. And of course there was the 2-star one in *The List* I mentioned in the Introduction, where Charlotte Runcie criticised me for giving my audience nothing but farts in exchange for money. It's worth noting here that there were only three farts in the entire hour-long show. I played them in, on a sound cue, right at the end of the show, as the audience filed out. So saying I'd 'only' given them farts, after I'd been speaking for nearly sixty minutes, is misrepresenting me slightly.

Having said that, if I'd read that review that said I only gave people farts, I would've DEFINITELY gone to the show in a flash! It sounds hilarious! And much funnier than the actual show ended up being, to be honest. Also, I would have thought that Charlotte Runcie, being the granddaughter of the Archbishop of Canterbury, wouldn't have been so dismissive of farts, bearing in mind how obsessed Martin Luther, the head of Protestantism, was with them. Charlotte Runcie needs to do a bit more research into comedy and farts and their relationship to the theological imperatives of her grandfather's forebears if she's to be taken seriously as a comedy critic.

Martin Luther had some great quotes. None as good as Jesus's tax-paying one, but he had some great shit-based ones in his repertoire, which Jesus deliberately avoided as he thought they'd only be edited out of his book anyway. Luther was driven mad with irritable bowel syndrome in later life. Some scholars think it was this health issue that caused his anti-Semitism, rather than it being down to something like racism, which is a bit like when Nigel Farage[18] blamed immigration for congestion on the M4, which caused him to miss a UKIP reception. These scholars' theory is that because Luther was in so much pain and discomfort, and so angry all the time, that he became very intolerant of people from different places. Now I've got IBS, but it wouldn't cross my mind to blame an entire race of people for it. Even on a really bad day. I can't imagine saying, 'Oh, my poor old guts are bad today…it's those bloody Poles again! Coming over here, giving me IBS.'

Luther did a lot of his writing sitting on the toilet and he was obsessed with keeping the Devil away. One of his most famous quotes is: 'I resist the Devil and it is with a single fart that I chase him away.' But my favourite Luther fart quote is: 'I have shit in my pants, and you can hang them around your neck and wipe your mouth with it.' He said that to the Devil, by the way, not his wife.

Dr Rowan Williams didn't use any of Luther's quotes at the royal wedding of William and Kate. Shame. More people might have watched it if he had. I heard the viewing figures weren't great. And now, back to Dr Rowan Williams: 'Thank you. The response to the psalm is, "I have shit in my pants and you can hang it around your neck and wipe your mouth with it."'

See? Now I'm past page eleven I'm happy to talk about farts and shit and religion and the royals. I have fart carte blanche. Like the homeless. And the Swedes.

---

[18] If you're in any doubt about Farage being racist, have a look at the *Telegraph* article by Dan Hodges from March 2015.

Near the end of the Edinburgh Fringe run of *War Donkey*, the notorious BBC Radio 4 producer Alison Vernon-Smith came to see the show and persuaded the controllers at BBC Radio 4 Comedy to see it. A four-part comedy series about feminism was commissioned without a pilot. 'Great news!' I said to Alison when she told me. 'Oh, but hang on, it's for radio. I'll have to drop the costumes and props, and concentrate on the writing side of it, won't I, Alison?'

'Yes. Yes, you will, Bridget,' she said.

Ah, shit. Now there was nothing to hide behind.

CHAPTER FOUR

'In fact, there are so many knockers on show now in all sorts
of different environments, that some days I can't see the deeply
unequal society that objectifies, demeans and trivialises women,
for the tits.'

Looking back, the time between *War Donkey*, in August 2012, and my first radio series, recorded in March 2013, was probably the last time I was known, if indeed I am even known at all beyond a small circle of comedy fans, as Bridget Christie the comedian rather than Bridget Christie the feminist comedian. I was also sometimes known as that unfunny twat from Gloucester with no chin. But that was mainly just by my cosmetic surgeon.

Of course what this now means, looking forward, is that I have the gargantuan task of trying to disassociate myself from an ideology that supports gender equality, and the people who subscribe to those politics, if I want to branch out into other markets. Which is exactly what I'm planning to do.

I'm not interested in playing to people who agree with me any longer. What's the point in that? Where's the challenge for me? It doesn't interest me to have rooms full of people all nodding in agreement and clapping. It was nice at first, but now I just find it really annoying. I don't care about being liked. I'm going after all the *other* lot now, the people who *don't* believe in fairness and reason and equality.

I've done feminism now, remember: that's what the broadsheet journalists, writing to a tiny minority of comedy-literate Fringe-goers, said in 2014. So what now? I don't want all the lefty lot coming in again, wearing hats made of solar panels. I want the other lot, sitting down and plugging themselves into the mains and eating endangered species in front of me. I want all the corporate tax evaders and the public farters. I want to have people nodding and clapping at *un*fairness.

I've got to try to shake off all the hairy, fair, lefty, BBC-left-wing-biased, indignant-lefty, *Guardian*-reading, lentil-eating, sock-wearing, hat-wearing, bleeding-heart liberal, do-gooding, equal-rights-believing, pinko, recycling, Jeremy Clarkson-sacking, door-opening, Red Ed-and-Red Ken, Red Ed Ken, hairy, Marxist, lefty-liberal, communist, solar-eclipse-enthusiastic, hairy, Red Ken Ed Ken, BBC-left-wing-biased, hairy, anti-establishment, Marxist, lentil-eating, walking-boots-wearing, fully waterproofed, solar-panelled, lefty, Marxist, offshore-wind-farm, sustainable-fishing, vegan, sandal-wearing, sock-mad, Jeremy Clarkson-sacking audience I've managed to build up over the last three years and try to branch out into other markets.

Although, on second thoughts, I might want to hold on to them for a bit longer, and pick up new people, rather than shaking them all off, because I'd really like to do bigger rooms on my next tour and so I'll need the old lot.

I am writing this chapter in a very comfortable hotel room in Glasgow in March 2015. There's a wardrobe, a window and some pictures on the walls. A man has just brought me a burger and chips and a glass of wine and I'm really looking forward to not being woken up in the morning by being shouted at to wipe a bottom. I hate it when the postman shouts through the letterbox like that! I have just performed my solo show *An Ungrateful Woman* at the Glasgow Stand, one of the loveliest bespoke comedy clubs in Britain, for the Glasgow Comedy Festival.

As I was leaving, the venue staff told me that I have the nicest, tidiest audience and that although they enjoyed my show, the real stars were the crowd, because they hadn't made any mess, the legends. This meant they didn't have a stressful turnaround to get the room ready for the next show.

In fact, they said that my audience is as nice, if not nicer, than Daniel Kitson's audience! And Daniel Kitson's audience are so nice they look like they've been shipped in from Great Ormond Street Hospital, where they've been volunteering for the last fifty years, without stopping for toilet breaks.

So I think I probably need to build on my current audience, rather than having a cull and starting again. I'm thinking of using the Glasgow Stand's feedback as publicity for my next tour: 'Bridget Christie has the tidiest audience. We would not hesitate to have her back. Especially in the 7.30 p.m. slot, when we have another show on afterwards. She makes what would normally be quite a tight turnaround actually quite enjoyable' (Glasgow Stand).

And then I'll follow it up with 'Unfunny woman' (the *Sun*) or 'As funny as lung cancer' (Twitter). Or 'Bridget Christie deserves to be raped' (Cooked and Bombed – an otherwise perfectly fine and good comedy website for people who genuinely love comedy).

Anyway, the British comedian Robin Ince has been allowed

to work the 'people who read books' market *and* the 'people who like science' market (even though he was replaced by Dara Ó Briain when the 'people who like science' comedy market was being primed for TV, perhaps because he hadn't slept with as many people as Dara). But of course Robin Ince is male, biologically speaking, and so he can do whatever the fuck he likes.

Just to be clear: I am very happy and honoured to be called a feminist comedian. I love women and I love my job. But I will talk about things other than feminism at some point, so I hope people aren't confused if they come to see Bridget Christie the feminist comedian and I don't talk about feminism. Or Bridget Christie. Or comedy. I hope loads of angry feminists don't start asking for refunds. Or for my head on a stick. Oh, they love heads on sticks, the feminists. I forgot to mention that in chapter 1.

Not everyone's cool with calling themselves a feminist though. When I performed *War Donkey* in Edinburgh, a bunch of teenage girls came by mistake and sat in the front row. They were just passing the venue and liked my poster, where I'd superimposed my face on to a donkey's. They had loads of H&M bags each and when I told my joke about misogyny and shiny leggings coming back into fashion, they all took shiny leggings they'd just bought out of their bags. This all came much later on, after I'd won their trust.

They weren't embarrassed at all at the sight of a woman dressed as a donkey pretending to be blown up by an Improvised Incendiary Device (IID). They weren't even embarrassed when I took off my donkey costume to reveal an inflatable ballerina costume underneath. Or when I slowly inflated the costume, while looking at them with a neutral expression on my face without saying anything. They weren't embarrassed then. But they were embarrassed when I said I was a feminist. They sank into their chairs and looked at the floor. I thought they might even get up and leave, they looked so mortified. Even though I had deflated the inflatable ballerina costume by this point and had put my donkey costume back on over the top of my normal clothes.

To these girls, feminism was embarrassing. It was like the diaphragm, Burberry or Myspace. And you know what? I don't blame them at all. I would've been embarrassed at their age. My forty-year-old self would've been my fifteen-year-old self's worst nightmare. They didn't want anything to do with it. The social connotations were too damaging.

But the problem is that misogyny, like those girls' shiny leggings, has made an unexpected comeback. And neither of them do ordinary women any favours. I blame the hyper-sexualisation of our culture, the mainstreaming of porn, organised religion and H&M.

Of course misogyny never went away. All that happened was that misogynists who worked in IT invented better ways for other misogynists to publicly express their hatred and contempt for women, especially for famous women (fair game) or for women who didn't particularly want to be famous but whose jobs meant that a certain amount of media coverage, however unwelcome, was unavoidable (still fair game).

Better still, the misogynists could contact these awful, speaking, achieving women directly and tell them all the different amazing ways in which they would be raping and killing them. Not really. I'm sure these IT geniuses thought Twitter would be a fantastic, safe, effective and instantaneous medium for the 2009 Iranian presidential election protestors to utilise and communicate with the rest of the world, and it was. But it has also facilitated scum. Of this there can be no doubt.

Twitter and Facebook have put twats and bigots and racists and homophobes and transphobes in touch with each other, given them a sense of camaraderie and allowed them to flourish. Before Twitter, a twat had to go to all the trouble of getting their hands on the BNP membership list to be in touch with other twats. Now all they have to do is come up with 140 characters of racist, homophobic, transphobic, misogynistic banter.

So advances in technology, combined with post-feminism, lad culture, ironic sexism, the backlash against political correctness, the martyrdom of publicly shamed bigots, the embarrassment of watching a comedian with genuine passion, the success of UKIP, the hijacking and misrepresentation of the concept of free speech, and the hashtag 'I am not a feminist because...' (where women posted photos of themselves holding signs giving all the reasons they're not feminists, including, 'I am not a feminist because I like taking care of my husband'), have all contributed to the feeling that the women's movement has taken a step backwards.

Feminism never went away. But what exactly is feminism and what's the point of it today? Well, feminism is the belief that women should have equal social, economic and political rights. We don't have these yet, and so that is the point of feminism.

But it's not all bad news, not for British women. According to a recent poll of British sexists in the *Lady*, British women are currently enjoying some of the best sexism in the world, and if there's one thing British sexists know about it's which type of sexism British women enjoy the most. And it's theirs, apparently, and we should all be grateful.

So I'm very grateful I'm allowed to 'hector' people about how damaging and effective gendered language is, how it's designed to demean and undermine what women do, and how it is so widespread and so common and applied all the time to women that we don't even notice it any more.

Gendered language is used everywhere and it takes many different forms. It's so ingrained we don't even notice it. It's used in the media, in courts of law, by critics, judges, police officers, television presenters and journalists.

I had a review once, a very positive review, by a good journalist, so I hate to bring it up, but my review began with the following sentence: 'Feminism has ruined my life!' yelps Bridget Christie, at the beginning of her show. (Definition of yelp: a sharp, shrill bark or cry, as of a dog or turkey). I don't have a very high-pitched voice, and it wasn't a cry. I might have shouted the line. I do have a history of shouting sometimes. But I have never yelped. I don't think a male comedian's review would include the word 'yelp'; that's all I'm saying. I don't think it was deliberate, but by using the world 'yelp' – a word that is more commonly used to describe the noise dogs and turkeys make when their foot is stood on – it demeans what I do.

Likewise, when a female comic talks passionately about issues, she is perceived as 'whingeing' or 'moaning'. A male comic doing the same thing is principled, committed and passionate. Mark Thomas, for example, didn't 'bleat on' about the arms trade. He spoke powerfully, bravely and emotionally about an issue that was important to him. I look forward to a time when a woman's voice, publicly expressing an opinion, isn't compared to that of a sheep or a goat. I don't know what

I'll be doing in five or ten years' time (I'll probably be dead), but for now, there's still plenty to be 'banging on' about. To quote Helen Lewis the journalist, 'the comments on any article about feminism justify feminism'.

So that kind of gendered language is designed to undermine and devalue what women do. But there is another, more sinister way of manipulating language that benefits patriarchal or 'dominant' systems.

Jackson Katz, an American anti-sexist activist, did an extraordinarily brilliant and insightful TED talk about the way in which 'men's problems' have been spun to make them look like 'women's problems' by switching the focus on to victims rather than the perpetrators. He explains how 'men are rendered invisible in large measure in the discourse about issues that are primarily about themselves, especially when it comes to domestic or sexual violence.' He goes on, 'men are largely erased from so much of the conversation about a subject that is centrally about them.' He illustrates on the 'sentence structure level how the way that we use language conspires to keep our attention off men', drawing on the work of feminist linguist Julia Penelope.

He uses the example of the sentence 'John Beat Mary' turning into 'Mary was beaten by John' and then 'Mary was beaten' to 'Mary is a battered woman'. John has been removed from the story completely. Katz argues that we are now 'entirely focused on Mary. Why did she stay with John? Why didn't she leave, etc., etc., etc. Surely the story is WHY did JOHN beat Mary?' This doesn't mean that we should forget the victims, obviously, but we are not going to get to the root of male violence if we don't focus on why so many men beat, rape and kill women.

Domestic violence campaigns are rightly focused on securing or ring-fencing money for shelters and raising awareness, but we also need to focus on the perpetrators; why they do it, and how they are punished. The whole of society suffers from male violence, so the whole of society needs to address it. Education, the law and our judiciary system all have an equal part to play.

Katz argues that gender-based violence is currently seen as a 'women's issue' that 'some good men help out with', and he has some problems with this. In order to deal effectively with gender-based violence, Katz says that a paradigm-shifting perspective is needed, that gender violence needs to be seen for what it is, i.e. a 'men's issue' that 'some good women help out with'. Calling gender violence a women's issue is part of the problem.

I've often thought about this paradox. Feminism is about men, and how they view and treat women. So don't we need to start marketing it that way? Make it for men? Rather than for women? Take women *out* of feminism? How did we all fall for it? They've managed to make something that's about *them* look like it's about *us*. Absolute genius!

I think we need to re-think our approach. Perhaps women's charities and the government should stop focusing so heavily on victims for poster campaigns, but shine a light on the perpetrators instead? Maybe the prospect of having their face on the side of a bus or on a poster above the hand dryer in ladies' toilets would serve as more of a deterrent? I think we should at least try it for a bit, see if it makes any difference.

Anyway, we should all be grateful for British sexism, because, as they said in the *Lady*, it's the good type of sexism.

I hadn't realised this at all, but then in April 2014 Rashida Manjoo, a South African human rights lawyer and the UN Special Rapporteur on violence against women, came to Britain to deliver her report on gender equality in the UK, and in a 4,000-word report she said that the UK had an 'in-your-face, boys' club sexist culture'.

British sexists were absolutely affronted by this insult and they went on Twitter – now a designated sexism conservation area – to defend themselves. They called Manjoo old and ugly and suggested she went back to South Africa where there are far more rapes than there are in Britain, thereby proving her point beautifully. Manjoo then followed up her original report with a much shorter one that simply said, 'See?'

Then a right-wing male columnist, who I don't want to name because I think he'd like that, defended British sexism by saying that Manjoo's report was utter nonsense and that yes, we might be a bit sexist here but it's only light-hearted, cartoon sexism. It's not the proper stuff that they have in other countries. If anyone's oppressed in Britain, it's the men! Then he went on to prove this by saying that when he went to drop his wife off at her yoga class all the women took the piss out of him.

Oh yes, silly Rashida Manjoo, getting the Home Office to organise her itinerary, making it the first UK visit of its kind by an independent expert charged by the UN Human Rights Council to monitor violence against women. She should've just visited a yoga class in an affluent area of London, then she'd have got a much better idea of gender-based violence and female oppression and sexism in the UK.

And anyway, the columnist said, we weren't nearly as bad as the Saudi Arabians. It's not a competition! Also, I'm sorry,

I didn't realise we had to be grateful for British sexism and misogyny because it's worse in other countries. Perhaps next time we're followed home late at night, ladies, we should get little Union Jack flags out of our bags and start waving them around with national pride.

Woohoo! Yay! British sexism! Best sexism in the world! I mean, I am quite intimidated because it's dark and no one's around, but thanks for not stoning me, yeah, guys? I mean, I am still pretty scared because I'm only thirteen and on my way home from school, but at least I'm allowed to go to school, eh, guys? Not like in Nigeria! Hooray! I might start running, actually. Oh, brilliant! There's only nine of you. Phew! That's lucky, isn't it? If I was in India there'd probably be about fifteen or twenty of you, wouldn't there? Those cowardly Indian rapists, going round in gangs! Not like our brave British rapists, working alone or in pairs or for football clubs! Just be grateful, just be grateful... oh, taxi! Thank heavens you arrived then, those men are following me. You are licensed, aren't you? No? Oh dear. I mean hooray! Unlicensed British minicabs! Much safer than travelling in Taliban-controlled areas!

This is a non-argument. The columnist was comparing the UK to totalitarian states, or countries run by despots or religious fanatics, countries with appalling human rights records. The UK's supposed to be a democratic, civilised society. He should be comparing it to other civilised societies. Like the Sealed Knot – the English Civil War re-enactment society – the Royal Horticultural Society, or the Village in *The Prisoner*.

The columnist says his only wish is that feminist activist groups and lefty Special Rapporteurs would just stop whingeing, because British women are amongst the most privileged, liberated women in the world. They can vote, they are well educated, have control over their own assets and their own bladders. But we only have these rights because loads of women whinged and moaned for them in the first place. Sometimes I think these men posing as journalists are just being stupid on purpose to try to drive traffic to their websites.

Either way, here's a quick reminder of how easy British women have it.[19]

> In the UK approximately 100,000 women are raped each year, and just 6 per cent of reported rapes end in a conviction.
>
> Men outnumber women in the UK Parliament by 4:1, and just four of the twenty-three Cabinet members are women.
>
> In the UK women working full-time earn 16 per cent less than men, and two-thirds of low-paid workers are women.
>
> Sexual bullying and harassment are routine in UK schools. Almost a third of girls experience unwanted sexual touching in UK schools, and close to one in three (28 per cent) of sixteen- to eighteen-year-olds say they have seen sexual pictures on mobile phones at school a few times a month or more.

[19] According to UK Feminista as of April 2015.

* * *

Feminists are constantly criticised for tackling everyday sexism, which some people believe is just a bit of harmless fun. Page 3 is just banter with tits. Banter, banter, banter. This argument is also used to excuse racism, homophobia, transphobia and team-building activity weekends in Center Parcs. If I had a pound for every time I heard 'Why are these bloody feminists bothering with Page 3 when there's female genital mutilation and domestic violence and rape for them to sort out?' I'd have £5.63.

The argument is irritating. It's like anti-environmentalists saying, 'Why are you bothering about convincing one person to cycle instead of using their car when there are ice-caps melting and we're running out of oil? You need to concentrate on the big issues, you idiots.' Yes, we do need to sort out the big issues, but that doesn't mean ignoring the less complicated ones.

In case you don't know what Page 3 is, I'll just quickly explain. In 1969, a man called Rupert Murdoch bought the *Sun* newspaper. At the time, there weren't any bare tits in newspapers. Or on the news. Or on *Question Time*. Or *Panorama*. Or on any election coverage. It was almost as if they didn't exist at all.

You had to be a bit more enterprising and determined to see some bare tits back then. You couldn't just be confronted with a pair while trying to find out what the key points to the Chancellor's Budget were. Oh no, you had to go to an art gallery or a porno shop, or bribe a nice lady at the bus stop with your half-eaten Highland Toffee to see some. Or eat loads of nuts in a pub. Or pretend there was something up with your car, find your nearest car mechanic, then feign interest in all the months of the year.

It's not like nowadays. Now we live in a tit ubiquity. There are literally bare boobs everywhere. You can just log on to the World Wide Web for your boob fix now, or nip down the shops for some bread and milk and see a load on a shelf, or drive into a petrol station and see some massive ones on the cover of the *Daily Sport*, next to a pile of reduced CarPlan Blue Star De-icer. Because that's where bare boobs belong. Next to a blue chemical that helps you get ice off your windscreen. Bare boobs are now as omnipresent as God, rats and diesel particles. In fact, there are so many knockers on show now in all sorts of different environments that some days I can't see the deeply unequal society that objectifies, demeans and trivialises women for the tits.

The position on publicly displayed bare boobs is very confusing. For example, the boobs are allowed inside a newspaper that is stocked inside the Houses of Parliament, but they are *not* allowed when they are attached to a breastfeeding woman in Claridge's.

So, Murdoch put tits on Page 3 of the *Sun*. Forty-four years ago. And they've been in the *Sun*, on Page 3, ever since. Not the same pair, obviously.

Then an ace woman called Lucy-Anne Holmes started the No More Page 3 campaign. She thought that a newspaper shouldn't feature young topless women in it, because the message that sends out about women's place in society is a wholly negative one. The tits are out of context. Look, none of us have any problem with tits. Holmes isn't going around art galleries and museums, smashing up all depictions of boobs? She's not a feminist version of ISIS. It's not that breasts exist, it's that they shouldn't exist in a *newspaper*. She's not Oliver

Cromwell. Naked women in newspapers is demeaning and trivialises women. Women's bodies aren't cartoons, or a bit of a laugh. They're not the same as a story about a hamster that lived in a man's hair for forty-five years without anyone noticing, even though it was still going round in its hamster wheel and had learnt how to play tunes on the man's head. Also, I always hated the girls' unrealistic expressions. They're always smiling and chuffed to bits. Can't they sometimes look quizzical or confrontational or melancholic or cold? Anyway, Holmes won. The paper version of the *Sun* no longer shows bare breasts. The *Sun* does continue to exist though, and still employs columnists, so there's still much to do.

Sexism and misogyny are two separate things but from the same family, a bit like garlic and leeks. Their ideology is the same, but one smells a bit stronger than the other. You can be a sexist, i.e. 'I don't recognise you without your apron on, love', and not a misogynist, which is a person who hates women. A misogynistic comment wouldn't be so light-hearted and friendly. It would normally include violence and/or passive-aggressive behaviour, or big ideas. Something like, 'Whoops! I just dropped my wallet. Pick it up, there's a love. You like my wallet, don't you? Why don't you take a tenner out of it and treat yourself to a shoe. *Your kind* love shoes. Oh, and while you're down there, suck on this.'

I guess British sexism is easier to understand than foreign sexism, though, isn't it? For example, I was hissed at by a man the other day. He just stood there hissing at me, like a snake would. I know this isn't technically 'sexism', it's more 'reptile-themed harassment', but I think I can include it in this bit because a) it happened, and b) I don't have anything else about snakes in the book. I had the kids with me too. Anyway, I'm not sure which country he was from, but he was wearing a dishdasha. It must've been a country whose womenfolk fancy snakes. Or men pretending to be snakes. Why else would he be hissing at me? Hissing, as a chat-up line, must have a pretty high hit rate in his country, because it's quite a bold move, isn't it? Hissing at a stranger? Either that or he was a children's entertainer – Mr Snake-o the Amazing Snake Man – and was pimping for business. I did have the kids with me.

I didn't know how to respond to Sir Hiss. I didn't know if the hissing was a question or a statement. He'd been hissing at me for so long that he'd hissed himself into a corner and didn't know how to get out of it. You know what it's like, we've all been there. You keep hissing at someone for ages, raising your eyebrows and looking them up and down, then communication breaks down and no one knows where to go from there. It's very hard to just revert to speaking again. I could see his mind doing overtime, trying to think of a way out of it. I wanted to say to him, 'Come on, mate, stop hissing now. Every time you hiss you're just digging yourself a deeper hole.' But I thought with the language barrier he might misinterpret what I said about holes and then we'd be in even bigger trouble. I could see him thinking, Oh God. I've been hissing at this lady for so long now, I'd better just totally commit to it and pretend to be a snake. Oh, damn, this shirt is clean on today, it's going to get all dirty now, slithering around. I'd better watch out for all the dog shit and spit as well. I've obviously not managed to either intimidate her or seduce her, which is odd because hissing at strange women normally always works.

Anyway, in the end I had to say something. I said, 'What do you want? Why are you hissing at me and raising your eyebrows?

Do I have to be a snake as well? Am I supposed to hiss back at you? Are you going to suddenly shed your skin to reveal another sexist underneath? A British sexist? Look, I don't care where you're from, because I'm not a racist. One of the main reasons I have stayed in London, even though the pollution is killing me, is because of its cultural and ethnic diversity. I want my children to know men like you. Well, not like you, because you're hissing, but you know what I mean. Welcome to my town. But let me give you some advice. If you're going to come over here and be like our decent British sexists, you're going to have to learn the sexist language. I don't know what a hiss means in your country. In Britain, doing reptile noises, in a foreign accent, to a woman with children you don't know, means you're a children's entertainer, not a sexual predator. Now go and listen to those British builders over there for a couple of hours and learn how to do it properly.'

I did a UK tour of *War Donkey* in the autumn of 2012. During a show in a former strip club in the back room of a pub in the northern town of Grimsby (which hadn't been properly cleaned up after it stopped being a strip club and before I performed in it), a drunk man walked between me and the first row of the audience on his way to the men's toilets, getting his penis out of his trousers. I presume he was getting it out early so that it was ready to be urinated out of when he arrived at the urinal, thereby saving valuable drinking time. I don't think his penis asked to watch my show. Anyway, that was one of the highlights of the tour, to be honest.

CHAPTER FIVE

*'Yes, we have the vote, but we can't get ourselves down to
the polling stations because we're crippled with malnutrition,
slaughtered by low self-esteem and irritated by vajazzle adhesive.
Plus we forgot to fill in the Electoral Register form.'*

*B*ridget *Christie Minds the Gap*, my first radio series, was
broadcast in March 2013 on BBC Radio 4. I'd written
and performed seven solo Edinburgh Fringe shows and been
gigging for nine years. I had a very small, very loyal fan base
but wasn't making any money. It was broadcast in the 11 p.m.
'alternative' comedy slot, so I hoped it would cause lots of
arguments between couples listening in just before they went
to bed.

The series was about feminism, so I had weeks of fun thinking about all the different ways people would want to kill me
for talking about it. And that's just other feminists. I thought
other feminists might hate it because it wasn't clever enough,
or serious enough, or didn't solve anything, or because it didn't
fit in with their idea of feminism, or because it didn't cover
the subjects that they themselves would've talked about had
they been commissioned to write a four-part comedy series

about feminism, or because it didn't delve deeply enough into any one subject, or because I didn't represent enough different types of women (this I agree with) or because it had all been said before, and said much more wittily by *Caitlin Moran*. CAITLIN BLOODY MORAN! You know, that other funny feminist. Misogynists would hate it because I was speaking in their kitchen and not even cooking anything. Dogs would hate it because there weren't any dogs in it. Tables would hate it because there wasn't enough stuff about tables in it. I put my one silly joke about Margaret Thatcher turning around in it and the *Telegraph* accused me of 'Thatcher-bashing'. One joke. That's hardly a bash. More of a poke. One joke about Margaret Thatcher turning around. I don't know what the problem is. She's not going to hear it, is she?

I was being predictable, apparently, and because I believe in a woman's right to be treated equally and with respect and I've been on Radio 4, I am an example of the BBC's left-wing bias. 'Why don't these lefty commie feminist comedians make jokes about how left-wing women turn around, like Clare Short, Harriet Harman or Polly Toynbee?' That's the general thing, isn't it? Well, because they didn't make speeches about turning, that's why. There are no famous speeches by left-wing women that involve turning. I wish there were. Thatcher gets enough publicity as it is.

Anyway, it was just one tiny light-hearted joke about women turning. It's not like I ruined Britain for ever or anything. Apparently there are too many left-wing comedians on the UK comedy circuit at the moment. It's absolutely swamped with them. I didn't know this. I thought there were only about six. Then, in November 2014, Nigel Farage, the comedian, finally wrote an article in the *Independent* newspaper about all the left-wing comedians. The country's overrun with them, apparently.

Speaking of 'politicians', I have something to share with you about George Osborne, the Chancellor of the Exchequer. Apparently he only eats off plates with Margaret Thatcher's face on them. His butler said that he insists upon it. He bolts his food really quickly so that he can look at her, according to his estate manager. Then he cries on to the plate and likes to pretend that she's swimming in his fallen tears. That's what his groom said, anyway. His footman said he's drawn a tiny body under her face, wearing a swimming costume and arm bands and holding a cocktail, and he likes to imagine she's on holiday in his plate. His seamstress says it's quite uncomfortable to watch. Then, according to his housekeeper, he licks all his salty tears up, like a dog, with his sad, hot, forked tongue, until it's spotlessly clean. His gillie said it makes him feel a bit sick. Then he dries the plate with a small piece of the Turin Shroud he cut off and stole just for drying his Maggie plates with. The burial cloth of Jesus is the only thing good enough to dry George's Maggie plates with, according to the small boy who goes around lighting all his lamps. His scullery maid said his Maggie plates are never touched by anyone except him. The whole thing is meticulously timed, too, according to his chauffeur. His head gardener timed it once. He said George cries for exactly three minutes, imagines the holiday thing for seven, and then licks for two. The Turin Shroud drying part takes fifty-four seconds. His parlour maid said that he then puts the plate away in a locked cabinet, along with his latex human costume that he wears for work, and the whole thing starts all over again in the morning. Anyway, enough about George Osborne's eating habits.

I thought I needed to head off all the inevitable knee-jerk reactions to my series straight away so I opened the first episode like this live, in front of a confused studio audience of Radio 4 free-ticket types who probably thought they were coming to see Nicholas Parsons anyway:

> Hello and welcome to Bridget Christie
> Minds the Gap! A four-part radio series
> about feminism. 'Oh God,' I can hear the
> listeners saying, 'not another boring Radio
> 4 programme about women.' And that's just
> the women! They've already got Woman's
> Hour. They don't need another 30 minutes
> out of the week's 168 hours of broadcasting.
> Well, it gets better, because not only am I
> a woman on Radio 4 with her own series,
> I'm an uneducated woman with a regional
> accent talking about feminism. And yes,
> this is what you pay your licence fee for,
> Richard Littlejohn. Oh, and if any Islamic
> fundamentalists are listening, don't worry,
> I am not a threat to you. In many ways,
> I'm your ideal woman. I haven't had an
> education and you can't see me!

Both series of Minds the Gap were produced by Alison Vernon-Smith and Alexandra Smith – horrible bitches the pair of them. All they did all day was criticise my outfits and call me fat. Awful women.

Anyway, we decided that each episode would focus on a particular issue and that we'd stick to feminism in Britain today. It's only four 28-minute episodes! There's only so much you can talk about. Episode 1 would be a generic look at feminism in Britain today, then for the following three episodes we'd focus on certain areas. Episode 2 would be about bodies and the objectification of women.

We'd talk about the issues for hours, decide what we thought about them, and then I'd go off and try to make them funny. The difficulty is that in an hour's show or in a twenty-eight-minute episode or in a book, there's only so much you can talk about. You can't cover everything. People will always criticise you for stuff you didn't talk about. The stuff you left out. Like in this book, there's loads of stuff I've not talked about that I wanted to but I can't even list them because someone will say I've missed something off the list of things I'm not even meant to be talking about. I tell you, feminism is a minefield. Is it any wonder more people don't talk about it? And there's another thing. I thought about not writing this book because many women don't have a voice or a platform, especially women from black and minority ethnic groups and immigrant women and transwomen. With a few exceptions they are very rarely asked on to TV debates or news programmes or asked to write columns about British feminism in national newspapers. British feminism in terms of TV and media coverage at least looks very white at the moment. So I felt bad that I might be taking an opportunity away from one of these women, but then I thought that that was ridiculous, and that I couldn't possibly be, because I'd been commissioned to write a funny book, and women aren't funny, no matter how oppressed or silenced they are. So actually, I'm completely clear on that one.

I tried to adopt gender-blind casting in my Radio 4 series, and use a female actress to play the part of a man. If Phyllida

Lloyd can take on the RSC and stage an all-female *Julius Caesar*, I'm damned if I'm going to have Radio 4 force a man upon me. Especially in a comedy show. Everyone knows men aren't funny. But Radio 4 said, 'You can't have a woman, but you can have the next best thing. Fred MacAulay is available for all the recording dates.'

I'd worked with Fred MacAulay in Edinburgh years ago on a show called *Celebrity Autobiography* and it was quite clear to me, and to all the other people in the cast, that he was one of the funniest men from the island of Wyre, Orkney (population: 29). If I couldn't have Fred then I wouldn't have a man in it at all. So it was lucky he was available on the recording dates.

Everything about Fred was perfect for what I needed for the show. He's about five foot nine and often wears a hat. He's well dressed and has very good luggage and luxury stationery. Fred is also a keen walker and has dogs. And all this was a way to offset and balance out all the high-pitched, whinge-ing oestrogen in the show. In hindsight, I think his part was underwritten. And that's not a metaphor for the size of his penis. I regret now not writing more for Fred MacAulay, the funniest man in feminist comedy. I'm sure we'll do something together again. Perhaps we could write a BBC Radio 4 series about all the bad things women do to men? Just for parity.

Comedy is subjective and so is feminism so you literally can't win. You have to liberate yourself from the need to be liked or popular and do what you do. In fact, I even liberated myself from trying to be funny. And just started saying things that I thought. I find misogyny absurd and ludicrous, so that's what I try to focus on.

I write about things that annoy me, so for episode 2 of

series 1 we focused on women's bodies and the objectification of women in the media. At the time, Marks & Spencer had a really annoying 'Every Woman' advert that didn't have different types of women in it. They should've called it their 'Some Women' underwear campaign. Featuring at least two different types of women. Who fall within their very strict and narrow age and size restrictions. The M&S Every Woman campaign offended some of the women in the world, who rightly pointed out that some women were over fifty-seven or a size 18. The hideous freaks! How dare they even exist? Let alone HAVE UNDERWEAR?!

I wasn't offended by the campaign. I just thought it was a bit patronising and cynical. Plus, their strapline was rubbish. 'These are not just any normal real women; these are M&S normal real women.' We're not chickens! They made it sound like they'd reared their own women. 'Our organic, corn-fed women roamed freely on a farm in Gloucestershire. We pay a fair price to our suppliers.'

Also, if you're going to pretend to represent real women, you need to go for it. Show our cellulite and our stretch marks. Show us eating baked beans out of a tin while crying at *One Born Every Minute* and *Call the Midwife*.

Anyway, they scrapped that underwear campaign pretty quickly and replaced it with a new one, featuring the normal, real, womanly UK size 6, 25-year-old supermodel Rosie Huntington-Whiteley, posing on a bed in a push-up bra, reading the latest Fawcett Society newsletter, with her finger between her lips and frowning. That'll teach her to put it in her mouth after she's just dewormed the cat.[20]

---

[20] Have you noticed how much I like cats yet?

There's a difference between being offended and being annoyed. We feminists have to pick our battles wisely, because sometimes, when we say we're offended, what we really mean is that we're just annoyed. For example, Jeremy Clarkson's market-driven misogyny didn't offend me. It annoyed me because it wasn't genuine. He's just trying to get our attention. He might be a punching racist, but I don't actually think he's a sexist. I think he loves women. He just hasn't worked out how to interact with them, or talk about them.

It's important that feminists make the distinction between taking offence and being annoyed. We don't want to muddy the waters when it comes to the real issues. Otherwise we'll end up like the boy who cried Virginia Woolf. You know – Richard Burton.

This is the new fight, women, and one that even Charles Darwin didn't see coming. The Evolution of Cosmetic Surgery, or, as I like to call it, the Descent of Woman.

After I had my second child, I thought my vagina needed a bit of a boost, but I never considered labiaplasty. I know that a lot of women do; in fact, labiaplasty is one of the fastest-growing cosmetic procedures. I'm not judging those women. It is their vagina and they can do whatever they like with it, but I'm just going to offer up my alternative to surgery. I organised a naming ceremony for it. No one came. I burned some geranium oil and we shared a ham and tomato sandwich. I've felt much better about Brian ever since, and every man I've shown Brian to since that naming ceremony (mainly comedy critics and awards panel judges and bookers and promoters and comedy photographers and agents and TV commissioners who work in comedy) has felt better about it too.

Labial surgery is like pollarding a tree. All the birds' nests have gone, and the plastic carrier bags, and the wood pigeons. Vaginas go from being the trees of life to barren sticks. Leave them alone.

I didn't think you could legislate against designer vaginas, although Theresa May has just done exactly that. She has said that surgeons who carry out this procedure could be committing a criminal offence akin with FGM, unless there is a physical or mental health justification.

Women now have more power and money and opportunity than ever before, so how did we end up a generation of women crippled with self-loathing, eating disorders, body dysmorphia and agitated montes pubis? Something has gone badly wrong when 40,000 British women are walking around with industrial-grade silicone, used in mattresses, in their mammaries. Yes, we have the vote, but we can't get ourselves down to the polling stations because we're crippled with malnutrition, slaughtered by low self-esteem and irritated by vajazzle adhesive. Plus, we forgot to fill in the Electoral Register form.

The only thing I've had done is gum surgery. But that was because I was mugged and got my teeth knocked out (*by a man! So we can add teeth-smashing to the list as well*), so they needed a bit of straightening out. It wasn't because I'd succumbed to the relentless bombardment of unrealistic images of women's gums in the media.

I've always been quite sensible about my face and body. I don't go on silly fad diets or punishing exercise routines. I don't starve or shave myself so that I have the expression and body of a pre-op lab rat. And I don't allow myself to be treated like some sort of human dustbin or shape-sorter. I decide what goes into my body, and through which holes.

And I'm a mum now. I have two children. My body doesn't

need to be perfect, it just needs to work. As long as I can pick up my children, throw them into a bin and run away really quickly, that's all that matters. And I can't do that with enormous mattress-filled breasts, a frozen forehead or convalescing labia.

Katie Price (who I like, by the way, I'm just using her as an example of someone who has had lots of cosmetic surgery) has now had her breast size reduced, in order to be 'taken more seriously'. Perhaps I should have breast enlargement, to ensure people don't take me too seriously and criticise me for not having any of the answers. Yes. It might be nice to be judged by a different set of rules for a change. To not be held accountable for every single thing I say all the time, or for things I haven't said because I've been paraphrased or taken out of context or because someone just wants to have a go. Although by all means please do criticise me, it's the only way I'll learn. Don't take that as an invitation though.

So I'm fine with my body. And I'm fine with nudity. I even bought a house from a nudist. What I'm not so comfortable with is up-close nudity with a stranger, like when I was given a lap dance by Peter Stringfellow. Peter Stringfellow didn't personally give me a lap dance. That would've been very awkward. Especially if his mullet got caught in my rosary beads. But he was sat opposite me at the time, eating a steak and laughing at me. It doesn't sound good, does it? It sounds as though as well as paying for a lap dance, I also paid for Peter Stringfellow to watch me having one. Not only that, I made him his tea as well.

Basically, I'd been invited to dinner by Peter Stringfellow, along with some female colleagues from work. I used to work on a gossip column, and you get invited to all sorts of places when you work for a newspaper. Free publicity and all that. I mean, during my time there I'd been inside London's most exclusive private members' clubs, art galleries and celebrities' bins. Peter Stringfellow arranged for us all to have individual lap dances, as a treat at the end of the meal. To be honest with you, after eating a massive spicy fish, I'd have been much happier with some sorbet. (You know Peter Stringfellow, don't you? He's sort of 1980s-looking. Has a mullet, funny teeth and pointy ears. He looks like the result of a one-night stand between Nosferatu and Carol Thatcher.)

I didn't like having a row of women lined up in front of me at the end of my meal. It was like being presented with a human cheeseboard. And none of them were from Gloucester or Cheddar. I said to Peter, 'But I'd normally go for a more mature type, or a blue-veined one.' But you won't find any of those in Stringfellows, I can tell you that! The girls in Stringfellows are so young, they're still milk.

I didn't want a lap dance. I don't like anyone performing just for me, I find it very intimidating. That clown on my fifth birthday was bad enough, and he wasn't even naked. Or on my lap. And Peter Stringfellow wasn't watching me. My parents wouldn't have invited Peter Stringfellow to my fifth birthday party. Even in the 1970s.

But the biggest problem I had with it wasn't even necessarily a feminist or a Catholic issue. Having my own personal lap dance seemed like a waste. I'm from a big, Irish, working-class family. I'm the ninth child. I'm used to sharing things out. We shared everything. Food, shoes, sentences. We even shared our parents.

A whole woman all to myself was too much. We still had pudding and coffee to come. I always leave room for those. I'd had a whole Dover sole. Which still had its head on, by the way. If ever I'm served a fish with its head on, I always cover its eyes with a napkin. (Can I just say here that the food in Stringfellows is absolutely fantastic? Much better than it needs to be. I was expecting chicken nuggets or scampi. Definitely something in a basket. And Slush Puppies. Maybe a toffee apple or some candyfloss for dessert. I ate Dover sole. With a fish knife. I think my napkin had even been ironed. Peter Stringfellow's napkins were better turned out than I was. You don't expect *that* in a lap dancing club, do you? If you ask me, Peter Stringfellow is missing a trick here. He needs to look at his marketing. 'Dancing naked girls, nice fish and ironed napkins.' It would open up the club to a whole new demographic.)

I remember looking at my perfectly folded, bleached white napkin, tucked firmly under my plate, next to a glass of clean water, and suddenly feeling nostalgic for the old NHS, before cuts and outsourcing. The last thing I thought I'd be thinking about, as I sat in Peter Stringfellow's Club, surrounded by vaginas, was the sick and the elderly, waiting in corridors. With no napkins at all. Let alone crisp, white ones. I thought about being in A&E with my children and our feet sticking to the floor, and wondering if I should ask someone for a wet wipe to give it a going over. I remembered noticing the floor in Westfield shopping centre in Shepherd's Bush and thinking how much cleaner the floor was there than it was in some hospitals I'd been in. But I also thought about my love and admiration for the NHS. How they operated on my son when he had a hernia. How well they treated my daughter when she fractured her leg. I thought about my dying mother, and the care she had. I thought about my GP, who spotted I had a rare liver disease that can cause stillbirth, during my second pregnancy, on New Year's Eve, and how my celebrations were ruined because I had to go in for my baby's heartbeat to be monitored as my best friend, the man, writer and comedian Andrew Doyle saw the new year in on his own in a pub. I thought about how I didn't have to pay for all of this care. I thought about healthcare in other countries. I thought about how fundamental the NHS is to the lives and dignity of British people, and how our health system, although flawed and fallible, is the envy of the world. I thought about Nye Bevan. I thought that if only all the immigrants with HIV would stop coming over here to be treated and draining the NHS of vital resources, like Nigel Farage said they were, then the NHS might be as clean and as hygienic as Peter Stringfellows' lap dancing club.

Anyway, I was saying that I always cover a fish's eyes when I'm eating it. But you can't put a napkin over a fish's eyes in a lap dancing club, because that looks like a statement. It looks like you're trying to protect the fish's innocence. It's not really lap dancing club etiquette, to cover a dead fish's eyes. So I spent the whole meal trying to avoid eye contact with my fish, or Michael, as I called him. Then I had to do it all over again with my lap dancer. Who also made me feel guilty, and who I also named Michael. To make it seem more personal, you know. Anyway, you definitely can't put a napkin over a lap dancer's eyes. They don't like it. That's definitely not lap dancing club etiquette. Anyway, I'm sure that Michael's eyes weren't judging me, I was judging myself, but still...too many eyes. That night, all things considered, I think I managed to commit all eight of the seven deadly sins.

Two of the most divisive issues within feminism are the sex industry and Margaret Thatcher. Some feminists admire both, some feminists admire neither, and some admire one or the other. And never the twain shall meet. Perhaps we should put them together. Maybe Maggie should be the face of Rampant Rabbits in Ann Summers. Or of those funny bottom plug things? The strapline could be some sort of joke about buggering up our national assets and now our anuses or something. No, that won't work. Two wrongs don't make a right.

What annoys me about the sex industry, and particularly prostitution, is the way people often talk about it, using tired, old, hoary clichés. 'It's the oldest profession in the world.' Well, it's not. The oldest profession in the world is hunter-gathering, followed by subsistence farming, followed by web design.

The problem is that some feminists believe that the sex industry can be empowering to women and other feminists don't. I can see both sides of the argument. Depending on which feminists I'm out with at the time. Some of them can be very intimidating. When all the feminists meet up for a night out, all we talk about is the sex industry, hegemonic epistemology in feminist discourse, and the Minister for Women and Equalities's shoes.

I personally think that if a woman is of sound mind and has freely chosen to work in the sex industry, then fine. Like Brooke Magnanti, who said this about feminism:

> I genuinely do not get the third-wave
> bluestocking professional feminists in this
> country. Genuinely. I've tried to give a shit
> about maternity leave and who does the
> housework, and all I can come up with is, if
> your job doesn't give you as much time off as
> you want, suck it up or get another job. If your
> partner doesn't do the washing-up, same.

Suck it up? Suck it up? Why don't you s— Oh, hang on.

This is a great example of how complex the issue of the sex industry is within feminism. Luckily, I'm here to explain it to you simply and clearly, just like I did with the Vikings in my radio pitch.

Brooke Magnanti is obviously a feminist. She's a financially independent, strong woman who worked in the sex industry to get her through college because her doctoral studies didn't include enough sex, which she loves. If that's not a feminist I don't know what is. But Brooke won't call herself a feminist, because she feels that the 'British feminist community', whatever that is, slighted her by saying that some areas of the sex industry, like porn, prostitution and strip clubs, are contributing factors in female oppression. End Violence Against Women's position on prostitution is that although they do not condemn women who are involved in it, they argue that it is a patriarchal institution through which women are exploited, marginalised, abused and stereotyped.

So she doesn't want to be part of a community that says that, because she did that, and doesn't think it's all like that. She thinks the sex industry can be empowering, if you follow the manufacturing guidelines properly and do not exceed the stated dose. Now because of that, sexy feminist academics, who don't work in the sex industry, even if they could, or in science, and who don't think that the sex industry empowers women, won't call themselves sex workers, or sexy, because some sex workers, like Brooke Magnanti, who were paid for sex, said that they won't call themselves feminists, so the sexless feminists said, 'Well, if you won't call yourself a feminist, we're not going to call ourselves sexy, because we don't want to be part of the sexy community, not if the sexy community has said that we're not sexists.' And herein lies the problem. It's a complicated, volatile situation, and that's without even bringing Vikings into the equation.

As a political movement, feminism requires, on some level, for feminists to be able to decide and agree on things. My friends and I can't even decide whether to go for a coffee or a tea, let alone whether the sex industry objectifies women or not.

The problem is that, at some point, a political movement needs a leader, and the one thing feminists do not take kindly to is being told what to do, especially by other feminists. It had to be a man, didn't it? Although Jimmy Somerville from Bronski Beat is not enjoying having to wee sitting down. That was the deal. He could be the Head of Women, but we weren't installing a urinal at HQ.

It doesn't make economic sense for a woman to be the leader of the feminists. Leadership takes time and commitment, and after childcare and expenses, it just doesn't add up for a woman to do it. She's better off staying at home and filling out the feminist leadership application form for her husband. Ironically, the only women who are able to put in the time and effort to fight for equal pay and affordable childcare are women with independent wealth and no children.[21]

But maybe a woman shouldn't be in charge of the feminist movement. A very nice male comic said to me once, 'If only more men got involved in feminism, it might do much better.' And when high-profile men join in it can only be a good thing, and we should all be *very grateful*. In fact, one quite shit bloke feminist is much more valuable than, say, a million

---

[21] Read Virginia Woolf's *A Room of One's Own*. It's brilliant on this and funny and, crucially, not very long.

pretty good female ones. Especially in terms of media coverage. A male comedian, for example, simply has to say publicly, 'I don't think we should laugh at women being raped or killed by their partners,' and he is pretty much given the run of the UN. And as much pussy as he wants.

When Jimmy Somerville from Bronski Beat, the current Head of Women, dies, perhaps Russell Brand can take over? Brand's a feminist now, because he had a relationship with a woman he thought was brilliant, which made him think that there might be other brilliant women out there as well and that he should treat women better, which is great. It's really encouraging that more men are getting involved in trying to tackle issues that they are the root cause of. Brand then tweeted a photo of himself holding up a No More Page 3 campaign T-shirt with the words, 'And finally, through the love of a good woman, teenage, sexist me is slain.'

Which suggests that Brand's old-fashioned sexism from his past was down to the rubbish women he'd met previously, rather than it being down to his sexism. Which is a bit insulting to all the women in his life and THE WHOLE OF WOMANKIND. Don't get me wrong, it's good that Russell's trying not to be a sexist now, but we just need to keep it all in perspective. He's not supposed to be a sexist in the first place, remember. He wasn't supposed to brag to a woman's grandfather about her sexual behaviour, or prank call a rape hotline. I just think we need to hesitate before congratulating people for trying to not be something that they're not supposed to be anyway, because it sets the bar for humanity too low. It's like him tweeting a photo of himself next to Denzel Washington with the words, 'And finally, through the talent of a good ethnic actor, teenage, racist me is slain.'

I'm being hard on Russell. He's not one of the seriously bad guys. He does some good stuff, such as raising awareness and media interest for the Focus E15 mothers, whose passionate campaign for social housing came to symbolise the London housing crisis.[22]

And I agree with him on many issues – capitalism, tax evasion, skinny jeans – but Russell's type of sexism, which he once described as being 'a bit like his granny's racism; a bit 1970s and harmless' is still sexism. Even if he tried to distract us by coating his sexism in flowery language and calling it 'a cascading dichotomy of highly nuanced empiricism and the indefatigable needs of me old working-class winky', it would still be sexism. Also he encouraged young people not to vote, which is irresponsible.

Anyway, going back to the empowerment argument, my lap dancer didn't seem very empowered to me. For a start, she had to be picked by me, the 'client', and that made me feel a bit like a cotton plantation owner. And by the way, most lap dancing clubs have a pay-to-play policy. So the girls have to pay to be there, pay for their own clothes and tip bar staff to send rich clients their way, and then try to make the money back on the night. Over the weekend, the fees they have to pay can triple, and clubs are increasing the number of dancers they have in every night to increase their revenue, making the competition for dances even greater. So if they don't get a lap dance, they can actually end up quite a few quid down.

Maybe it might have solved the imbalance of power if I'd

---

[22] Twenty-nine young mothers were evicted from the specialist hostel Focus E15 and told they would have to relocate to Hastings, Birmingham or Manchester, away from their families, friends and support networks, to start all over again. Their story, far from unique, was just the tip of the iceberg in what many social commentators and activists are calling the 'social cleansing of the poor' from the capital.

been put in stocks. And she was allowed to throw my pudding and coffee at my face if I didn't look as if I was enjoying it enough. Or if Peter Stringfellow had a post-lap-dance self-flagellation room installed for all his Catholic/feminist clients. It's worth mentioning here that Peter Stringfellow is one of the coolest celebrities the Tory Party has.

Lap dancing is just one aspect of the sex industry, of course. It also has porn. I'm not a puritan. My problem with porn is just that it's too easily accessible, that children can find it by accident online, and there's too much sex in it. Where's the jeopardy? The suspense? You always know where porn's going to end. In sex. I don't find porn exciting at all. I tell you a porn film I'd like to see: one with no sex in it. That'd put the cat amongst the pigeons.

Personally, I'm excited by roller coasters, civil war re-enactment society events and waterproof jackets. I've got about thirteen rain jackets, in all different colours and styles. If only there were some way of combining porn with all my favourite things.

A survey for the Channel 4 programme *The Sex Education Show vs Pornography* found that 60 per cent of fourteen- to seventeen-year-olds agreed that 'pornography might give boys or girls false ideas about sex', and three in ten said they learnt about sex from porn. A BBC survey of eighteen- to twenty-four-year-old men found that 60 per cent said porn has harmful effects; 25 per cent said they were worried about the amount of porn they were looking at, while almost as many said they were concerned about the type of images they were viewing; and one in five men worry that porn is influencing their behaviour. And in 2007 Ofsted, the UK schools inspectorate, commended the sexually explicit content in lads' mags such as

Nuts, claiming that they offer a 'very positive source of advice and reassurance for many young people' despite 'at times reinforcing sexist attitudes'.

Sex is used to sell everything now, from PVC windows and camping equipment to sex. Sex sells, and women's bodies have been used in advertising since its beginning. Even before advertising began, they used sex to advertise advertising. But the images of women are becoming more and more explicit now. And they're everywhere. Just a normal women's magazine will have a photograph of a semi-naked woman on the front, in a pair of tiny patriotic knickers, bending over and looking shocked. Those magazines should be on the top shelf, not in with *Scooby-Doo* and *Doctor Who* magazines.

I don't want to see women portrayed like that, and I don't want my children to see them either. I want my children to see monsters and zombies. Dead people. Really dead. Not just dead in the eyes. I don't want to have to explain to my son why the poor lady on the front page of the *Sunday Sport* can't afford any pants. He thinks she was involved in a tornado and lost all her clothes.

We're bombarded by these images, often airbrushed images, and it's this commodification of women's bodies as objects, as highly sexualised objects, that contributes to women's poor relationship with their bodies. Ninety per cent of British women feel body-image anxiety. Ninety per cent! Which makes me wonder, who are the other 10 per cent? I'll tell you. Nuns, that's who. There are a growing number of young nuns in this country. They're not religious, they just want out of all this nonsense. And who can blame them? As a feminist, and a Catholic, I've thought about it myself. In fact, it was my husband's suggestion. He didn't exactly suggest I became a nun; rather, he said that living with me was like living in a convent, what with all the crucifixes and habits and huge, framed pictures of all the Popes there have ever been, going up the stairs, in chronological order, and all the rosary beads everywhere, and statues of Jesus and saints, and the altar in the front room, and the stained-glass windscreen on my car, and also because of all the nuns that live with us.

In many respects, now is the best time to be a woman: we've got the vote, we've got marriage rights, and we got rid of Page 3. Although don't say that to the *Sun*, or they'll bring it back again. It was an editorial decision.

So how are we using our freedom and opportunity and money?

Well, we are hoping to cater to everyone's tastes by slicing ourselves up like a Solihull Toby Carvery on pension day. We stick things on, and tuck other bits in, get hair extensions and have other hair removed.

We lie under lamps to be darker, and bleach ourselves to be lighter. We enhance our breasts, then reduce them again because they give us backache.

We freeze our foreheads and fill our lips. Once, we removed our ribs, then put them back in again because fashions changed. We break and bind our feet and paint our faces with mercury. Now we vajazzle our montes pubis and, if we work in musical theatre and have hairy hands, we hajazzle our hands too.

And we can't stop. We'll carry on until we become the human equivalent of a Fuzzy-Felt board. And until all that remains of our true selves is our low self-esteem.[23]

---

[23] As Mary Wollstonecraft wrote, 'indoctrinated from childhood to believe that beauty is woman's scepter, spirit takes the form of their bodies, locked in the gilded cage, only seeks to adorn its prison'. And it was ever thus.

Perhaps we need to have all our money taken away from us again, like in the good old days.

But it's not just young boys who are afraid of hair down there. In 1848, on his wedding night, the artist John Ruskin was so shocked at the sight of his bride's pubic hair that he apparently fainted and spent the rest of the night down the pub. Well you've all heard the joke, John Ruskin, socialist thinker and philanthropist, walks into a bar. The barman says, 'Why the long face?' Anyway, he couldn't consummate it so he had it annulled. His marriage. Not his wife's vagina.

Strangely, Ruskin's Wikipedia entry doesn't mention any of this. He obviously edits it himself like Grant Shapps doesn't. It just says, 'The complex reasons for the non-consummation and ultimate failure of the Ruskin marriage are a matter of continued speculation and debate.' Not amongst feminists they're not. It was her Victorian herb garden, clear and simple.

We think we have control of our bodies because we now have more money to spend on them, but is that control?

Surveys and polls consistently prove that women would rather lose weight than achieve any other goal in life.

Forty thousand women had cosmetic surgery in 2011. This figure does not include 'lunchtime' procedures, such as Botox.

Women had 90 per cent of cosmetic procedures in 2011. The most popular are breast augmentation, eyelids and face/neck lifts.

A third of women would have surgery to change their body shape.

Half of women aged sixteen to twenty-one would consider cosmetic surgery.

Demand for cosmetic vaginal surgery has increased fivefold

in the last ten years; almost all women referred for this have genitalia that fit within a normal/expected range of size.

Thirty per cent of female students aged eighteen to sixty-five would be prepared to die younger for a 'perfect' body; 10 per cent were willing to trade between two and five years of life.

1.6 million people in the UK are estimated to currently suffer from some form of eating disorder; 89 per cent of these are female.

Now those are the facts. But look. I've got two webbed toes on my right foot. Not fully webbed, just half webbed. It's a family thing. I'm from a family of ducks. And we're all very proud of our webbed feet. And yet, with these feet, I have managed to live a full and varied life. I even managed to have two children. Well, ducklings. I call them children. In many ways, not just psychologically, I'm damaged goods. And yet here I am, writing my own book (not with my toes, though. I am using my unwebbed fingers). A woman, a Gloucester woman, with webbed feet, and no formal education, was commissioned to write her own *book* about feminism. My editor didn't know I had webbed feet. She does now.

If we don't start valuing ourselves as more than just a commodity, and basing all our happiness and success on how we look, all the progress we've made will be a complete waste of time. What's the point in holding up a mirror to female oppression if we can't even look in it ourselves?

CHAPTER SIX

*'Women who behave in a certain way are sometimes called
patriarchal collaborators. They are also sometimes referred to as
dicks.'*

In episode 3 of *Minds the Gap*, my radio series from the spring
of 2013, I wanted to talk about how misogyny, over thousands of years, has shaped the way women treat each other in
their day-to-day relationships. Ways that are so complex and
subtle that when you try to explain them to another person,
they think you've gone mad. Over the next few pages, to prove
I am not mad, I will try to get to the bottom of all this using
an Organix herb puff snack, a church pew and a bag of dirty
laundry.

Feminist A is not better than Feminist B because she (or
he! Steady on!) knows who Ariel Levy is. It doesn't matter.
Something as fundamental and as basic as equal rights for
women is for all women. Not just for some of them who've
read more about it. Whatever your feminism is, that is the best
and the right type of feminism for you. You can make it fit in
around your lifestyle. Like exercise and alcohol dependency.

I am not a better feminist than you because I wear Dr

Martens. There isn't a hierarchy, although it does sometimes feel like there is. You don't need a degree in gender studies or feminist theory to grasp its ideology. Intellectual snobbery is just an erudite way of exercising your superiority over others. It's just sneering at a shell suit, cerebrally.

We should be united in our shared goals, not bickering about how we achieve them. We should be celebrating feminism's diverse voices, not mocking them. I was delayed for well over a year on this book, out of fear. Fear that I was doing it the wrong way. Fear of a backlash 'from within'. Fear of scorn from my feminist sisters. Ludicrous, isn't it? How a movement that fights for women's voices to be heard can also be the very thing silencing them. But then I thought, Well, this is my way so it's the right way for me. If I try to write it with the essence of me missing, it won't be a book for her, or for him, or for anyone. It wouldn't even be a book for me. Also, if I marketed it as a 'comedy' book, lots of feminists won't read it anyway.

We don't need to know who everyone is. The women who work for FORWARD in Kenya, educating local communities and trying to eradicate FGM, may not have read Alcoff's *Cultural Feminism versus Post-structuralism: The Identity Crisis in Feminist Theory*. Jenny from Hull, who is staying in a refuge with her three children after finally summoning up the courage to leave her abusive husband, probably won't ring her mum when the kids are down for a chat about hegemonic epistemology in feminist discourse.

Gloria Steinem once said in an interview: 'Listen to the voice inside you and follow that…The primary thing is not that they [young women] know who I am, but that they know who they are.'

I have absolutely no idea why we do the things we do. I'm not a feminist academic. I'm not even a feminist. I'm Bridget Christie. I heard that comedy needed some feminism in it and so I pretended to understand it. And now I'm up to my neck in it. I shouldn't be doing comedy about the complexities of women's minds. I don't even know my own mind.

Normally I just copy stuff off the internet for my material. For this episode I googled 'women explained'. Nothing came up. Then I did a search for 'scholarly articles on the complexities of women's behaviour'. My computer crashed.

But if we work together, we can't fail. Historically, us women haven't been allowed any actual power. We've had to make do with power's sickly cousin, status. And this constant jostling for position in the pecking order brings out the worst in us. It's either that, or God was right all along. We're just evil.

Now it might not sound like it at the moment, but I really am a feminist. There's nothing I like more than a big chunky slice of woman. And I'm always hugely relieved to find one waiting for me, holding a spatula and smiling, when I arrive for my cervical screening test. But we're not going to get anywhere by thinking that *all* women are great, *all* the time, because we're not. Some of those practice nurses can be butchers. Once, the nurse took so long and was so rough, I think her watch is still in there somewhere. And I'd have thought that it was better to find out how the speculum worked *before* inserting it. It's a shame. I used to really look forward to having a smear. But now, because of her, all the fun's gone out of it. The last thing you want to be thinking as your cervix is swept is, Ow! What happened to the sisterhood?!

To me women are beautiful creatures. Capable of incredible grace, dignity, strength, patience and resilience. But we can also be nasty, vindictive, vile, spiteful and cunning. And we can be all of these things, all at the same time. Because we are women. And are brilliant at multitasking. We've had to perfect the art of manipulation and cunning over thousands of years, so that not only do men not know we're doing it, we don't even realise we're doing it ourselves half the time. That's why women make such brilliant spies. Stella Rimington didn't even know she was the Director General of MI5 until the press leaked it.

You would not believe the lengths I have gone to keep certain women away from my fictional husband. And I'm not proud of this. Do you remember when that Icelandic volcano erupted and buggered up everyone's flights? That was me. His ex-girlfriend was coming over from America and she wanted to 'catch up'. So I just jumped up and down a lot until the tectonic plates fragmented. Some of my best friends said that eruption had my name written all over it. I did feel a bit guilty afterwards. Not because I'd been petty and insecure and did something that was beneath me, but because it mucked up President Obama's schedule. Women, we must learn that this type of silly behaviour can have serious consequences.

In the olden days, women didn't have many outlets for their dictatorial tendencies – apart from Catherine the Great, Elizabeth I, Joan of Arc and Boudicca – women really only got to decide on the family's religious beliefs and toilet paper. Traditionally, most of the power we derived came from within the home. That's why we take it so personally when people tell us we're bad mums, or bad wives, and that our wallpaper is 'too busy'. And yes. I am equating the importance of my children with interior design. I've got William Morris wallpaper. And there's nothing busy about it at all. In fact, it could do with getting out a bit more. And twas ever thus.

I wrote this 'Cave' sketch for the radio show to demonstrate what we can be like sometimes:

CAVE NOISES

A CAVE. AGES AND AGES AGO.

FRED: Bridget, would you like me to sound like a Neanderthal man for this sketch?

BRIDGET: Yes please, Fred, that would be great.

FRED: Righto. Erm...woman?

BRIDGET: Yes, Ugg?

FRED: I meant to tell you. A woman has moved into the next cave and she popped in earlier to borrow some flint.

BRIDGET: She wanted flint?

FRED: Yes.

BRIDGET: For herself?

FRED: Yes. I know, I thought it was odd, too.

BRIDGET: Well it certainly changes a few things. Anyway, go on.

FRED: That's it, really.

BRIDGET: That's 'it'? A strange woman comes round to borrow some flint and you think we're going to leave it at that?

FRED: Well, nothing happened. She came in,
           looked around for a bit and then went.

BRIDGET: What did you talk about?

FRED: Nothing really.

BRIDGET: What, you stood here in silence? That's a
           bit odd, isn't it?

FRED: Well, while I was finding the flint, she said
           some things.

BRIDGET: Such as?

FRED: Nothing really. Just chit-chat.

BRIDGET: About?

FRED: Well, she noticed our wall paintings and
           said they were more 'domestic art' than
           'fine art'.

BRIDGET: What does THAT mean? What's art?

FRED: Apparently domestic art is stuff that we're
           happy to have on our walls at home. You
           know, something that we can passively
           consume and not think too deeply about.
           Like a hunting scene, a bison, or something
           by Jack Vettriano.

BRIDGET: Oh, right. And she said all this the first
           time she met you, did she? How long was
           she here for? Where was she standing when

she said it? And what was she wearing? Did
you ask her about our wall paintings or did
she offer it up apropos of nothing? What
else did she say? When she wasn't speaking,
was her mouth slightly open, or completely
shut?

FRED: Erm…I didn't really notice…

BRIDGET: (INTERRUPTING) Did she ask where I
           was? Is she married? When she asked you
           for the flint, how did she say it? And how
           close to you was she standing? Which
           word did she emphasise? Because if it was
           the word 'flint', as in, 'Have you got some
           "flint" I can borrow?' rather than 'Can I
           borrow some flint?' – you're both in BIG
           trouble.

FRED: Oh, she forgot to take the flint, actually.

BRIDGET: She didn't forget the flint, Ugg! She didn't
           come for flint. It's not about flint! Or our
           wall paintings! Oh, she's good. This one's
           real good. She hasn't even met me yet, and
           she's already winning. Well, I'll have to pop
           round and see which animals she's got on
           her walls, won't I? And I'll bring the flint
           that she forgot. I'll say, 'Here's your FLINT.
           I think you must have FORGOTTEN it.'

FRED: I think she did just want some flint. She
           seemed very nice.

BRIDGET: No, Ugg! I know exactly what she was
doing. Because I did the same thing to
Wilma last week.

Now I don't live in a cave,[24] I live in Stoke Newington, which is in north London, obviously. Some of the women there can be quite judgemental. Especially the mothers. They judge you for things like if your baby's got a dummy in its mouth. Or a fag.

This 'competitive parenting' is a great way for us women to get status over one another. One day I was in a shoe shop and my son offered another little boy one of his Organix herby puff things. The boy's mother screamed. I mean, she actually screamed. A proper scream, in a shoe shop. At a tiny, inanimate piece of puffed wheat.

This is what middle-class London mothers do. They scream at the sight of an unidentified snack approaching their child. It was an Organix herby puff. ISIS didn't charge into the shoe shop. The ceiling didn't come down. She wasn't just told the price of the baby Converse. It was an Organix herby puff.

Good evening. The headlines tonight.
A mother is recovering in hospital today
with shock, after her child, who was being
fitted for a pair of baby Converse, was
offered a child's organic snack by another
mother with a regional accent.

---

[24] Although I did nearly buy one once. It was in Worcestershire and it cost £33,000 and had no electricity. This is true.

The snack-providing mother, who has
asked to remain anonymous, said that the
Islington mother totally overreacted,
like a complete nob.

The Health Secretary, Jeremy Hunt,
said that while parents do need to remain
vigilant when giving their children snacks,
they also need to remain calm. He then
added that the abortion limit should be
reduced, before quickly hiding behind a
bush again.

And in other news, the burlesque
performer Dita Von Teese has also
been hiding, but behind some feathers.
And calling it art.

The mother had clearly assumed, because of my accent and because I had sick on my clothes, and because my baby was smoking, that my baby would be eating something that her baby shouldn't. In other words, her child was better than mine. I didn't give my kids crisps when they were little because of the high salt content, but even if I did, that wouldn't necessarily make me a bad mother. Leaving them in Sainsbury's and not realising until I was nearly home doesn't even make me a bad mother.

I didn't hate that woman, I felt sorry for her. When you give up work and have children your world shrinks. No one talks to you, or asks you anything. Trivial things become big things. You have to get status from somewhere. Even if it's from screaming at an Organix herby puff. It might be that, or it might just be that she was a snobby twat. Like I said at the beginning, I don't know. It's complicated.

But this need to control every aspect of our home lives, and hold down a job, and still look great, has meant that we're all totally knackered. Now and then, I think that it might be nice to just die for a bit. Not for long. Just long enough to be able to read the paper in its entirety.

I get so little time to myself these days, I'm forced to take drastic measures. Every Sunday lunchtime, I pretend to have the runs, just so that I can read the church newsletter. When I'm at home I'm shouted at all the time. Can I have something to eat? Where's my shoes? Can you wipe my bottom? I've wet my pants! And that's just when my in-laws are visiting.

Anyway, back to women's relationships with other women, of which I have none. They're really complex and we'll never get to the bottom of why we do things. Some things become power struggles and you have no idea why. See what you think of this one.

When I was eight months pregnant I went to a nativity play, but I had to stand because all the seats were taken. This is what happened.

A MAN: (*quietly*) Oh, here have my seat. And congratulations!

ME: (*quietly*) Oh, thank you. That's really kind of you. Are you sure?

MAN: Yes of course, I insist.

Then the man's wife looked at me in utter disgust, and said to her husband, 'Why did you do that? You've lost your seat now. We came early so we could sit together.'

MAN: She's pregnant. We're at a nativity play!
Do you know the story?

And then she hissed, 'Well, that was very nice of you, dear.'

And she said all this while I was right next to her. It was like I was invisible. But we were so close, in fact, that every time she moved her head, her hair would brush across my face. Which was really annoying. I say hair. She didn't really have any hair. Just loads of snakes. I don't know why she did that – was it because she'd lost control of the chair situation? Or did it go much deeper than that? I think that when women behave like this, it's often because they are insecure or ... (pause) ... because they're just horrible.

But we don't just slight each other in shoe shops and churches. Offices can be an absolute nest of vipers. Because women are relatively new to the workplace, we're still negotiating our way around it. Lifts are especially problematic for us, with all their buttons and numbers and hydraulics and mirrors and bad lighting. Which remind us of our failings. We can't even go up and down inside buildings without being made to feel bad about ourselves.

Once, years and years ago, when I worked for a newspaper, an award-winning female columnist, whose demographic is middle-aged working mums and who often writes about women's issues and feminism, asked me to do her washing. When I say do her washing, she didn't hand me a bottle of Vanish and her husband's soiled undergarments and wish me luck. She gave me a Harrods bag full of washing to take to the dry-cleaner's.

Up until that point I had a good relationship with her. We had similar backgrounds, a similar education, and we both loved looking at photographs of poodles. It was all going really well. Then she asked me to do her washing. I was thirty-three at the time. I'd been working in offices for nearly twenty years and at the end of it all, I was reduced to this, to dealing with the dirty washing of another woman. It made me feel demeaned, and undermined.

Obviously, I said, 'What? I don't think so, do you?'

To be fair, she was very apologetic and embarrassed about asking me, and I thought that would be the end of it. Then she asked me to take it to one of the others girls instead. So I waited until one of them went to the loo, put it by her desk and then ran away. I hadn't solved anything! I'd just moved the problem along the floor a bit. Now – why did she do that? To remind me that we weren't actually equal? I have no idea. If even professional feminists, of which I am one, who make a living out of standing up for the everywoman, are not aware that they themselves are part of the problem, then something's up.

I never did find out what happened to that washing. I like to think that the other woman didn't do it either, and that she, in turn, slid the bag along to the next woman, and then that woman moved it on to the next, and so on and so forth, until eventually the bag ended up back in the female columnist's office. And it's still there. Festering away. Like an electrocuted rat in a fusebox.

Anyway, I don't have a problem with housework, or menial tasks. That wasn't the issue here. On the contrary, I quite enjoy them. Just because I'm a feminist, that doesn't mean that I can't also be domesticated. I love hoovering, washing, baking. Not all the time, obviously, it's really boring, that's why I pay other women to do it for me. But let me tell you, when I do bake, my chocolate roulade brings all the boys to the yard. Not that I want them there. By the way, you can be a feminist and have a cleaner. The cleaning is not the important part of the story. I pay my cleaners to do their job, which is cleaning, but I don't then ask them to do other jobs for me that aren't anything to do with cleaning, like doing my invoices, or book my gigs, or write this book for me. Not when I can just have sex with someone who will do that for me in order to get on in this business.

At least the female columnist didn't sexually manipulate me into doing the laundry, which is another way some women get what they want. Can I just reiterate here that I am a feminist? I believe in equal social, economic and political rights for women, and I don't believe that a woman should be oppressed simply because of her sex. She can be oppressed for other reasons, but not just her sex.

I used to work with a posh girl once, called Emily, who would to come in to work with her arm in a sling because blow-drying her hair the night before made her arm ache. So all the men in the office did her work for her. I just couldn't treat her as an equal after that. Mary Wollstonecraft, author of *A Vindication of the Rights of Woman*, published in 1792, worked in our office as a temp for a bit. It was after working with Emily that she wrote the following:

> Women are so much degraded by mistaken
> notions of female excellence, that I do

> not mean to add a paradox when I assert,
> that this artificial weakness produces a
> propensity to tyrannize, and gives birth
> to cunning, which leads them to play off
> those contemptible infantine airs that
> undermine esteem even whilst they excite
> desire.

I'd never sexually manipulate someone at work to get what I wanted. I'd do it for a charity, though. I made an ex-boyfriend pay me for sex once, but instead of taking his cash, I got him to set up a direct debit for the Fawcett Society. That foot rub has paid for itself in vital campaigning and hustings debates.

But being a coquettish imbecile is not the only option. Some women disregard other women by claiming honorary male status, and they take real pride in it. Once, a female estate agent said this to me as she was trying to sell me a property: 'I don't really have any female friends. I don't like women. The things they say annoy me. And I find their voices incredibly irritating. I'm more of a man's woman, really.' So I said to her, 'Well, I think we're all done here, aren't we? What with me being a woman and all.' Patriarchal collaborator.

When women do achieve real power they are undermined and demeaned by the press and the media. Whether we've won a gold medal, or we're a Cabinet minister, or we're a twice-winning Booker Prize novelist, it's all reduced to our pert bottoms, the heels on our shoes or our reproductive abilities.

And the media loves nothing more than inventing fictitious arguments between us to perpetuate the myths that this is what women are like, that we shouldn't be in a position of influence, and that there are only two types of women. Women with opinions, who are evil and dangerous, like Hilary Mantel, i.e. 'witches', and nice women who aren't allowed opinions, like Kate Middleton. Mantel's won the Booker Prize. Twice. She's a Dame.

Mantel's 'Royal Bodies' lecture at the British Museum, for the *London Review of Books*, explored the commodification of royalty across the centuries. Instead she was accused of launching an 'astonishing and venomous attack' on Kate Middleton, with the *Daily Mail* using the headline 'A PLASTIC PRINCESS DESIGNED TO BREED'.

It would be nice to think that all this came from men, but it doesn't. And women's magazines are full of nasty, vicious, facile criticism (I don't know why I write all these hateful pieces for them.) And yet these magazines are written by women, and read by women.

We don't often focus on how we treat each other, because we are still treated so badly by men. But we need to. My worst critics have all been women. The things they have criticised me for, and accused me of, have been the very worst things I've ever read about myself. Ever.

I've already said that I want this book to be a positive book and that I'm not really interested in dissing other women, because it's just a bit reductive, especially when there are so many rapists and wife beaters and bookshop farters for us to focus our energies on.

But not all men are oppressors and not all women are saviours. Society is made up of individuals. Some of us are shit and think shit things, and some of us are all right. And until Ipsos MORI conducts a poll of racists, homophobes, transphobes and misogynists, to find out what the gender split is, we'll just have to assume that there are an equal amount of pricks on both sides.

Although an idiotic survey by Ticketmaster in 2013 found that men were more likely to laugh at jokes 'based on race' than women were. Jokes based on race? What does that mean? Does it mean men were more likely to laugh at racist jokes? Or laugh at racists? I think Ticketmaster needs to go back and ask the question again, just to be clear. It's quite an important distinction to make.

So we can't say for sure whether the average woman is fairer than the average man. We just don't have those figures. What we *do* know, though, is that women haven't prevented men from having an education, voting, being a writer on *The Odd Couple*, wearing trousers to church, running the marathon, being in the Olympics, standing for Parliament, having a credit card, becoming an astronaut, being in the military or being admitted to private members' clubs.[25]

We do know that UKIP is less popular amongst women voters, but that could just be down to the fact that there aren't any attractive UKIP MPs for us slags to try to hump. Not now they've fucked off to Bongo Bongo Land with an owl and a jar of honey to look at some trees. And we know that David Cameron isn't popular with women voters. But that's just because they're worried that if they go to the pub with him to talk policy, he'll just drive off when they're in the toilet. And we know that Ed Miliband isn't popular with women because his brother's better-looking. And that Nick Clegg isn't popular with women because he didn't kick Lord

---

[25] This is all true. I promise you. Look it up!.

Rennard out after it was found that there was no basis for accusing him of leching and perving over female Lib Dem Party members.

But this kind of power is not actual power, but false power, because it involves either manipulating men, or seducing men, or the acceptance of men. When a woman has *real* power, men don't come into it at all! There are no men working in the women's real power shop. There are no men in portraits of powerful women. If half the population suddenly died out (the male half, obviously), these women would still have their power. Their power comes from a whole range of different places: from their expertise, their talent, their insight, or bravery or knowledge. Or it can come simply from respect. In matriarchal societies (of which there are about six), women are powerful simply because that culture decided they were. This is also fine. But a truly powerful woman is never in the debt of either 'the Man' or a man.

Of course, until fairly recently women and girls weren't afforded any of the freedoms that would give them the tools with which to gain real power – a formal education, reproductive rights, control over their assets or property – or instructions on plugs – and in many parts of the world women still don't have those basic rights, but many of us do. It seems a shame to waste them.

I'd like young women to feel empowered and liberated as a result of their own decisions, actions and achievements. I'd love it if, when women talk of empowerment and liberation, it doesn't involve them having sexual or emotional control over men. If the woman's power derives from something that doesn't involve men in any way, then she has real power. If her power is entirely dependent on the reaction, manipulation, acceptance or seduction of men, then she has fake power. It will blow down in the wind. What if he suddenly changes his mind? I'll give you some examples of women I consider truly powerful. You can pick your own. Remember – we are not the same.

Powerful women

Aung San Suu Kyi, Burmese opposition politician (no men or sex involved – just politics)

Lynsey Addario, photojournalist (no men or sex involved – just photos)

Marie Curie, physicist and chemist (no men or sex involved, just pioneering research on radioactivity).

Dame Sally Davies, Chief Medical Officer for England (no men or sex involved – just medicine and compassion)

Mary Beard. Classical scholar (no men or sex involved – just history and facts and ideas)

Ellen Johnson Sirleaf, Liberian President (no men or sex involved – just debt relief and war-crime investigations)

Janet Yellen, Chair of the Federal Reserve (no men or sex involved – just loads of money and decisions)

Not powerful

Most women in fiction (men and sex generally involved)

Kim Kardashian (okay, that is technically dissing another woman, which I promised I wouldn't do, but come on, the oiled-up ass thing was completely ridiculous. How is oiled-up ass powerful? It's not powerful, it's slippery, is what it is. Kim is an easy target and I didn't really want to use her as an example of a woman with fake power, but I had to, because she is considered powerful by many people and tried to 'break the internet' by oiling-up her ass, which is funny).

When I see a beautiful woman, who is respected and revered for her beauty ALONE, and for NO OTHER REASON, I see a beautiful woman who I can admire, but I don't see a powerful woman, because her beauty will fade, and with it, her power. But true power should fade when you're democratically unelected, or sacked, or you run out of film or ideas, not when your tits sag.

I'm not saying we shouldn't celebrate beauty. Of course we should. The world needs beauty. Beautifying ourselves is fun and makes us feel better. Beauty is great! Barbara Castle, she of the Equal Pay Act 1971, refused to be photographed without her make-up on, saying, 'I care about my appearance and I think that all women in public life should, for the fun of it, for their own satisfaction.' But she never used her sex as a political prop: 'I have never consciously exploited that fact that I am a woman. I wouldn't dare try that even if I knew how to. I have too much respect for my male colleagues to think they would be particularly impressed.' So of course we're allowed to look nice. All I'm saying is that we shouldn't rely SOLELY on our beauty to give us our sense of worth or purpose. We should judge ourselves by our characters and as valuable contributors to society, because once we get past forty, and fifty, and sixty and seventy, and beyond, we're going to need something other than our reflections and the adoration of men to make us feel powerful.

It's not just men who make women feel as though beauty is power. Women do it to each other all the time. Women who behave like this are sometimes called patriarchal collaborators. They are also sometimes referred to as dicks.

Think of it this way. One in four women will be affected by domestic violence in their lifetime. Do we really need to laugh at her fat ankles as well? Or glaze over when talking to a woman at a party and unglaze when a man comes over? Or save our best ideas for when in the company of men? Because we're *not* worth it.

One in three women will be sexually assaulted. Do we really need to pull the ladder up behind us when we reach the top of our industry? Or twirl our hair around our fingers and stand with our feet pointing inwards when we speak to someone else's boyfriend or husband, then stop twirling our hair and reposition our feet when he goes to get a drink? Even though his partner is looking at us with both of her eyebrows raised and wearing a T-shirt saying, 'He doesn't know what you're up to, mate, but I do, so stop it.

One in four women will be raped. Do we really need to cultivate the thinking that other women should toughen up and stop being victims? Or not laugh at another woman's joke and then laugh so much we develop emphysema when a man repeats that exact joke immediately afterwards? Or not support other women? In any way? Or value their input? On anything?

I once went on a date, and my date's ex-girlfriend came

along and he *massaged her bare feet*. So just to make that clear for you, in case you were a bit confused. I went on a first date with a man. The man's ex-girlfriend came along. He massaged her feet. It was when we were sitting on a picnic bench outside a pub (opposite each other; she sat next to him). She took her shoes off and said her feet ached and asked him to massage them. He did. At no point did either of them offer to massage my feet (which were inside my shoes and socks and on the floor, in case you were wondering). No one was paying my feet, or the rest of me for that matter, any attention whatsoever. It was another one of those situations where you think you've gone mad. Foot Woman wanted me to know that if she wanted to, she could *take this man and his hands from me*, but I didn't want him anyway. So the power she thought she had, she didn't have anyway.

If you feel threatened by a female colleague at work, because she's pretty, or popular, or waves loaded firearms about, try to remember that you're both being paid less than your male colleagues for doing the same job. If that doesn't provoke solidarity, I don't know what will.

And finally, if you are a female politician, please try to tackle women's issues, or even just highlight them a bit. And no, Nadine Dorries, that doesn't mean comparing the investigation into your personal expenses to the persecution of the suffragettes.

All women have encountered the Screaming Puff Lady, Medusa the Chairwoman or Madam Dirty Laundry at some point in their lives, and if you haven't, that's because you are those women. And you need to get your bitchy nose out of my book. Not really! Thanks for buying it. Tell all your bitchy mates!

And it's no good just half of us treating each other better. As a bitchy woman, I know we'll never stop being petty and vindictive and cruel about other women, because at the end of the day, it's just too much fun, but maybe we could try cutting back a bit, just until we've broken the back of gender-based violence. And that might be a while yet.

In the words of Wollstonecraft, 'In order for equality to take place, society must change its thinking.' Half of that society is us.

Feminism has had a great couple of years in terms of media coverage, yet still for a lot of teenage girls feminism is like their parents turning up at a nightclub. Ridiculous, embarrassing and likely to get itself locked in a cubicle.

Many people still believe that feminists are all a bunch of butch, humourless, man-hating lesbians who stomp around academia in their DMs, using words like 'intersectionality' and drawing trousers on ladies' toilet signs. Remember, from chapter 1?

The only famous feminist they know about is Millie Tant from *Viz*, who has arguably done more to put feminism on the map than Germaine Greer. How many men have read *The Female Eunuch*? And how many men have read *Viz*? Exactly.

You don't need to be ashamed to pronounce yourself a feminist. There is never any need or justification for someone to begin a sentence with the caveat 'I am not a feminist, but...', because a feminist is not the same as being a racist. Whatever follows that is going to be something in support of women, or women's rights. You don't have to flag it up because you're afraid you're going to be socially ostracised or outcast from your social group. You never have to say: 'I am not a feminist, but...that stoning's a bit much, isn't it?' I'm not a feminist, but...that rape in Delhi was absolutely appalling.' Or 'I'm not a feminist, but...I can't believe the Taliban shot a little girl just because she wanted to go to school.'

I think we need to change the debate on this. So the question is not 'Are you a feminist?' but 'Are you *not* a feminist?' Being a feminist should be our default position. A given.

Maybe that's where we're going wrong. Maybe we need to approach it in a different way. There are so many anti-feminists out there, many of them financially independent, contraceptive-taking, voting, educated women, that perhaps we should stop fighting for more women's rights, and start fighting for less of them. Maybe we should try to have all the hard-won rights taken from us again. Perhaps that might end the debate once and for all. Obviously, our aim would still be gender equality, so men wouldn't have any rights either. It'd be like living in Iran. Perhaps then everyone would stop being so stupid and reactionary about feminism.

Part of the problem is that the word 'feminist' has become so stigmatised over the last twenty years that it's almost become a social taboo to admit to being one. This is partly down to the media, who try to discredit feminism by coming up with silly insults for feminists.

The insults are never intelligent or insightful critiques, because you can't intelligently criticise a movement whose only objective is gender equality. Not without looking like an utter tool. They are always petty insults about a particular feminist or how irrelevant certain campaigns are compared to others. You're basically trying to argue against reason, fairness, logic and fact, so people have to resort to petty insults. The suffragettes were called 'unnatural and unladylike'. I can't imagine that dampened their morale much.

EMILY WILDING DAVISON: Excuse me, Emmeline, I'm sorry to interrupt you, but I have some very bad news for the campaign.

EMMELINE PANKHURST: What is it, Emily?

EMILY: I don't really know how to tell you, Emmeline. Perhaps you should sit down.

EMMELINE: No, it's okay, I'll stand, like a man, thank you, Emily.

EMILY: The *Daily Mail* have said we're…they've called us…

EMMELINE: Come on, Emily, spit it out.

EMILY: They've said we're…un… un…unladylike (*bursts into tears*).

EMMELINE: (*screams*) Oh! Oh no! Oh, how awful! Oh, I'd hate to be thought of as unladylike. Oh dear. Perhaps we should just forget about the vote. We had a go, but I don't think it's worth it, actually. Not if men who write for the *Daily Mail* think we're unladylike.

The stereotype of a feminist is a woman devoid of humour and sexuality. But I'm not, and neither are any of my feminist friends. We're only devoid of humour and sexuality when we're told to cheer up or to have sex.

I wasn't aware feminism had to be funny, anyway. Why do people keep going on about all these 'humourless feminists' all the time? When did having a sense of humour and being up for sex all the time become an integral part of the fight for equality?

People don't say, 'Oh, Amnesty International. Aren't they marvellous? Protecting human rights worldwide. They really are great. They could protect humans in a funnier way, though. They just need to gag it up a bit, that's all, then maybe lots of people wouldn't find human rights organisations so alienating. And more men might join in.'

Or, 'This Martin Luther King fellow looks promising. He has some very good ideas. He's incredibly charismatic. Shame his "I Have a Dream" speech wasn't funny. I mean, ideologically it was sound enough, and he made some good points. It was even quite moving and poetic in parts, but there just weren't enough jokes in it, I'm afraid. The first five minutes got nothing at all. No. Unfunny civil rights is not for me. I think I'll carry on being a racist.'

Mary Wollstonecraft said, 'I do not wish women to have power over men, but over themselves.' We don't want more than men, we just want the same.

Incredibly, lots of women still reject feminism, even though it is personally responsible for many of those women's own rights, because they don't really understand what it means. These women don't feel that feminism has anything to do with them. They neither need it nor want it. They hate it for destabilising the status quo and for challenging 'the natural order of things'. They hate it because they think it means perceiving women as victims and they don't identify themselves as victims.

I know that upholding feminist beliefs is a luxury, and that many women around the world don't have this freedom and I do understand why many women might reject feminism, and I don't judge them. Many women reject feminism and all it stands for, they hate it because they just want to get through life with the least amount of trouble.

This is from Andrea Dworkin's *Right-Wing Women:*

> From father's house to husband's house to
> a grave that still might not be her own,
> a woman acquiesces to male authority
> in order to gain some protection from
> male violence. She conforms, in order
> to be as safe as she can be. Sometimes it
> is a lethargic conformity, in which case
> male demands slowly close in on her, as
> if she were a character buried alive in an
> Edgar Allan Poe story. Sometimes it is a
> militant conformity. She will save herself
> by proving that she is loyal, obedient,
> useful, even fanatic in the service of the
> men around her. She is the happy hooker,
> the happy homemaker, the exemplary
> Christian, the pure academic, the perfect
> comrade, the terrorist par excellence.

But for women who are free and who reject it because they don't like the name of it or because they think it's a club with rules, it really isn't. They can have their own version of feminism. In the words of Jessica Valenti, 'Feminism isn't a monolith. It's a constantly shifting discourse.' But it's good to remember that women would not have the vote without feminism. Without feminism, women would not be educated, have sexual freedom, reproductive rights or control over their own assets, bodies or destinies. We would not have access to birth control without feminism, and we could be fired from our jobs for becoming pregnant. If we were raped, our father would be paid damages, because his 'property' had been damaged. We would not be allowed to sit on a jury.

That is why I identify as a feminist. I also identify as a feminist for marketing purposes.

CHAPTER SEVEN

'Because I thought I'd be taken more seriously if I pretended to be a man, I had dressed as King Charles II. I wondered about wearing the robe all the time, perhaps even during childbirth as well.'

Were it not for the Edinburgh Festival Fringe and a man called Tommy Sheppard, I wouldn't have worked out how to talk about feminism in comedy. Or how to talk about farts. Or how to talk. Or fart. I'd still be forcing people to watch me gurning, pretending to be various chemical compositions or viruses, and doing impressions of how TV historians walk. Probably.

So if there're any furious sexists out there still reading this book (which you shouldn't be, as the cover clearly states that this book is not for you) then you can blame Tommy Sheppard. The Northern Irish former Scottish Labour councillor and candidate, and now SNP parliamentary candidate, owner of the Stand Comedy Clubs. I don't mean Tommy Shepherd (aka Speed), a fictional character, superhero and member of Marvel's Young Avengers. He did not facilitate feminist-based comedy at the Edinburgh Festival Fringe.

Tommy Sheppard has given me a venue at the Edinburgh

Stand since 2010, when I did my *A Ant* show. Before then, I was making a financial loss every year by taking a show to the Fringe, but the Stand's deals are fair and favour the acts in a festival where most performers actually lose thousands of pounds, though no one seems to believe this.

I'm lucky enough to live in London, the stand-up capital of the world. If you want to be a stand-up, or to watch stand-up, you come here. There are so many comedy gigs in London that the comedy website Chortle has to list them by area (north, south, east, west or central London). In New York, acts pay for stage time to try to get parts in sitcoms. In London stand-ups want to be stand-ups, and acts from other countries come to work here because they admit it is the best stand-up comedy city in the world.

Whether you're a physical clown who doesn't speak (Holly Burn), a ventriloquist (Nina Conti), a sketch/improv group (Austentatious), a character comedian (Jo Neary), a musical act (Isy Suttie), a double act (Anna & Katy), a political act (Josie Long), or a socio-politico-feminist act (Kate Smurthwaite), there is a gig you can do.

But this diversity of comedy acts and voices from different backgrounds and creeds and nationalities will start to diminish as London house prices and rents continue to rocket. The sums just won't add up, and as writers from ordinary backgrounds are being priced out of the capital, so too will their audiences.

And it's the same in the Edinburgh Fringe. Most stand-ups will consider going to the Edinburgh Fringe at some point. I don't think it's presumptuous to say that. Whether to perform in a showcase, or to do their own solo show, they will want to go. And it's not just to create long-form arty-farty stand-up shows with narratives and through lines and messages and artistic integrity, beloved only by broadsheets. Jim Davidson, Jimmy Carr and Jeremy Paxman have all taken shows to the Edinburgh Fringe as well.

The Fringe is seen by some comics as a trade fair, a place to be spotted for other things. A route to fame, and when that fame is achieved, Edinburgh is nothing but some Scottish offal to be scraped off their shoe. To others, it's where they get better. It's where they work out what they're doing, what they want to do, and what they DON'T want to do. It's where they take risks and fail.

In the last few years, it's ended up being the place where you definitely do not experiment. Sky-rocketing rents for accommodation and for venues combined with the sheer volume of acts taking shows to the fringe now has meant that we're all competing for space and coverage against impossible financial odds.

At the Stand, if your show doesn't sell a single ticket, all month, the cost of your venue is absorbed by the Stand. So you might not make any money, but you won't lose anything either. Of course you still have all your other costs, like rent and travel and advertising and PR and tour posters and publicity photographs and haemorrhoid cream and beta blockers, which you have to pay for. Luckily I'm having sex with ticket inspectors, landlords, chemists, photographers, critics and producers and tour promoters and journalists and awards judges and Nica Burns, the director of the Foster's Awards, to get on in this business. But you won't incur extortionate venue hire costs as well. In fact, Tommy Sheppard at the Stand insists that comedians who play at his venue DON'T have sex with him in order to get on in this business.

My Edinburgh shows weren't generating any work for me

outside of Edinburgh. None of my ideas were being developed and the shows didn't tour. I've always talked about things that interested me, but until that thing was feminism, the shows didn't generate much interest. Plus they were a bit shit, if I'm honest. Apart from my *Charles II* shows. I still quite like those. I don't feel bad about being shit for a long time, because if I'd started good, I wouldn't have worked out how to be better. I wouldn't know how to deal with bad gigs, or hecklers or the feelings of self-loathing that come after hecklers and bad gigs.

Having said that I don't think I've worked out the best way of delivering my material yet. I'm still figuring it out. I used to have more ideas and concepts in my shows. There were more things to look at. It wasn't just me, with a microphone, droning on for an hour. Or maybe I should just write better material. I recreated the Ascension of Christ into heaven once, using a fishing rod and a tiny plastic Jesus. I did it at the end of my show about Catholicism. I was given Catholicism by my parents, who I love. But it's like being given a three-legged dog. I'd rather have gone to the dogs' home and picked a dog myself, which had four legs, but we've made eye contact now. I can't just leave it there. I'm a Catholic: the guilt of it would kill me. All I will say is that people found Catholicism as awkward and embarrassing and alienating to listen to as they did feminism. If not more so.

I know what you're thinking: 'What??!!! Catholic? *But she's a feminist?!*' Yes, you can be part of an organised religion and a feminist. But it's complicated. It just takes a certain amount of ethical and moral accounting and a certain amount of wilful ignorance. It doesn't make you a hypocrite. It just means you're trying to make everything work. It's like I was saying earlier. We're all individuals who can hold contrasting belief systems that would appear to contradict one another. For example, not all scientists are atheists and some feminists are Muslim or Christian. Even though some feminists tell them they can't possibly be. Anyway, at the end of my show about being a Catholic (in which I tried and failed to clarify my complex and admittedly contradictory position), I'd kill the lights and go to a blackout. Before the show started and the audience were seated, I had already set and hidden a tiny plastic Jesus at the back of the stage on the floor. I normally concealed him behind a small black box. People don't notice something like a small black box on the floor at the back of the stage, and if they do, they just assume it's some kind of safety thing covering a plug. Not very many audience members would think there was a tiny plastic Jesus attached to a fishing line behind it. Or a tiny plastic feminist.

So it worked like this: I'd attached the end of a fishing line to the tiny plastic Jesus and then fed the line along the stage, up the back wall and then along the ceiling, threading it through hooks along the way. The audience couldn't see the line because it was so thin and far away. The rod that I used to reel Jesus up to the ceiling was normally hidden just behind the curtain. Or at the side of the stage. To be honest, even if they noticed the rod, I don't think they've have worked out what I was going to do with it.

I then gave an audience member a powerful torch, and instructed them to follow the tiny plastic Jesus as it ascended to the ceiling, which, although 'lo-fi' sounding, actually worked a treat. I had also attached a tiny wooden wardrobe to the tiny Jesus, which, I told the audience, was a gift he'd made for his father. Just to prove to him that his carpentry apprenticeship and time on earth had all been worth it.

On the ceiling, I'd rigged up a small piece of cloth, which Jesus then disappeared behind when he reached the top. I thought about using cotton wool balls instead of cloth, to make it look like he went behind some clouds, but actually, using a little piece of cloth gave it a duality of meaning, an extra dimension, a finality – for both Jesus and me. For Jesus, he'd ascended into heaven. Curtains down. End of the first act. Jesus, for a lot of Christians, is currently in the interval. They're all waiting for the second act. For the Second Coming. I hope they're not still waiting in Norwich Arts Centre, where I did the show in February 2012.

By the way, I was nearly arrested at Belfast airport when I did the show there. They searched my suitcase and told me I couldn't board the plane with fishing wire (which could be used to garrotte someone with), and they weren't too chuffed when I explained what the little Jesus and fishing rod were. Anyway, once I'd proved to them that I was a comedian, by telling them some long-winded, confusing jokes about gravity and sausage rolls, they let me off.

I returned to Belfast three years later, as a feminist, on International Women's Day weekend, to perform at a pro-choice fund-raiser organised by Mark Thomas for an extraordinary and inspiring woman called Dawn Purvis and the Belfast branch of Alliance for Choice, who campaign for abortion rights for women. Also on the bill were Mark, obviously, Robin Ince, Josie Long and Gemma Hutton, who were all the best that I had ever seen them. In fact, it was one of the few times in my career when I genuinely felt proud of myself. I was so proud to be on a bill with this bunch of genius clowns. I'd given up travelling with loads of props by then, which is probably for the best, as I don't know how the customs officials at Belfast would've responded to finding a tiny plastic baby attached to a fishing rod. Especially if they also knew I was a feminist over there supporting pro-choice activists.

Just to reiterate, because I know you'll be thinking, What? A Catholic did a fund-raiser for a pro-choice alliance?! Yes. Yes, I did. I like Jesus and women having control over their own bodies. That's my feminism.

What do you think about THAT?!

Anyway, what I'm trying to get at is that although some parts of my shows were interesting and original, they didn't appeal to a mass audience. Or even a minor one. If I ran a provincial arts theatre that was about to lose all its funding, for example, and the local council was planning a visit to decide whether culture and the arts had any place in communities or society, I wouldn't reveal me from a curtain and say 'Ta-da!' I'd get someone off the telly in.

So I had lots of unsuccessful Edinburgh shows, and went on depressing tours. I talked about Catholicism; about working at the *Daily Mail*; I did characters of the dead kings and Dan Brown and Louise Mensch and Nick Clegg. Nothing really took off, creatively or financially, until I talked about things that mattered to me, but I wouldn't have been able to talk about things that mattered to me before, because I didn't have the confidence.

In 2006 I did my first ever debut solo show, *The Cheese Roll*. But cheese didn't really matter to me. It wasn't an hour of comedy about cheese rolls that you eat, by the way; even I wouldn't attempt that. Not unless I dressed up as a piece of cheese and the whole thing was about the objectification of cheese in advertising. It was about Gloucestershire's annual cheese-rolling competition. I wasn't writing about feminism back in 2006, because a man hadn't farted yet. I was mainly writing about people chasing cheese down a really steep hill, which is an event that genuinely happens every year in my home county. I suppose I could've written about the cheese roll from a feminist perspective. I suppose I could've talked about how unfair the women's race is, about how women competitors have to hurl themselves down the hill (which is so steep it has the same gradient as a cliff), wearing tight skirts and high heels, holding parasols, or umbrellas if it's raining, doing the washing-up, and giving male spectators hand jobs on the way down, thus putting themselves at a distinct disadvantage.

They're obviously going to have slower race times than the men if they have to incorporate all that into their downward trajectory. The men, on the other hand, are allowed to just somersault their way down the hill, half pissed and wearing gorilla costumes.

Now before someone tells me to check my cheese-chasing privilege, I do realise that the women's race at Gloucestershire's annual cheese-rolling competition is a far cry from multiple interlocking oppressions.[26] I know that. I do know that. But I've been told to keep it in by my editor, who is going through this book line by line and taking out anything too substantial in order to keep the book light. I keep trying to trick her, and I've snuck a few serious bits in, but the other day she just went nuts. She took out the word 'androcentric'.

'Pretend you're writing *The Ladybird Book of Feminism*! It's

---

[26] Intersectionality is the study of intersections between forms or systems of oppression, domination or discrimination.

going to be in the Humour section, remember. If you're going to write light-hearted witticisms about things that fall outside of your jurisdiction then I'd leave all that for the second or third book that I'm not offering you. You can't possibly talk about all women's experiences and you don't represent all women. You don't even represent yourself, although you did for a few years when you were between agents, so just concentrate on farts and cheese for this first book and don't worry about all the stuff you've left out and issues that deserve their own chapters.'

'So I can't win then?' I asked my editor.

'No, you literally can't,' she said. 'Just go on holiday when the book comes out and don't read anything.'

'Oh, OK,' I said. 'Do you say that to everyone?'

'No. Just to you and Russell Brand,' she said.

The cheese roll takes place every year on the late May bank holiday in Gloucester, where I grew up. I have Irish Catholic parents and I'm the youngest of nine children. I didn't choose Catholicism, by the way, I inherited it, as I said, along with alcoholism, two webbed toes on my right foot, and a large collection of Pope memorabilia, all of which I have already passed on to my son.

The webbed toes are a Christie thing. I know I keep going on about them. It affects the second and third toes on the right foot. A lot of my siblings have these webbed toes. I hope they don't mind me mentioning this. Sometimes you just have to do the right thing. I owe it to other women with webbed toes to speak out. It's nothing to be ashamed of, and my sisters are no less beautiful because they have webbed toes. We're like an amphibious version of the Nolans. Who can't sing.

I did a gig recently and mentioned I was a Catholic and

my webbed toes and a drunk man shouted out, 'Well, I'm an atheist – take your sock off and prove it.'

I said to him, 'I said I was a Catholic. If you want me to take my sock off, you'll have to marry me first. And even then I can't guarantee anything. In fact, once we're married, I'll probably wear even more socks. Or just one massive sock, covering my entire body, like a woolly sleeping bag. All your mates would think you'd married a frigid, Catholic version of Lowly Worm from the Richard Scarry books. But without the hat. Or *joie de vivre*.'

(This was at the Latitude Festival. I was doing a gig in a tent in the daytime. The man responded to this by just wandering out of the tent. Then some kids starting throwing small coins at me, giving me more than I made in my first eight years at the Edinburgh Fringe.)

I wasn't allowed to doubt anything about my religion when I was growing up. Mum and Dad told us just to accept things without question. So when my dad came to stay with me in London recently and couldn't grasp the price of a sausage roll in the West End, I said, 'Look, Dad, don't question the sausage roll, because you will never understand the sausage roll. The sausage roll is too complex. Even the sausage roll makers don't understand it fully. That's the beauty of it, the mystery. Just accept the sausage roll. Like I had to when I asked you about Christ's Ascension into heaven.'

When I was a kid, I asked my dad if gravity would have stopped the Ascension. He told me not to be blasphemous, and that there was no such thing as gravity. If there was it would have been mentioned in the Bible. I can't believe I'm forty-three and I'm still not allowed to mention physics.

When my friends' parents stay with them they have to hide their collections of porn. When my dad comes to stay I have to hide my collection of books about Isaac Newton. I hid it up a tree in my garden. But I'd forgotten I'd put it there and one day, my dad was sat underneath it and the whole lot fell on him. And squashed his sausage roll. And it was an expensive London one too. And he was still trying to work out the mystery of it.

I met Richard Dawkins, the Head of Atheism, at a benefit at the Bloomsbury Theatre once, and because he was wearing sandals I called him Jesus, for a joke. He said to me, 'Why have you called me Jesus for a joke? Don't you know who I am? I am Richard Dawkins. The Head of Atheism.'

'The Head of Atheism?' I said, 'Well, you say you are. Have you got any scientific evidence to back that up? Look, Rich,' I said, 'I'm a Catholic. If you say you're Richard Dawkins, I believe you. I'm just trying to be as annoying as you are. Also, they're called Jesus sandals. You can't expect to be the Head of Atheism and yet go around in footwear popularised by the son of God, unchallenged. You're lucky you can wear sandals. I've got webbed feet.[27]

What I'm trying to say is that growing up in my big Catholic family, we didn't have much. But every year Mum and Dad would take us to see a massive cheese being rolled down a hill, so, you know, we didn't go without. The world is divided into people that go to the cheese roll, and people that go to Glyndebourne. The only people who might go to both are people from devised theatre, journalists, paramedics and St John Ambulance.

In case my fictional husband forgets, when I die, I'm having my ashes put inside a seven-pound cheese and at my funeral

[27] I didn't meet him. This is a lie.

everyone has to chase me down the hill, regardless of age, ability, health or fitness. There won't be separate races for different genders, though.

The format of the cheese roll hasn't changed since the Iron Age. It started as a pagan ritual and locals just carried on the tradition. There are categories for men and women (as I've already explained). There's even a separate race for local celebrities. One year, Eddie the Eagle went head to head with EMF, Doctor Foster, Fred West, Richard Reid (the shoe bomber), Simon Pegg, Saajid Badat (the convicted terrorist), Robin Day and the Tailor of Gloucester. I hope I never qualify as a 'local celebrity'.

Cooper's Hill is beautiful and sacred. Our Gloucester ancestors have celebrated the onset of summer there for hundreds of years. It's where they worshipped nature and the changing seasons by throwing some cheese down the hill and running after it. Now, I don't know about you, but I think that's pretty inspired. It does make you wonder which ideas they rejected, though. Throwing some fish at a cow? Or riding a blindfolded pig across the river?

I'm very proud to be from Gloucester and I'm very proud of our traditions. And even though I left Gloucester when I was seventeen and have lived in London ever since, I say to people, 'I'm from Gloucester and we chase a cheese down a hill. I bet you don't do that where you're from, loser.'

And they say, 'Gloucester? You're from Gloucester? Isn't that where Fred and Rose West, the mass murderers, are from? Aren't they from Gloucester?'

And I say, 'No, they weren't. They moved there from Herefordshire. It's not the same thing at all.'

Then they say, 'Gloucester? You're from Gloucester?

Isn't that where Saajid Badat, the convicted terrorist, is from?'

And I say, 'Yes. Yes, it is.'

Then they say, 'Gloucester? You're from Gloucester? Isn't that where Richard Reid, the shoe bomber, is from?'

And I say, 'Yes. Yes, it is.'

And then they say, 'Isn't FKA twigs from Gloucester, as well?'

And I say, 'No. No, he absolutely isn't.' (I don't know who FKA twigs is, as I am forty-three, but it is typical of Gloucester to have a rapper named after some broken wood.)

I always feel like I have to defend Gloucester's violent reputation but sometimes it can be quite difficult. I remember the first time my fictional husband met my dad. We were driving round the city and Dad was pointing out all the landmarks and places of interest. We'd already covered all the horrific murders and the terrorism. Then as we drove past the county court Dad explained that Gloucester had the highest number of rape cases in the country, but the lowest amount of convictions, so if my fictional husband wanted to get away with any of that raping, he'd come to the right place. So that broke the ice. I hope the Gloucester Tourist Information Centre doesn't read this book. I think they'd be upset.

So the winner of the cheese roll gets to keep the cheese, second prize is a fiver, and third prize is £3. That might not sound very much these days, but £3 was a lot of money in the Iron Age. You could get a cow and a wife. And some iron. I'm worried about the cheese roll's future, because it's now hit the mainstream. And when things hit the mainstream, they tend to go downhill. Apart from pornography, obviously, which seems to be going from strength to strength. The cheese roll has even made it into *Hello!* and *OK!* magazines!

Even more worrying than the mainstreaming of the cheese roll was that the People for the Ethical Treatment of Animals (PETA) tried to ban it. They thought it was unethical to roll a dairy cheese down the hill and they were campaigning for a non-dairy-based soy alternative to be used instead. They even picketed local cheese shops. So I wrote PETA a letter. It said:

Dear People for the Ethical Treatment of Animals,

Re: the cheese roll, Cooper's Hill, Gloucester

In regard to your proposed banning of the above event, I'd like to advise you that we are not throwing a cow down the hill and chasing it, merely the product of a cow, i.e. cheese. No animals are treated unethically at the cheese roll. In fact, lots of dogs come along and they seem to really enjoy it. Some families aren't as well off as the People for the Ethical Treatment of Animals, and don't have much fun in their lives. They can't afford to take time off from work to disrupt the Milan fashion show, or to break into pet shops to release hamsters into the wild. They can't afford to take their children to expensive theme parks and festivals like EuroDisney, Alton Towers and Gay Pride. These people take their children, just once a year, to see some cheese being rolled down a hill. And they don't even have to pay. It's free. To deny these little children the magic and beauty of the cheese roll is unethical treatment of children.

Best wishes,

Bridget Christie, a vegetarian [which I was at the time], a friend of cheese and hills.

No one really came to my *Cheese Roll* show. One day, four people came. One paying punter, plus Nica Burns, the director of the Edinburgh Comedy Awards, along with two judges. So that wasn't very intimidating. I couldn't even hide behind the fourth wall, because I'd incorporated lots of audience participation into the show, like an idiot.

In the entire run, I only got a decent-sized audience once. It was my last day so I sent a text around. Simon Amstell, who wears jumpers in his show posters, came, and so did Dan Antopolski, who is Jesus in the film of *The Da Vinci Code*, and my sister Eileen, who'd come all the way from Gloucester on a train for one night to see the show. But the show was cancelled. The woman whose job it was to open the Holyrood Tavern slept in because she had been out drinking late. My audience, the only audience I ever had that year, and the largest I'd had in my career to date, were all standing outside on the pavement, all twenty-three of them, waiting for her to turn up. She didn't, and everyone went home. Like I said, not all my Edinburgh shows did well.

I first started doing stand-up in 2003. In my Edinburgh shows, from 2005 onwards, because I thought I'd be taken more seriously if I pretended to be a man, I had dressed as King Charles II. I wondered about wearing the robe all the time, perhaps even during childbirth as well. I thought the midwives wouldn't patronise me so much if they thought I was a man. But if you went into labour in Hackney, and you were dressed as Charles II, you wouldn't get any special treatment. You would at the Chelsea and Westminster, as he built it, but not at the Homerton.

Anyway, I only did two shows about Charles II because all my costumes and props were destroyed by an infestation of fly larvae. What are the chances of that? Only Charles's shoes and hat survived. I got an email from the producer of the first Charles II show I did, saying that they'd had a fly infestation in their offices in Wardour Street for about a month, but couldn't find the cause of it. Then apparently someone saw a fly coming out of a red suitcase with 'Bridget Christie – the Court of King Charles II' written on it. Now, I had a red suitcase, and I did a show about King Charles II, and my name is Bridget Christie. Not only that, my producer didn't produce any other shows about Charles II, with any other women called Bridget Christie, who had red suitcases, so I assumed it was my suitcase. And it turned out that it was.

Anyway, in the first show, I did an Oliver Cromwell character who used to eat a banana really slowly (easier to eat than celery). When they packed up all my things, they'd left a banana in the case and some flies or other sort of fruit-eating insect had got in there and had laid loads of eggs and all the baby flies had an English Civil War-themed fancy dress party, where there were only bananas to eat, and the costumes were too big for all the guests. Because they were flies.

Although something quite wonderful came out of my Charles II character. I found out about it when my friend, the comedian, writer, actor, musician and mother Isy Suttie, texted me to say, 'Oh my god, look up "Charles II Malmesbury House" on the *Daily Mail*'s website now and scroll down to the photos before they realise what they've done and correct it!! DO IT NOW!' The *Mail Online* wrote a piece about a Grade II listed property that had come on to the market for the first time in 600 years. Malmesbury House in Salisbury was where King Charles II lived in 1665 after fleeing London to escape the Plague. Underneath an official portrait of Charles II, a reporter had used this picture of me, superimposed on to a horse, that I used as the poster for one of my Edinburgh shows. He obviously just searched for 'Charles II' and picked a picture at random, an easy enough mistake to make. Although:

1. It's obviously a woman, with a drawn-on moustache, superimposed on to a horse, in a handmade costume. Look at the rip under my armpit where I've just crudely cut up some old curtains.

2. It's a photograph. They didn't have cameras back then.

3. It's clearly not Charles II. It's me.

Loads of other friends spotted it too and subsequently emailed me. Luckily, the clever chap who does all my website and internet stuff, James Hingley, took a screenshot of it before the *Mail Online* spotted the error and changed it. Sportingly the *Mail* kindly gave me permission to use it. Look!

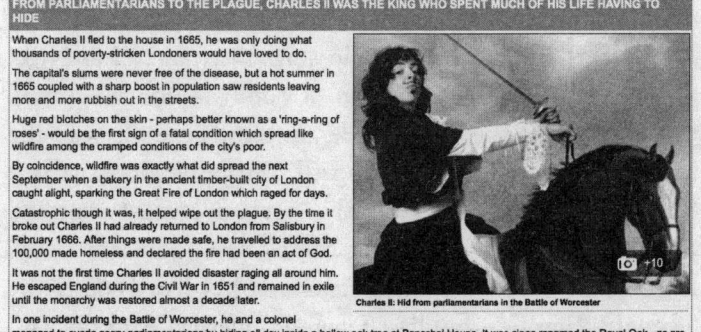

FROM PARLIAMENTARIANS TO THE PLAGUE, CHARLES II WAS THE KING WHO SPENT MUCH OF HIS LIFE HAVING TO HIDE

When Charles II fled to the house in 1665, he was only doing what thousands of poverty-stricken Londoners would have loved to do.

The capital's slums were never free of the disease, but a hot summer in 1665 coupled with a sharp boost in population saw residents leaving more and more rubbish out in the streets.

Huge red blotches on the skin - perhaps better known as a 'ring-a-ring of roses' - would be the first sign of a fatal condition which spread like wildfire among the cramped conditions of the city's poor.

By coincidence, wildfire was exactly what did spread the next September when a bakery in the ancient timber-built city of London caught alight, sparking the Great Fire of London which raged for days.

Catastrophic though it was, it helped wipe out the plague. By the time it broke out Charles II had already returned to London from Salisbury in February 1666. After things were made safe, he travelled to address the 100,000 made homeless and declared the fire had been an act of God.

It was not the first time Charles II avoided disaster raging all around him. He escaped England during the Civil War in 1651 and remained in exile until the monarchy was restored almost a decade later.

Charles II: Hid from parliamentarians in the Battle of Worcester

In one incident during the Battle of Worcester, he and a colonel managed to evade angry parliamentarians by hiding all day inside a hollow oak tree at Boscobel House. It was since renamed the Royal Oak - as are countless pubs.

Lots of comedians and actors start out doing characters. There's a new one going around the circuit at the moment who I mentioned earlier, called Nigel Farage. The comedian behind the character Nigel Farage (the leader of UKIP as at March 2015) is fantastic. He never lets it drop for a minute! The level of commitment he puts into that character is astonishing. He's like the Daniel Day-Lewis of character comedy. It's very hard to do that. I know. When I was an ant, I'd say, 'Hello, I'm an ant.' Wink wink! But he never does that. He never breaks the fourth wall, ever. I keep looking for a glimmer in his eye, for some little telltale sign, but nope. Nothing. If I'm honest, I think the comedian playing Nigel Farage is a bit out of his depth. I know exactly what's happened here. He had ten minutes on immigrants that went down much better than he'd anticipated, then a big agent or comedy promoter heard there's this new bloke storming it down the racist clubs and now he's expected to fill two hours on tour with jokes about issues other than immigration, and he's finding it a bit of a struggle. We don't even know if he's British, this comedian. He might be Bulgarian for all we know, and be really good at posh English accents. I wonder if he stays in character as Nigel Farage when he goes to the toilet or not. Or whether the comedian stays in character as Nigel Farage and sees the expulsion of bodily waste, while still in character as the UKIP leader, as some kind of cleansing ritual, a urinary purge, if you will, before he clocks off for the night. 'Goodnight, comedy Nigel! See you tomorrow! Pssssssssssssssss... byeeeeeee... there you go... into the toilet. With all the other human waste.' I like to think he goes in character, holding a fag and a beer. And that his mate, who is also a comedian, called Paul Nuttall, holds his fag and pint for him while he does a wee-wee.

I'm being silly about Nigel Farage because this is a comedy book and Nigel Farage is silly. What I should be focusing on is the fact that UKIP allowed a far right MEP to join their group from a Polish party whose leader believes that women shouldn't be allowed to vote and that the differences between consensual sex and rape are too subtle to bother with.

Another male character of mine, in Edinburgh in 2006, was Dan Brown. The conceit was that he was over here performing excerpts from his latest book, *The Laughter Code*. His jokes were really laborious and long-winded and not suited to live comedy at all and were written in his style of writing. Here's an example of a few of 'Dan's' jokes (written by me, obviously):

> The mysterious chicken crossed the busy
> inner city road. But why? It was rush
> hour, and it was pushing forty degrees.
> As the weary commuters sat in their air-
> conditioned mobile prisons, Bob Carter, a
> security guard from North Dakota, looked
> at the chicken with apprehension and
> curiosity. What was it doing on Highway
> 504 at 1700 hours? He thought of calling
> John, his overweight high-school friend,
> now a world-famous cryptographer, but
> there wasn't time. The lights had changed
> and the gridlock nudged forward, like
> the barrel of a gun in a game of Russian
> roulette.

'God damn those fucking lights!' he
hissed.

Bob was thirty-eight and tanned. Bob's
Alfa Romeo tore toward the chicken,
but the lights changed again and he was
running out of options fast. The Rhode
Island Red Rooster was getting away.

'Hey!' Bob shouted, his desperation
furrowing his sunkissed sweaty brow. 'Hey,
Rooster! For Christ's sake! Why are you
crossing the road?'

As Bob held his breath, the mysterious
chicken slowly looked over its muscular
shoulder, and with narrowing eyes, it
replied sinisterly, 'To get to the other
fucking side, asshole.'

Do we have any door-to-door salesmen
in here tonight? No? Anyone got a door?
Okay, here's a joke for my English buddy
with a door. This is fun, dudes!!!

'Knock knock,' said the albino voodoo
assassin.

'Who's there?' replied Sister Margaret
cautiously. She didn't like meeting people
in the middle of the night, it wasn't a habit

of hers and she was in no mood for silly
jokes.

'Doctor,' said the assassin, with a heavy
Arabic accent.

'Witch doctor?' replied the clever Irish
nun, hoping to close it down.

'No, you're wrong,' said the assassin. 'It's
not witch doctor, it's doctor who, actually,
you fucking asshole.'

None of these characters or ideas worked. So after my radio
series and a few tours, lugging suitcases of costumes around
and years of talking about things I didn't care about, I wanted
to concentrate solely on pure material. I wasn't going to go up
to the Fringe again, but then, in the spring of 2013, I decided,
after going to Edinburgh all these years with donkey costumes
and explosives and celery and cheese rolls and false beards
and papier mâché hills and not getting much of an audience,
I might as well write one more show where I just spoke. No
props, no costumes, no paraphernalia. Just me speaking about
things I care about and see if the people who liked the radio
series bought tickets for the show.

And they did.

CHAPTER EIGHT

'I was going to do a big list of women's words, but I can't think of any I'm afraid. Because I am a woman and words aren't really for us, remember? Either for speaking or for writing down.'

All I had in May 2013 was the title (*A Bic for Her*), and the routine I'd written for the first radio series, in the summer of 2012, about these 'Bic for Her' biro pens I'd seen in Ryman.

They amused me. I'm not *that* bothered about gendered products, to be honest. I find them funny at best and annoying at worst, but they are very good pill-sweeteners. If things start to get a bit 'uh-oh, here comes the serious bit', I can always chuck in the odd male tea bag or female earplug to give the audience a break. So I talked to the Swedish woman behind the till in Ryman about the pens and we laughed about them. She said you wouldn't really get a product like that in Sweden. I told her not to be so smug, and that if Sweden was so *great* and so *equal* then perhaps she should go home. I then bought her entire stock of Bic for Her pens as I thought I might give them out in my show. Or not. My routine started with me

talking about feminism in general, a rewrite and expansion of
my 'I am not a feminist, but...' bit.

> I'm not a feminist. Oh, God forbid, no.
> Horrible, hairy, humourless, bra-less lot.
> No, no, not one of those feminists from
> the bloody UN. God, no. In fact, in many
> ways, I'm the exact *opposite* of a feminist. I
> have no hair anywhere on my body at all,
> not even on my head. I even pulled out
> all my eyelashes and shaved my eyebrows
> off in case anyone mistook me for one of
> the bloody feminists. And I've thrown out
> most of my Day of the Week dungarees. I
> just kept my Saturday and Sunday ones.
> So I just wanted to say that *I am not a*
> *feminist. But...* I'm not sure that Bic the
> biro manufacturers needed to have brought
> out a pen specifically for women, called
> a Bic for Her, that's gender-specifically,
> ergonomically designed for a woman's
> hand, and comes in a series of bright pastel
> colours, presumably to cheer us all up.

> *But I'm not a feminist.* I just don't think
> we need our own pens, do we? I mean, in
> all the years I've been writing, since I was
> forty-one, and I'm forty-three now—

Yes, I do look young on the cover, thanks for that – com-
pliments about my appearance are always welcome and

appreciated, and yes, even though I am a feminist I can still enjoy someone paying me a compliment (see chapter 1).

> —I have never, *ever* once thought,[28] God, this pen is uncomfortable, and the colour is all wrong for me! It's extremely heavy as well. And the colour? Why on earth would a woman want to write with a black or grey or blue pen, for heaven's sake?
>
> And it's very difficult to hang on to, because it just goes straight down. It's not contoured in the middle.
>
> Well . . . this is a man's pen, really. How am I supposed to write with a man's pen? Why can't someone invent a woman's pen? That's easier for us to hold? And comes in a series of bright pastel colours that would help us to get out of all of our moods? Why can't a man invent a woman's pen for us? Oh, I'd find writing about feminism much easier if I was using a pink, gender-specific pen that had a rubbery grip on it.

---

[28] At this point I'd get a black Bic biro from my pocket, drop it and then spend ages crawling around on the floor trying to pick it up. I'd then plead with a male audience member to come and pick it up for me. But they never would, so this bit would take ages, with me pleading more desperately as time went on to the man to pick it up for me. Sometimes it would go on for so long that I would lose the audience, but I knew that a bit about domestic violence was coming up, so I always had to make sure that this bit worked, so that I had earned the right to do the next bit. I would disregard any notion of self-respect or dignity in order to achieve this.

This one I'm using keeps slipping out of
my hands—

It doesn't . . . I'm using my laptop.

—Perhaps if a man could invent a pen
especially for me, I could write ladies' words
with it. Like 'chocolate' and 'jewellery'
and 'big divorce settlement'. All the
women's words. I was going to do a big list
of women's words, but I can't think of any
others I'm afraid. Because I am a woman
and words aren't really for us, remember?
Either for speaking, or for writing down.

Only they are now! We have been
recognised at last, ladies! Now we are
allowed to write! Because Bic said so!
One wonders how Mary Shelley managed
to write *Frankenstein*. Perhaps she was
lactating at the time, and sprayed her work
of genius on a wall in her own milk. Like
some kind of breastfeeding graffiti artist
who specialised in horror. Or maybe she
just used a quill and some ink, like the men
did.

Perhaps that's why the Brontës were so
shit at writing. Because their pens were too
uncomfortable and drab.

I'd then perform a sketch where I was all three Brontë sisters, talking to each other.

> 'Oh, Charlotte, I'm having terrible trouble
> writing Heathcliff. I think it's my pen, you
> see, it doesn't fit my hand properly. I think
> it's because it's a man's pen. Men can hold
> pens so much easier than us, can't they?
> Although our brother, Branwell Brontë, is
> a man, isn't he? With man's hands. And
> he hasn't managed to write much, has
> he? Even though he has man's hands. I
> went through his notebook the other day,
> Charlotte, and it's just page after page after
> page after page of spunking cocks. I mean,
> some of them are very funny, and let's face
> it, when is a drawing of a spunking cock
> *not* funny? But there's not much thought
> gone into them, Charlotte. They all look
> pretty much the same. Anyway…I don't
> think I will be able to finish *Wuthering
> Heights*. Not unless I can find a pen with a
> textured, rubbery grip.'

> 'Oh, Emily [the other one], I'm so glad
> you said that. I thought it was just me! My
> pen is also causing me massive shit. Poor
> Jane Eyre, she is so one-dimensional at the
> moment. I think it's because the pen that I
> use only comes in men's colours. If only it
> was pink or purple, or lime green, or a nice

yellowy colour, perhaps, I'm sure I could
make Jane Eyre a more rounded character,
rather than the tedious, one-dimensional
one she is at the moment.

'Anne [the third one]? Anne? Anne,
where are you?...Oh! Anne, I do wish you
wouldn't keep standing directly behind me
like that. It's very disconcerting, and I can
feel your breath on my neck.'

For some reason, I made Anne Brontë really weird and
intimidating and threatening. It's just how I imagined her to
be. Wracked with jealousy and rage, for having less attention
than the other two. Skulking around the parsonage and trying
to put them off their writing, by banging pans together and
breathing loudly.

'Anyway, Anne...we were just wondering
how you were getting on with *The Tenant
of Wildfell Hall*? With your man's pen.
Us two are having a bit of trouble holding
them.'

'Oh yes, fine, thank you, sisters. But as
you both well know, I've always had man's
hands.'

I started doing this routine live in about October 2012,
and then it went into the radio series, which was broadcast in
March 2013. When it went out, people got in touch to say that

Ellen DeGeneres also had a funny routine about the pens, and that there were some hilarious reviews of them on Amazon. I looked them all up, and they were all hilarious. None of them mentioned the Brontës, though.

Still, this didn't stop people from the online nob community from accusing me of winning the Edinburgh Comedy Award with a show that I didn't even write myself. A show that was 'entirely constructed around things that other people had said on Amazon about Bic for Her pens', as if all I did was stand onstage and read out things other people had said. For an hour.

The irony of being accused of not writing my own feminist show, in which I discuss the merits of gendered pens, was not lost on me. Also, the entire routine lasted around five to six minutes. So that still left fifty-four to fifty-five minutes unaccounted for. I don't know for certain, but I'm pretty sure the Foster's Award panel judges wouldn't have chosen a show in which a person just read out some Amazon reviews other people had written, for sixty minutes. Not when there were 500-odd other comedy shows on the Fringe they could've chosen.

So I had the title and the pen routine. I just needed to get another fifty-five minutes together before August. I remember doing a terrible work-in-progress show at the Machynlleth Comedy Festival. Apart from the pen stuff it was awful.

Every year, around April/May, when I'm starting to write a new show for Edinburgh, I look like I've never been onstage before. It's disconcerting but also thrilling. It reminds you of the precariousness of it all and it keeps you grounded.

Luckily, not long after the work-in-progress gig, Sir Stirling Moss, the icon of British motor racing, said the following stupid thing on the radio about female drivers in F1: 'The mental stress I think would be pretty difficult for a lady to deal with in a practical fashion. I just don't think they have aptitude to win a Formula One race.' Sir Stirling basically said that women didn't have the right sort of brains for racing cars. The problem, he said, was that women's brains were female, rather than male, and this was what was wrong with them.

By pure chance, I'd just watched an inspiring and moving documentary about Susie Wolff, the Formula One racing car driver. There was footage of Susie as a little girl, she must've been only about four, my own daughter's age, driving around a field on a tiny quad bike. Apparently she got her first one aged two. Her dad owned a bike shop and raced bikes and Susie and her brother would go around with him. Motor racing was clearly in her menstrual blood. I just thought how angry and upset I'd be if someone said my daughter didn't have the right kind of brain for doing something she was clearly brilliant at, like pulling hilarious faces, and that the specific problem my daughter's brain had was that it was female.

So I was annoyed when Sir Stirling said women couldn't drive fast cars, because I thought about all the professional female racing car drivers and about all the obstacles they'd have faced to be able to compete at the top level of motor racing. I thought about female fighter pilots, and commercial airline pilots, and scientists and mathematicians, and about engineers and architects and politicians and surgeons and police officers and all women working in predominantly male or at least perceived as male professions, who've had to fight every step of the way, who've had to prove themselves to be better than their male peers, even to be considered as equal to them. And it annoyed me.

Also, Moss's younger sister, Pat Moss, was one of the most successful female rally drivers of all time, so he obviously knew full well that women could drive fast. In fact in 1960 she won Liège-Rome-Liège, beating all the men too.

So. I looked up Moss to see if he'd said or done anything else that might fit with his sexist comments and enable me to construct a routine around. Fortuitously for me – less so for him – Moss had previously fallen down a lift shaft in his own house and really injured himself. Moss has a lift inside his own house. One day, he didn't check to see if the lift was there before he stepped into it. It wasn't. And he fell down the shaft. Stirling Moss was shafted by his own shaft. I appreciate this is not, in and of itself, a funny story, but when told in the context of his sexist comments, lots of women laughed. I wrote it in a way that suggested that Moss said the sexist comments about women not being able to race cars because their brains weren't up to it, then immediately fell down a lift shaft. In reality, he fell down the lift shaft about three years earlier. This is the routine:

> In April this year, the former British
> racing driver Sir Stirling Moss said, 'I
> think women have the physical strength,
> but I don't know if they have the mental
> aptitude to race cars.' Before stepping out
> on to a lift that wasn't there. Falling fifty
> feet down a lift shaft. Breaking both his
> ankles and ending up in intensive care.
> The female firefighter who rescued him
> said, 'I think that men have the physical
> strength, but I don't know if they have the
> mental aptitude to use lifts.'

Poor old Sir Stirling. He really hurt himself. Did you read about it in the papers? It was a big news story. His wife, Lady Moss, could hardly contain her concern. Although in her statement to the press she gave it a really good go.

Anyway, he was seriously injured, Stirling Moss. It's such a shame when a misogynist ends up in intensive care, isn't it? Because he'll be well looked after. In my opinion, a former racing driver shouldn't be allowed to make a sexist comment and then be a burden on the NHS. The British taxpayer should not be paying for a sexist to get his broken ankles cast. This country has gone to shit, I tell you. First the privatisation of the railways, and now free healthcare for misogynists. You know they all come over here, don't you? All the foreign sexists? To get all their ankles fixed. They get their teeth done as well while they're at it! There are signs in Iran saying, 'Sexists of Iran! Get your broken ankles and rotten teeth fixed in UK.' We're a bloody joke. They don't do that in Sweden or Finland or Iceland or Norway, which have some of the best equal rights records in the world. They just leave all the sexists hobbling around with black teeth.

By the way, I am not a spoof of a 1980s feminist comedian. I'm not a character act. This is what I'm like in real life. All the time. It's exhausting. I'm like it at home, in shops, at children's parties. Parties that I go to with my two small children, by the way; I'm not a feminist children's entertainer. Though some of the shit five-year-old boys can come out with, perhaps I should be.

So it's not a character that's glad Sir Stirling Moss seriously injured himself. *I'm* glad. Now, I don't consider myself a radical feminist by any means, I'm not one of those feminists who hate all men. How could I possibly have met all men? I don't think that a former racing driver should be able to say that the whole of womenkind can't drive fast cars because their brains aren't up to it – and then be allowed to live.

What should've happened with Moss, if we lived in an equal and fair society, one that encouraged and supported and respected women instead of one that demeaned and objectified and patronised them all the time, was that the female firefighter who rescued Moss would've left him there, on top of that lift, in agony, going, 'Ahhh, ahhh, my ankles, my ankles, my poor, old, brittle, sexist ankles,' until he starved (just like the suffragettes did to get us the vote), and after he died, on the day of his funeral, the driver of his hearse would be the Formula One test driver Susie Woolf. She's allowed to test drive for F1, just not race for them, what with having a woman's brain and all.

And so she'd drive the hearse to the cemetery, at 190mph, and Sir Stirling Moss would be being all flung around in the back, in his car-shaped coffin, made of moss, and all the car-shaped wreaths and car shaped sponge cakes placed on top of the coffin by all of his fans would be thrown everywhere, and be all squashed and ruined, and there'd be buttercream and jam and hundreds and thousands all over the windows, and it would all just be this massive mess of moss and flowers and cake ingredients and a dead sexist. And this would be called Moss Mess – a bit like Eton Mess but without the strawberries or cream or meringue – and this would be served up to all of Sir Stirling Moss's posh friends at the wake, and they'd think that it was delicious and amazing and all planned, and they'd be gobbling it all up and rubbing it in their faces and they'd think that the billionaire sexist Sir Stirling

Moss must've left very specific instructions in his will for his catering to be done by Heston Blumenthal. They'd be saying, 'Mmmmm, this Moss Mess is so delicious and post-modern. Heston is so clever. Only Heston would think to fuse moss and buttercream with a dead sexist. Mmmm. Yummy.' Stick it in your ears, Tarquin! That's how posh people eat. They're disgusting.

And then when Susie Wolff got to the graveside first, there'd be all objectified grid boys stood around the grave, dressed in tiny red and white shorts, waving little flags about, making demeaning poses, sticking their bums out and putting their fingers in their mouths like this – because the men in my Sir Stirling Moss funeral routine aren't allowed to drive any of the cars, but they can advertise them, lie all over them and fondle them. Look at all this plastic and metal that has more value than me!!! Oh, I wish I was an inanimate object like this, with wheels and an engine, rather than just a sexual one.

(*It's still not finished, this routine, so I'd get on board if you're not already*)

Then just as Sir Stirling Moss's dead sexist

body is lowered into the ground, Susie
Wolff would get some champagne (that's
what racing drivers do, isn't it, when they
win? They shake up a massive bottle of
champagne and they put it between their
legs and squirt it all over everyone, like
this – as if the bottle is a symbol of their
manhood or something. It's like they're
saying, 'Look at me! Look at me! I'm the
fastest! I'm a racing car driver and my
semen is so manly it's from a French wine
region! Look at my French fizzy sperm! I've
got the fastest, fizziest spunk on the track!
Le Coq Sportif!' Oh, just grow up and die
and let the women have a go.

But Susie Wolff wouldn't have a big
phallic bottle of champagne, she'd have
two of those little half-sized bottles that
she'd hold by her breasts. She'd squirt
that all over Sir Stirling Moss's dead sexist
descending body, saying, 'Look at me!
Look at me! I've got the fastest, fizziest
breast milk on the track! My milk is so
womanly it's from a French wine region!'
And while she was doing that, behind her
there'd be loads of feminists, all dressed up
as Emmeline Pankhurst and Emily Wilding
Davison, in Edwardian clothes, holding
placards saying 'RACES FOR WOMEN'
on them, and someone would take a

photograph of that scene and *that* would be the front cover of the new F1 calendar!

What happened to Moss was that the doors of the lift opened but the lift hadn't arrived at his floor yet, but he got in anyway. Happened to me once, in a shopping centre in Gloucester. My immediate thought was, there's something missing from this lift. Oh yes – the lift. I won't get in it. Because it's not there. But that's me and my woman's brain for you. Able to tell when the lift part of a lift isn't there. The lift was in Stirling Moss's house, by the way. He has a lift inside his house. Who has a lift inside their own house? Apart from Sir Stirling Moss and Batman? How did Moss discipline his children if he didn't have any stairs?

'Right, that's it! I've had enough! You will sit in the lift and go up and down until you've learnt some manners!'

Now, I know what you're thinking. It's not funny to laugh at an elderly, vulnerable man who's had a fall. And you're right. In real life, I would not laugh at anyone falling down a lift shaft, let alone an elderly man. But this is not real life. This is stand-up.

Sir Stirling Moss said that women didn't have the mental capacity to race cars, which is ridiculous and annoying. He also fell down a lift shaft by not checking to see if the lift was there first, which is extremely unfortunate and not funny in isolation. Obviously I don't wish him dead for his silly comments, I was taking an extreme position in order to make myself look ridiculous for comic effect. In a show about everyday sexism and misogyny, you can see how a comedian might link those two things together. Most audiences and critics seemed to get that. Except for the *Telegraph*, which wrote:

'...the routine goes on for far too long, and – especially during a show fired by a passion for reason and fairness – a younger person poking protracted fun at an injured octogenarian leaves an unpleasant taste.'

The Times didn't make the routine sound particularly generous either, but understood my motives:

'True, she does call for Stirling Moss's slow death by starvation, followed by a deliberately botched funeral that humiliates him and all his friends, but as a comedian, of course, she is allowed to say anything at all as part of a democratic audit of social morality.'

I read these reviews out in the show and suggested that the routine wasn't 'too long' at all, within the context of patriarchal systems, and that I might write another Stirling Moss routine, in my next show, that was 200,000 years long.

But I'm obviously not glad that an old man fell down a lift, am I? I'm not an animal. But his accident worked nicely with his comment about women's 'lack of mental aptitude'. I don't know *any* woman who would get into a lift backwards, or looking somewhere other than towards or into the lift. Unless they have a fear of them, of course. But if they had a fear of lifts, wouldn't they just use the stairs? Rather than avoiding eye contact with them?

I had a much longer routine about John Inverdale, the veteran BBC presenter who announced live to the nation just before Marion Bartoli took the women's title at Wimbledon that she was 'not a looker', which involved him having a tennis ball served into his anus at 163mph by the world's fastest server, Sam Groth, and then sustaining internal injuries as none of the ballboys or ballgirls would retrieve the ball. But the problem was that I genuinely dislike John Inverdale, so I couldn't perform the routine with any sense of fun. It just looked like a really ambitious tennis-ball-related fatwa.

Anyway, John Inverdale recently far outdid his Marion Bartoli comments when covering the Cheltenham Festival this year, by saying, 'This is looking at it through rose-cunted – rose-tinted glasses from the past...[I] apologise there for a slip of the tongue, but Lizzie, your love of the sport just shines through.'

Inverdale's undoing was that he immediately apologised, drawing attention to it, when anyone who accidentally says 'cunt' a lot knows that the best thing to do is to move on as if you haven't said it at all and hope no one notices. Although it does make you wonder what Inverdale was thinking about when he said it to Lizzie. Does he like her? In which case, it was bad. Or does he hate her? In which case it's even worse.

But back to that other silly man from sport, Moss. I was slightly worried the routine would upset Moss if he came to the show but luckily he'd read some reviews that mentioned the routine and he was really pleased. From what he said in his email, I think he must have read these two reviews. He even emailed me to say so. Although he did leave Caps Lock on, which made the whole thing look more like a death threat.

I wanted to touch on serious issues but not go too deeply into them. Even though I was growing in confidence all the time, there were still subjects I didn't feel equipped to tackle. I was running a lot of this stuff in at regular club nights, in front of people who'd just come for a nice night out, and it didn't work out of context, which it should do, really. Believe it or not, I don't always just play to rooms full of lefty, *Guardian*-reading feminists who are already on board. I do all kinds of gigs, in all kinds of venues, and I very often bomb. In Salisbury, where I performed my solo show; where people had bought tickets to SEE ME AND ME ALONE, I wasn't clapped on to the stage. I came out, at the top of the show and about five people clapped. The room was full, by the way. I was the person they had paid to see, but for some reason, they had collectively decided that they would not welcome me on in the traditional manner, of clapping, as has been the custom for many years. Just to clarify, in case you're thinking, 'Well, maybe they didn't know you were coming out' I had just received clearance from front of house staff and the technician that everyone was seated and ready, and also I had just introduced myself in an enthusiastic way using an off-stage microphone, ending with the sentence '...please will you welcome to the stage, Bridget Chrიstie!!'... nothing. I went off stage and came back on another two times until they clapped, which sounds confrontational, but had to be done. When you're performing a solo show on tour you are the compère, opening act and headline act. A compère's job is to create a good vibe in the room. A compère would assume the audience would applaud an act when he or she introduced them, and if they didn't, he or she would insist that they did. I just had to do that for myself, that's all. You can't begin a two-hour show without being clapped on. A room of people who haven't clapped you on hold the power, and you have to get it back off them. It's not their job to have the power, it's mine! I had to be SEEN to be in charge, even if I wasn't. If I didn't take control of the room, there and then, the night would be a complete waste of time, so that's why I ordered them to clap, and to look like they were enjoying the clap as well. I was very charming and nice about it all, don't worry about that. I think I may have said something like, 'Clap, you weird twats, or you can all amuse yourselves for two hours.'

My point is that whoever you are, it's never a done deal. People assume that now I am that 'feminist comedian', I just preach to the converted, that I'm not a 'proper' stand-up (whatever that is) and that I couldn't cut it in the 'proper' comedy clubs (whatever they are) where comedians do actual jokes. Well, I do write jokes, it's just that at the moment they're about things that you might not normally hear about in a comedy club, and I've gigged in all sorts of different venues too. I've gigged amongst the exhibits at the Museum of London, inside an inflatable bowler hat (where a noisy generator kept on during the entire one-hour performance because it was keeping the inflatable hat inflated drowned out my own amplified voice). I've gigged at a weekenders' night club night like Glasgow Jongleurs and in half-empty rooms above and under pubs, I've even performed my show to about fifty babies at the Soho Theatre in London for their 'Soho Screamers' series for mothers and babies. I think even my harshest critics would struggle to call a massive noisy generator drunk Glaswegians, museum exhibits and fifty screaming, soiled babies 'the converted'.

I remember when I was working in the new stuff for *A Bic*

for Her in the winter of 2012, a nice friendly bloke came up to me after a gig at the Piccadilly Comedy Club near Leicester Square, run by Mike Manera, and said, 'That was good, mate. Bit too serious for a Saturday night, but I enjoyed it. You're brave to be talking about equal pay and that sort of stuff on a weekend.' And you know what? He was right. He wouldn't have said that if the material was funny enough. He would've just said it was funny. I had to make it funnier. I reminded myself that there were no unfunny subjects, just bad material. If what I was doing was 'a bit too serious for a Saturday night' then I'd failed. I had to be able to work on a Saturday night, which is when most people go out.

I had to find a way of counteracting the seriousness of the subject matter. A key part of this was my on stage persona. I had to be a much more extreme version of the real me, some-one a bit ridiculous, and confused, and angry about the wrong things. As well as highlighting the absurdity of misogyny, I also had to make myself absurd. If I was absurd, then I could say anything, and really have some fun with it. I also wanted to find ways of sneaking information into the show.

For example, immediately following the pen routine, I decided to pretend that an audience member had heckled me, demanding I address more complex feminist issues in greater depth. I wanted to sneak some of the more serious content into the show at that point, but by making the heavy stuff look like it had come from the audience's own demands, and not from me, it took the curse off it. I'd contrived a situation that made it look like I was trying hard to entertain them, but they were dragging me down and killing the night. Without want-ing to sound like an arrogant nob, it always worked. Audiences are suckers for a bit of interaction. They love it. They think they're getting something no one else is. Not knowing, of course, that you do the same thing every night, give or take. So I'd single out a man in the front row and say:

> Sorry, what was that, sir? Why am I so
> angry about silly pens for women when
> there are much more serious issues I should
> be talking about? Sorry, what? What's
> that you say? Why don't I get angry about
> domestic violence or female genital
> mutilation? Well, I have to hand it to you,
> sir, in nearly a decade of doing stand-up,
> I've never had a heckle like that!

Then I'd ask him his name.

> No, leave him alone, everyone. Don't
> laugh at him. He's right. And even though
> he's completely thrown me, and thrown
> the show into chaos, I'm glad he's brought
> it up.

> Listen, [WHATEVER HIS NAME WAS],
> I don't do those serious issues, because
> what I do is defined, in the loosest possible
> terms, as comedy. And however much *you*
> want me to talk about those terrible things,
> I'm not going to. I'm sorry. What? It was
> a brave heckle, yes, yes it was. You don't
> often hear the heckle 'Tell us about the
> cultural complexities of domestic violence',

but there is a time and a place for that
kind of subject material, and it's not a
comedy club. People have come out to
enjoy themselves. Look what you've done
to the room, [MAN'S NAME]. You've
completely killed it. You did that.

Then I'd pretend that another man had heckled me as well.
And I'd go and speak to him too.

What? What's that? Oh, no, not you as
well! Look, [MAN 1], you've started them
all off now.

[TO MAN 2] Yes, sir, yes you're right,
sex trafficking and honour killings are as
important as female genital mutilation and
domestic violence, but like I said to [MAN
1] over here, there is a time and a place.
Yes, you're brave too [TO MAN 2], your
heckle was as brave as [MAN 1's] heckle.
Honestly! Men are so competitive, aren't
they? Even when they're heckling about
women's rights!

Look, guys, I know what you're trying to
do. You're just trying to raise awareness
for these terrible things. And that is
admirable, it really is. Someone in this
audience might go home and look those
violations of human rights up, and be so

angered or moved that they dedicate their
entire lives to trying to make a change, but
guys, this is a comedy show, come on. Also,
to be honest, I just don't have the skills yet
to be able to do that kind of stuff justice.
I don't want to risk misjudging it. I'm not
Dapper Laughs.

I can't remember whether it was in a review of the show, or on social networking or a blog, but someone had written somewhere that I was completely 'thrown by a heckler' and that I just ended up saying I didn't have the skills to be able to talk about that difficult stuff, and that it was embarrassing and all the audience were laughing at me. Shame when your performance skills, hard won over years of genuine stage deaths, are mistaken for genuine errors, isn't it?

I put this reverse-heckle routine at around the midway point of the show, about thirty minutes in. I wanted just to remind the audience that we were going somewhere, and that I really wasn't all that bothered about silly sexist sportsmen and silly pens for women.

Certain topics, such as pointlessly gendered products, are easier to joke about. The humour comes from the fact that they exist and you don't need to put too much of a spin on it. People will be laughing anyway because the core thing is funny in itself. *Haha!!!! Pens for women's hands! Hahaha*! Easy. Done. Next!

You can't do that with horrible things. You need a way in. An angle. You need a unique perspective, which can come from a personal anecdote, or you can put a funny and unusual spin on it. You can talk around the subject or, if you're really talented, you can go into minute detail about the terrible thing in a mechanical, detached way, as if you are describing something else.

Obviously, gendered products would be pretty low down on any self-respecting feminist's list of things to sort out, but from a comedy perspective, they give the audience room to breathe. That's why I hope capitalist societies continue to thrive.

I find misogyny absurd. Every single thing about it. Even the word 'misogyny' is ridiculous. *Miso-jinny?* I genuinely do not know how people express sexist or misogynistic ideas or opinions with a straight face. I don't know how they do it. I have never, ever, once, in my entire life, heard a logical, reasonable justification for gender inequality. It makes *absolutely no sense whatsoever*. If you ask a young child what the difference between boys and girls are, they don't know. My son thinks the difference between men and women is 'slightly different voices and a couple of different body parts. That's all.'

I got into an argument with a bloke once who said that feminism was ruining everything and had 'gone too far' because when he moved into a village with his wife he wanted to go to the bloke's curry night which took place on Thursdays, but couldn't, because his wife felt left out and wanted to go too. This was feminism's fault, he said, because she wouldn't have felt like she had a right to go to the curry night without feminism. Feminism had ruined this man's life. Well, his Thursday curry night anyway. I didn't say a single word to this man. I didn't afford him the luxury of a response. I just laughed and laughed, and laughed, like a witch, until he walked off, confused.

I wanted to address domestic violence in the show as well.

One incident of domestic violence is reported to the police every minute. On average, two women a week are killed by a current or former male partner. I'd previously met Lisa King, Director of Communications and Fundraising at Refuge, to ask her how I could help raise awareness. As with most charities, the thing they need the most is media interest and money. So I had an idea and asked Lisa for as many blank direct debit forms as she could spare.

Just after the reverse-heckle routine, I told the audience I was now going to do some 'men's comedy', 'for the men in the house', which was a joke about the notion of gender and comedy, which I don't believe exists, because to assume there is 'women's' comedy and 'men's' comedy assumes all men have the same sense of humour and all women have the same sense of humour, and that men and women laugh at different things, which is stupid. So I told them we were going to have a general knowledge quiz, in which there was only one question, and whoever shouted out the right answer first won a cash prize. The question was, 'Which lads' mag has the best tits in it?' They would always shout out. *Birdwatching Magazine* or *RSPB Monthly*. Anyway, it didn't matter, I would just pretend that they'd shouted out *Nuts* or *Zoo* and declare that man the winner. He would then receive his Refuge direct debit form and a stamped addressed envelope, I'd set off a party popper and the audience would clap. Sometimes the men would come up to me after the gig, laughing, and give me the form and the envelope (i.e. 'my props') back, misunderstanding the whole thing. I'd then have to explain to them that they had to take the form home, fill it in and send it off.

Anyway, I haven't just been writing jokes, and not going on marches. In my spare time – which I don't have – I've taken activism to a whole new level by throwing inappropriately displayed lads' mags into bins. Like many women who speak out, my actions have ostracised me from my own community. When I say ostracised from my own community, I mean that my husband and children won't go shopping with me any more.

It all started when I went to the supermarket with the kids one morning, around May 2013, for some gendered products they'd seen advertised on Boomerang, the kids' cartoon channel. Yes, well done, Boomerang. As I entered the shop, I noticed that on the bottom shelf of the magazine display unit there was a cosmetic surgery magazine that had a naked woman with arrows and lines drawn all over her face and body in a marker pen, which made it look like she'd forgotten which bits of her body went where; which was next to copies of *Zoo*; which were next to a stack of *Dora the Explorer* magazines (a little girls' magazine); which was next to a magazine called *Front* that had on the cover a completely naked woman except for a pair of strategically placed trainers, where a pair of pants should've been. No one should have to see a strategically placed trainer at eleven in the morning. Not when they've just popped out for bin bags and olive oil ear drops for shifting stubborn wax. I was so upset I sent for the shop manager. This is what happened.

A supermarket near me in north London.

ME: Hello. Thanks for coming down. Can you see anything wrong with this bottom shelf display here at all?

MANAGER: Oh, I know, it's all jumbled up. We just get a grid from head office which tells us where to display everything. Look, it's all numbered.

ME: No, I don't need a grid, thanks. I am asking you,

as a human being, with two eyes, if you can see, please, anything not quite right about the bottom shelf display there. Do any of these magazines look like they've been put in the wrong place?

MANAGER: I don't know what you mean. Is there anything else I can help you with?

ME: Look. I'll help you. (*Pointing to each magazine in turn*) Woman having her face cut up, naked breasts, *Dora the Explorer* magazine, trainer on a vagina. Which of those magazines is in the wrong place? I'll give you a clue. It's the one with glitter all over it that's aimed at girls aged four to six.

It wasn't the image as such. It was the normality of the image. Displayed in a supermarket, on a bottom shelf, next to a little girls' magazine. I'm not ashamed or embarrassed to tell you that I cried in the supermarket. Like a baby. I cried because no-one else seemed bothered by these images. I cried because I was frustrated. Highly sexualised images of women have become so embedded in our culture that most of us don't even notice them any more. I wasn't just upset at this one photograph, in isolation, of course I wasn't. It was the cumulative effect of seeing thousands of them, everywhere, and thinking about the societal implications. We consume objectified images of women in the same way we would a hub cap or a pie mould. When society dehumanises women, when it reduces a woman's body to an object, we are creating a climate where the exploitation of women is tolerated and even encouraged. By making women objects it makes it easier for them to be mistreated. We are not seen as individuals, with rights. And it's not about being a prude or a 'stick in the mud' either. There is a difference between a woman's sexuality and a woman as a sexual object.

So, we've become completely immune to objectified images of women. Also, it's not just about having kids. Lots of people don't have children and they don't want to look at objectified images of women, for all sorts of reasons, but if you do have kids it's an added annoyance. You have to explain everything to kids. Gravity, space, religion, God, why there's a trainer on a mons pubis. I don't know, ask your priest!

My son said, 'That trainer should be on her foot, shouldn't it, Mummy?' I said, 'Yes, dear, it should be. Although on this occasion, I'm very glad that it's not.' There was another little boy there, about my son's age, flicking though *Front* while his mum looked through a cycling magazine. She didn't even notice it, and he didn't bat an eyelid either – and why would he? He'd probably just seen some dentist porn or cheese porn on his iPad. What's a trainer on a vagina to a seven-year-old boy now? It's nothing! By the way, I made up cheese porn and dentist porn as a joke, but then I googled them and guess what? Now I'm on the dairy products' offenders' register.

The manager didn't do anything about the magazines. So after she'd gone, I picked up all the copies of *Zoo*, *Front* and the cosmetic surgery magazine and I threw them in the bin which was just behind the security guard. I was nervous that first time I did it, but I'm not nervous any more, and I've been throwing inappropriately displayed magazines into bins for about two years now, and I've never been stopped or caught once. I'm not encouraging you to do that in your local shops – that would be irresponsible, I don't want you to break the law on my behalf – what I am saying is that I've been doing it pretty much every week for two years and I've never been stopped or caught once. But I'm not encouraging you to do it, I'm just saying that I've never been caught. I wish I would get stopped by the police, because I'm getting a bit bored with it, to be honest.

It's statistically likely that I'm going to get caught, so I thought I'd check the legal position on what I was doing. I searched 'throwing lads' mags into bins' and nothing came up except me. I thought, Yes, I know what I'm doing – but is it theft or criminal damage? I couldn't find anything. Then I was in Costa Coffee and two policemen came in after me. I thought I'd check the law on it with them, save myself a bit of time.

A Costa Coffee in the motorway services on the M1.

ME: Hi, guys! Can I ask you something? If I move that muffin from there on the counter, to there underneath that shelf, that's not theft, is it?

ROZZER NUMBER 1: Why, what are you planning?

ME: What, with muffins? I'm not planning anything with muffins. Who are you? The Muffin Police?

ROZZER NUMBER 1 AGAIN (*he did all the talking, actually*): It's a very suspicious question. No one's ever asked me about the position of a muffin before.

ME: They might have. You just might not have heard them properly.

He was very aggressive with me, actually. The other one was nice, though. It was like that saying, you know.

Anyway, I was caught off guard. I wasn't expecting him to

ask me any questions, even though asking questions is quite a big part of his job. I had to think on my feet:

ME: Oh, well, I'm often shopping with the kids and they move stuff around. I'm just wondering if they can get into trouble.

THE FUZZ: Well, if they hide an item so that it can't be seen, then it's technically theft, because they've prevented a sale.

ME: No it isn't. All they've done is move something from one place in a shop, where it's seen by people who don't want to see it, to another place in the shop where it's not seen. That's not theft, it's just a bit of ethical filing.

OLD BILL: How old are your kids, anyway?

ME: Four and seven.

BACON: Well, you have to be twelve to be prosecuted, so you should be okay.

ME: Ah, so what you're telling me, Officer, is that I need to get the kids to do it. Gotcha.

So I get the kids to do it now, while I have a coffee and look at niche cheese and dentist porn.

So, by the summer of 2013, fate had been kind to me by throwing all sorts of stupidity in my way, which I could exploit for comic effect. I had my routines about Stirling Moss, gendered pens and silly sexist comments; I'd sneaked some serious issues in via a fake heckle and a 'pub quiz for men'; I had a real anecdote about stuff I was doing in real life. What I had to do next was work out how to talk in a funny way about feminist icons and one of my modern-day feminist heroes, Malala Yousafzai, the fifteen-year-old schoolgirl shot by the Taliban.

Since I had taken up feminism the year before, as a marketing device to boost my profile, lots of other people had taken it up as well. Like Beyoncé. Who has now become our new feminist icon. And thank God she did, because we've all been flailing around a bit since Margaret Thatcher passed over. Geri Halliwell, of course, said that Margaret Thatcher was the original Spice Girl. Privatisation Spice. But my targets here are not Beyoncé and Margaret Thatcher themselves. They did not hail themselves as feminist icons. Both women have been shoehorned into the role of feminist icon by people who can't read. This is what Beyoncé said about feminism: 'The word "feminist" can be very extreme. I need to come up with a catchy new word for feminism, right? Like . . . "bootylicious"?'

Eh? Bootylicious? I'm sorry, but we're talking about the systematic and prolonged oppression of women across the whole of society here, for thousands of years. We're not talking about a new ass-flavoured bubblegum.

Thatcher and Beyoncé are icons of politics, of pop, of individualism. They're women who reached the top in predominantly male professions. Margaret Thatcher becoming Prime Minister, at that time, is an extraordinary achievement. So we must respect and celebrate him for that. Which we do. So they are great role models. But icons? I don't think you can be an icon of something that you've publicly distanced yourself from or actually said you despise. That would be like asking Nigel Farage to host the Eurovision Song Contest. Live from the EU. (Jay Z, Beyoncé's husband, has also been hailed as a feminist. This is because he dropped the word 'bitch' from his songs after his daughter was born. So that's nice.)

And to be fair, since I wrote A Bic for Her in 2013, Beyoncé has now identified as a feminist, by performing in front of a huge neon 'FEMINIST' sign at the MTV Video Music Awards in August 2014. We had Malala Yousafzai as our feminist icon for about a week in October 2012. As far as I know, Malala can't sing and dance, but she was shot in the head at point-blank range on her way to school in the Swat Valley in Pakistan, for speaking out for a girl's right to an education. She was flown to England, to the Queen Elizabeth Hospital Birmingham, for brain surgery and survived. She's now at Edgbaston High School for Girls in Birmingham. Bit boring that, though, isn't it? A fifteen-year-old schoolgirl taking on the Taliban and winning? It's much better to have Beyoncé as our feminist icon, because she's beautiful, rich, can sing and dance and therefore embodies the four main tenets of feminism: capitalism, vanity, pitch and rhythm.

Anyway, Beyoncé is a good feminist icon in a capitalist society because she can boost circulation figures and generate sales. And Malala, with the best will in the world, isn't going to do that, is she? As far as I know, Malala isn't the body of an H&M bikini campaign, she doesn't have a lucrative sponsorship deal with Pepsi, she doesn't endorse Nintendo and L'Oréal, and she doesn't have her own perfume called Education. For Women.

All Malala has to offer is courage, inspiration and strength. She endorses basic human rights, fairness to all girls, everywhere, and activism. And where's the money in that? What sales would that generate? Sales of placards? Sales of loudspeakers?

And if you lived during the Arab Spring, sales of gas masks?

I hadn't really thought about any of this stuff before. Then I was asked by a women's magazine to write an article about my own personal modern-day feminist heroes. I emailed them and said I'd like to do my 400 words on Malala. They wrote back and said, 'Well, you could do Malala, who is obviously amazing, and we love her, but we're going to use a photograph of Lena Dunham so can you make her your feminist hero instead?' Even an article about modern-day feminist heroes has to be able to boost circulation. So not only are women's bodies commodified, even feminism itself was becoming a commodity! And thank God for that! I've got to get the car serviced!

Just to clarify, this is nothing to do with Lena Dunham. She is a hugely talented writer/actor/producer/director and is a feminist icon for a lot of young women. My point is that I wanted to write about Malala on this occasion, but a magazine would've preferred for me to write about Dunham so that my article matched the photograph they'd already chosen to go with the piece. I hadn't had any personal experience of media exposure before my radio series and so I didn't appreciate how it all worked, despite having been on the other side of it at the *Daily Mail*. This made me question everything. I thought about why some women had huge media profiles, while others didn't.

I wanted my audience to leave the show thinking about Malala Yousafzai. Hers was such an uplifting, inspiring story.

Now, I don't know if Malala knew at that stage that I didn't have an ending for my show, but either way, I am extremely grateful to her, both for her brilliant and timely speech and also for providing me with an ending. On 12 July 2013 Malala addressed the UN in New York, on her sixteenth birthday. Look it up. It's really great. Try to ignore Gordon Brown the Labour Party politician, former Prime Minister and UN Special Envoy for Global Education, sitting behind her and smiling all the way through it, because it ruins it a bit. I genuinely like Gordon Brown. He's doing some very good work at the UN (unpaid) and I think he is a genuinely decent man. I really do like him. He's just never cracked smiling, has he? All I'm saying is, try to concentrate on what Malala is saying, rather than trying to work out what emotion Gordon Brown is trying to convey with his face. It's a bit distracting. Anyway, I read out her speech, adding three extra words, so that it read like this:

> On 9 October 2012 the Taliban shot me on the left side of my forehead. They shot my friends too. They thought that the bullets would silence us. But they failed. And out of that silence came thousands of voices. The terrorists thought that they would change my aims and stop my ambitions, but nothing changed in my life, except this: weakness, fear and hopelessness died. Strength, power and courage was born...I want education for the sons and daughters of the Taliban...The extremists are afraid of books and pens...They are afraid of women...Let us pick up our books and pens. They are the most powerful weapons...Education is the only solution. Education first...One child, one teacher,

one book and one [Bic for Her] pen can
change the world.

What? Hang on?! No, Malala, no! Not you as well? I'd rather
have lost you to the Taliban than capitalism, Malala!

Then I played in Malala talking to the BBC's World Service
before she was shot about why her and her friends defied the
Taliban, which I'd heard earlier in the year and had been
extremely moved and inspired by. This was followed swiftly by
my walk-out music, Jay-Z's '99 Problems (But A Bitch Ain't
One)', a call back to a joke earlier in the show about Jay Z.
Then I left the building through the door behind the audience. And that was that.

I thought the show would bomb. I went on holiday to
France for the last two weeks of July with the kids and chilled
out. Well, when I say 'chilled out', I mean I was abused and
shouted at and was a slave in a *different* place for two weeks. It
was all very calm and enjoyable and relaxing and I managed
to read about two pages of a book. Then in August I went to
Edinburgh with A *Bic for Her*, and it went fine. I won a crate
of lager, some champagne and what is rightly, or wrongly, perceived as the most prestigious award in stand-up.

I thought, Ah, shit. I'm probably going to have to write
another bloody show now.

CHAPTER NINE

'Before the fart, I didn't see the links. I had trouble making connections between anything to be honest. I couldn't even make the connection between door keys and access to buildings.'

A *Bic For Her*'s Edinburgh 2013 success was inadvertent and unexpected. I was forty-two and had developed a weak bladder after two labours. Labour as in childbirth, I mean. I don't mean that two terms of a Labour government interfered with my ability to retain large amounts of urine. That's Jeremy Hunt the Health Secretary's fault.

I just thought that perhaps I'd left it too late. If I hadn't managed to write a successful show *before* I had kids, when I'd had lots of available writing and thinking time, I wasn't going to do so now, when I'm constantly being shouted at from different rooms to paint faces or wipe arses or find underpants. And that's just from all the other people working in Stoke Newington Library. Actually, what happens when you have kids is that you just make the most of the time that you've got.

Some critics said that *A Bic for Her* was me finding my voice. I'd been looking for it a long time, having lost it by the pork roll van up town in Gloucester sometime in the early eighties. I've been writing and performing since I was about thirteen, writing sketches and plays at school, then joining amateur dramatics groups until I went to drama school aged twenty-three. In about 1987/88, I was in a local production of *Daisy Pulls It Off*. The High Sheriff of Gloucester, who is an actual human person and not a hare or a toad or a fictional character in a children's book, saw me in it and said I had real comic potential. Mind you, I did have sex with him in order to 'get on in this business', like the critic said. I didn't just have sex with him, though; I also had sex with hares and toads and fictional characters in children's books, just to be sure I'd 'get on in this business'.

I remember being in the local newspaper, the *Gloucester Citizen*. I was really chuffed to have my photo in the paper, along with a good review. Mind you, I did have sex with the editor and everyone who worked at the paper to ensure this, like the critic said. I was so excited, and showed my mum and dad and everyone. But then my ex-boyfriend's sister went and ruined it all by saying, 'Next time you're in the paper, brush your hair, will you?' Women. Fucking bitches.

What I'm trying to say is, I didn't think it would take me another nineteen years and loads of sexists being twats day in, day out for me to finally find my voice. I suppose I should thank them all, but they'd only think I fancied them, misread the situation, and then sexually assault me. Then the judge would blame me, for sending mixed signals and wearing a blue T-shirt and jeans instead of a hooded, floor-length hessian sack with dog shit smeared all over it. Oh yes, I was gagging for it, with all my sluttish good etiquette.

So I'd written an hour of jokes about feminism. Everyone then agreed that there wasn't really anything else to say on the subject. I'd pretty much single-handedly ended all female oppression, in all its forms, on a global level. All the women are very grateful. Yes, all of them. No woman has ever disagreed with anything I've ever said about women, ever, because we all agree on absolutely every single thing (see chapter 1). In fact, I don't like to brag, but I recently had an email from the Head of Women, Jimmy Somerville from Bronski Beat, who I've mentioned previously, saying he'd been inundated with emails and texts from all 3.2 billion of them, saying how great I was.

I just hope feminism doesn't get too fashionable or popular. When something hits the mainstream, it normally signals its demise. Thank God David Cameron won't have anything to do with feminism. He thinks it's absolutely shit. Cheers, Dave, yeah. Thanks for not giving a hoot about 51 per cent of the people you're supposed to be responsible for. Yes, we all know you held a Girl Summit in July 2014, to highlight forced marriage and female genital mutilation, because you did loads of press and publicity for it, but you won't ring-fence funding for women's shelters; instead you cut tax credits, reduce housing benefit, cut public services and social security entitlements, shifting employment from public sector to the private sector, make cuts to local services, changes in Universal Credit, cuts to the National Scholarship Programme, extend waiting times on benefit claims and freeze child benefit.

Yeah, you stay away, mate. Feminism's toxic. Don't wear the T-shirt. Don't call yourself a feminist. Leave your daughter in a toilet. We all know what happened to Mumford & Sons after he jumped on their bandwagon.

In fact, Cameron, who is very unpopular with women

voters – surprisingly, given the above – appointed a woman to advise him on women's issues. Why he couldn't just ask his wife Samantha is beyond me. If my fictional husband came home and told me he was employing a woman to advise him on women, I would absolutely hit the glass ceiling.

But I haven't ended the patriarchy all by myself, not entirely. I nearly have, but not quite. I have had a little bit of help along the way, and while I'm very pleased these other brave women are being recognised, we need to keep their achievements in perspective. It's all very well Malala Yousafzai, as previously mentioned, speaking out about a girl's right to an education, and becoming the youngest person ever to win the Nobel Peace Prize, but let's not forget, I was the oldest woman ever to win two Chortle Awards in one year.

I'm not saying it wasn't courageous of a fifteen-year-old girl to put her life at risk for freedom and democracy by standing up to armed terrorists, but I did a gig in Hull in the winter of 2013, and there was no backstage toilet. I had to queue up with my audience in the interval and listen to what they were saying about me. And then the toilet wouldn't flush, so I had to come out of the cubicle and say to the next woman that it wouldn't flush. When I went back onstage for the second act, she was in the front row. I'm not saying Malala wasn't brave to carry on going to school even though she knew she was risking her life to do so, it was brave, but it's not as brave as being stared at for an hour by a woman from Hull who is not laughing at a single thing you say and who has just seen your wee, and carrying on regardless. Then on top of the toilet situation, a fruit fly kept flying around my face during the entire first half of the show, so I had to deal with that in an amusing way too. The venue was in an old fruit market, though, so one might argue that the fly had more of a right to be there than I did. Anyway, my point is, I think we all know who the true feminist hero of our times is.

After its Edinburgh run, *A Bic for Her* then transferred to London's Soho Theatre for nine weeks. My dad came with my sister and her daughters and her daughters' friends and they all liked it, which was a huge relief. I'd always tried to put family and friends off coming to see me in the past in case they saw a terrible show, but I remember hearing my dad laugh, and it being a pivotal moment for me. I didn't die on stage in front of my family. It was a huge breakthrough.

What I try to do is join up the dots, the dots between silly gendered pens and reproductive rights. Before the fart, I didn't see the links. I had trouble making connections between anything, to be honest. I couldn't even make the connection between door keys and access to buildings.

When I was sixteen I was a biker, as I've said, nicknamed Leather Arse by the others, and I went to the Isle of Man TT Race with loads of other Gloucester bikers. Even though I was the youngest person in the group by quite a few years, I was considered the most sensible, probably because I hadn't killed anyone yet and didn't have an incredibly impractical beard. We'd hired out this big chalet-type place with loads of bedrooms in it. We got there quite late and were all starving, so once everyone had unpacked we set out for something to eat and to get absolutely hammered somewhere. The main biker – let's call him Badger, although his real name was Stoat – handed me the only key to the place and said, 'This is the only key to the flat. Put it in a safe place.' So I hid it in my suitcase under my bed and then we all went out. He didn't say, 'We are going out now. We need to not lose this key. You don't get as pissed as everyone else, so you hang on to it and put it somewhere safe.'

'Badger' then had to break back into the flat through an air vent and get the only key from my suitcase. We all watched him do it wearing our night vision goggles.

I wouldn't do that now, because of feminism. I don't think I would ever be locked out of a building ever again. Not since the man farted.

After *A Bic for Her* in 2013, I knew I had to do another show straight away. I was also curious to see if people would come back and I thought that if they did, it might mean that I finally had a financially viable live career. I could do London runs and tour. I booked in a lot of previews to get the next show together, in little clubs through the spring and summer of 2014. I knew the show would be scrutinised and compared, probably unfavourably, to the previous one, which had been thought of as good. The things I wanted to talk about were more challenging for the second show, and I needed to get them right.

Appalling violations of human rights are not easy to listen to at the best of times. Ban Ki-moon, the UN Secretary General, for example, always calls me from children's parties being held in an underground indoor play area that's made entirely out of aluminium, when some free jazz improvisers are on. Or from the orchestra pit of Stomp. He only ever calls me from one of those two places. I think he does it on purpose. On top of that, he insists on speaking in tongues. Ban Ki-moon needs to start thinking about how he communicates bad things, otherwise we're all just going to start switching off.

Huw Edwards, the BBC's harbinger of doom, has pretty much nailed it. He pretends to be Welsh to deliver his bad news. It just takes the edge off it. And I don't need to remind you of Anthony Hopkins in *Silence of the Lambs*. He was not at all menacing, not with that lovely Welsh lilt.

I don't have a very wide vocabulary. I can't remember nouns – which I'm convinced came out of my brain during childbirth, along with afterbirth – and I am often drunk. This means I can sometimes come across like a younger, female Jethro who has been asked to explain to an alien what the point of *Candy Crush* is.

I don't enjoy making people nervous by talking about serious things. That's not my main objective. It is some comedians', but it's not mine. I'm not interested in just shocking people. 'Saying the unsayable!' is not something I'm interested in. It doesn't mean anything, does it? Everything's sayable, isn't it? You can literally say anything! Unless the unsayable thing you want to say something about hasn't got any language attached to it yet.

I'm a stand-up comedian. The only thing I am required to do is make people laugh. I'm a fun facilitator, someone's idea of a night out. I'm 'The Entertainment', as an elderly usher referred to me once when I arrived at an empty arts theatre in the depths of the Welsh mountains, on my sparsely attended *War Donkey* tour in 2012, and carrying the weight of being 'The Entertainer' in a small and economically depressed Welsh town was a sobering thought, a declaration of duty and responsibility, which I have never forgotten.

The comedians Mark Steel, Josie Long, Mark Thomas, Jeremy Hardy and Paul Sinha are brilliant at domesticating big ideas, like lion tamers with mic stands. They'll take a political issue and humanise it. They'll put themselves, and us, into the narrative, making it easier for us to understand what the fuck they're going on about. It's a real skill. If you're politically unengaged, they never make you feel alienated.

There's no short cut to finding out how to do this. You just have to gig and find out what works for you. Working the stuff up into coherent routines is the hardest part. A lot of people think we just pluck routines out of thin air, or just make it up when we get up onstage, but most comedians will have spent months, sometimes years, working stuff out.

I did an Edinburgh preview in 2013 in a room above a pub on Essex Street in Angel. The show included not yet properly worked-out material about labia minora reduction surgery, domestic violence, female genital mutilation, and farts. There was no stage and the room was very narrow, so I was within touching distance to the front row. Also, I'm quite short and a man in the front row had a very long upper body, so we were pretty much in each other's faces.

The audience were allowed to bring food up from the bar downstairs, but there weren't any tables so they had to try to balance their dinner on their laps. The man right in front of me with the long upper body was eating a curry, noisily and sloppily, all the way through my show. He didn't seem to think there was anything wrong with this at all. I was just another thing for this man to consume. Call me sensitive, but it seemed like a passive-aggressive act to me. It riled me. I wouldn't do something like that, because I'd think it was rude. I wouldn't polish off a banana split in the face of an archaeologist who was giving an emotional speech about the discovery of the Alfred Jewel.

So towards the end of my set I said to him, 'Nice, was it, mate? Enjoy that, did you?'

And he said, 'Yes. Yes, thanks, it was lovely. Bit spicy, though.'

I said, 'Well, never mind. There's a frozen yoghurt cafe over the road; why don't you nip across in the interval and get yourself a nice cold yoghurt? You could slurp your way through that while the next act is on.' He did, which meant that the next act had to do their preview with him eating frozen yoghurt right up in their face. And it was all my fault.

What I'm saying is, you just have to gig and gig and gig and you find a way of making your material accessible, even in the face of yoghurt and curry.

Another time, at the Edinburgh Fringe, a man sat in the front row of one of my shows eating a Chinese takeaway. When I challenged him about it, he seemed genuinely affronted and baffled as to why I'd brought it up. He said he was seeing dozens of Fringe shows back to back and didn't have time to eat it between shows, so had to have it while the performer was onstage.

The funniest experience I've had with audience members was when a dog came in once. Not just a dog. It didn't come by itself. It came with its owner. I didn't know what it was at first, because it was in a woman's handbag. I thought it was a wig. Because it had a little bow in it and everything, I thought, Well, I'd better not say anything, in case it's a spare. It's normally a wig on a head you have to avoid mentioning, not a wig in a bag. But then it moved.

I said to her, 'Is that a dog in your bag?'

She said, 'Yes.'

I said, 'Has it bought a ticket? This is the Fringe, you know, I'm not a charity. Does it want to see the show or is it just waiting for you?'

She said, 'I thought it might put you off.'

Maybe. But not as much as a moving, growling handbag would. It was a nice dog, a little Yorkshire terrier, so I picked it up and continued doing my show as normal, carrying the dog around with me, and every time I got to the end of a punch-line, it did a massive yawn followed by a big shake, you know how dogs do. Of course, everyone thought it was hilarious and much funnier than all my prepared material, which had taken me a year to write. Then a bloke in the audience waited for me after the show and said, 'Was that dog a plant?'

I said, 'No, it's a dog.'

He thought the whole thing was planned. Yes. I've had no budget for costume or props or press and marketing, because I spent all my money training a dog to yawn on cue. Twice.

Misogyny is as baffling to me as an industrial-sized tin of baked beans and I find that incredibly baffling. When I was pregnant with my second child, I stood at a baked-potato stand in Gloucester and stared at an industrial-sized tin of baked beans. For about twenty minutes. In the end, my son said to me, 'We really have to go now.' Why did I do that? Because I couldn't believe how big it was? Because I thought there might be something else in there, other than beans? Or maybe I stared at it for so long because I was so very, very tired and hormonal. I don't know. We do odd things.

So I try to incorporate this aspect of my personality into the act. I try to focus on the stupidity and senselessness of it all. With *A Bic for Her*, I had already liberated myself from the need to be liked or popular, and that freed me up. I wasn't thinking, Oh, that's a bit extreme, better water it down so that more people like it. It wasn't a conscious decision to write something I thought would have greater appeal. I just thought some people like me might like it. Some, it seemed, did. And I wondered if they would all come back to see the 2014 show, *An Ungrateful Woman*. As far as the critics were concerned, who'd never noticed me before, this was the Difficult Second Album.

CHAPTER TEN

'Every single vagina in the world is completely unique and magical.
Vaginas are like snowflakes. Made of gammon.'

As you know, I am a white, working-class woman, of Irish descent, who grew up in Gloucester and then moved to London and became a stand-up comedian. You might think I don't really have a right to talk about female genital mutilation. You might think this because, unless I've been involved in a series of incredibly unlikely events, resulting in a catastrophic case of mistaken identity, I am not, and never have been, in any danger of being directly affected by FGM. You might think I don't have a right to talk about FGM because in the late nineties I had a bikini wax before I went on holiday. But I don't agree with you if you think this, so in case you didn't already know, I'll just quickly explain what FGM entails.

Female genital mutilation has four main types.

Type One is the partial or total removal of the clitoris and/ or the prepuce.

Type Two is the partial or total removal of the clitoris and the labia minora, with or without the excision of the labia majora.

Type Three is the most extreme form, involving the creation of a covering scar seal by cutting and stitching together the labia minora and/or labia majora, with or without the excision of the clitoris.

Type Four refers to all other harmful procedures to the female genitalia for non-medical purposes. This can include pricking, piercing, scraping and cauterising.

Female genital mutilation is a real thing. It's a real thing that someone, a very long time ago, thought was a good idea. I don't know what he[29] looked like or what he was wearing when he first suggested FGM, I just don't know. I'm sorry, it was 5,000 years ago. I did have a nightmare about the inventor of FGM once though, and he looked a bit like this:

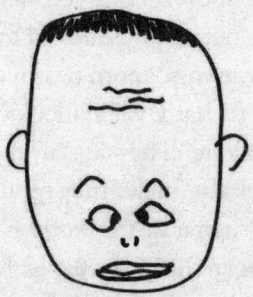

I don't know what traumatic experience he had been through that meant that he was working from a different set of rules to the rest of humanity. I don't know which of his *other* ideas were deemed too extreme and turned down. Whatever happened at that meeting – for there must surely have been some kind of meeting – no one called him out on it. The chair of the meeting didn't say, 'Erm … yes … I think I know what you're

---

[29] We can't be certain it was a man who first came up with the idea to mutilate female genitalia, but I think it's reasonable to assume that it was.

trying to achieve here ... and I admit, the women are getting a bit out of hand. I'm just not sure you're going the right way about it. I don't think you've thought it through properly. It just seems a little bit extreme, that's all. It's a *bold move*, I'll give you that. I'm just not sure it'll catch on. Tell you what, why doesn't everyone sleep on it? Have a word with the bitches in the morning when they've finished doing all their chores. See what they say. But I wouldn't get the company seal printed up just yet. I think you're going to get a lot of shit for this, mate.'

That didn't happen. That was about 5,000 years ago. And as of May 2015, an estimated 130 million women worldwide are living with the consequences of FGM. These women had no choice in it whatsoever. And yet, here in the West, we are choosing to have our genitals altered by cosmetic surgeons because the mainstreaming of porn has given men and women an unrealistic idea of what a vagina looks like. Ladies please, leave your vaginas alone. They are all magnificent. They're not all meant to look the same, they're supposed to look different. Every single vagina in the world is completely unique and magical. Vaginas are like snowflakes. Made of gammon.

When you learn about FGM for the first time, your brain can't process it. I remember my own reaction of disgust and shock and disbelief and I see this same reaction in others. People can't believe it happens, but it does. It's not some hellish thing made up. It's not from the world of fiction.

It wasn't invented by the Riddler or the Penguin as a patriarchal tool to threaten Batman with after he came out as a feminist and vowed to rid Gotham City of all forms of female oppression. It's not an urban myth. Or a Greek myth. Or even a Norse one.

Female genital mutilation is not a Swiftian satire. Type 3 FGM doesn't follow the rules and structure of a Latin satire. FGM wasn't in Jonathan Swift's *A Modest Proposal for Preventing the Children of Poor People from Being a Burthen to Their Parents or Country, and for Making Them Beneficial to the Publick*. Swift didn't suggest FGM be introduced to Ireland's poor, as an effective way of controlling the population and easing Ireland's economic problems, after his controversial 'baby-eating' idea didn't catch on.

In the whole gamut of female oppression, with gendered pens at one end of the spectrum, FGM sits firmly at the other. I would not suggest for a moment that one act of violence is worse than another. Every woman's pain and suffering and abuse is equal and relative. But what sets FGM apart from all other gender-based violence (with the exception of honour killings) is that FGM is considered a *good* thing by the communities that practise it. Both men and women from FGM practising communities respect the ideology behind it. They believe that FGM benefits girls and women, both physically and psychologically. It's a deeply entrenched tradition, which is why it's so hard to eradicate. Also, the cutters are paid well, so there is a financial incentive for them to continue doing it.

There are countries whose own governments are pro-FGM, who actually endorse and legitimise a practice that has been banned by the UN. In 2012, Azza El Garf, a prominent figure in Egypt's Freedom and Justice Party, the political wing of the Islamist group the Muslim Brotherhood, called FGM 'beautification plastic surgery' and didn't think FGM should be banned, saying it was a woman's personal decision. But it's not a woman's personal decision, is it? Little girls are held down, against their will, and tortured in the most inhumane and barbaric way imaginable, by the people they trust the most. Unless by 'a woman's personal decision' El Garf means it's a mother's personal decision to breach UN contraventions by violating the human rights of her daughter? In which case, that's not *really* the same thing at all, is it? I'm not sure a government official should be saying that committing child abuse and torture is a decision for parents. It's like Jeremy Hunt, the Health Secretary, saying that if parents want to cut their children's ears off and pull their eyeballs out, then that's their personal decision, really, it's not up to governments to intervene in that sort of thing.

FGM was banned in Egypt in 2008 but is still widespread. More than 90 per cent of Egyptian women are living with FGM, according to government statistics. In November 2014 the doctor and father of a thirteen-year-old girl who died after allegedly undergoing FGM were acquitted in a landmark trial in Egypt. Suhair al-Bataa died in June 2013. Her doctor denied carrying out FGM on her, and blamed her death on an allergy.

We cannot say we live in a civilised world until we have eradicated FGM. How can we have made all sorts of medical and scientific breakthroughs, and yet still tolerate this practice? How can we have the Rosetta spacecraft? Which was carrying the Philae probe, launch into space in 2004, using the gravity of Earth and Mars to slingshot its way towards comet 67P, land on it, bounce off it, and then land on it again, AND FGM?

On 24 October 2013 I read a piece by Maggie O'Kane and Patrick Farrelly in the *Guardian* newspaper about a couple of film-makers, Shara Amin and Nabaz Ahmed, who'd made a documentary about the prevalence of FGM in Iraqi Kurdistan. I've still got the article. I can't bring myself to throw it away.

Amin and Ahmed spent ten years on the road, talking to women and men about the impact of FGM on their lives, their children and their marriages. Sometimes it took them months to get people to speak about it. In the end the women spoke out. Their film, A Handful of Ash, not only managed to change fiercely conservative opinions, it also helped to change the law. Amin and Ahmed joined forces with WADI, a small German–Iraqi non-governmental organisation dedicated to eliminating FGM in Iraqi Kurdistan, and took their film to Parliament, which sparked a campaign by the Kurdish parliamentary Women's Committee to outlaw FGM, and the law was implemented in 2011.

A key turning point was when a leading Kurdish cleric, Mullah Omar Chngyani, told a conference that 'Female circumcision is an injustice. It is a crime against women.' A fatwa was declared against it and word filtered down into the villages. One midwife who practised FGM said that without this, she would still be performing FGM for Islam. Now normally I'd be quite sarcastic about a man speaking out and everyone listening, but on this occasion I'll let it go. It's crucial that Muslim leaders and tribal elders speak out. Female genital mutilation is not a requirement of Islam or Christianity and banning it isn't going to make much difference if communities stick together. FGM's nothing to do with religion; twats are just using the name of religion, once again, to justify the subjugation of women.

So this was a positive story, no doubt about that. These brave and brilliant film-makers had made a huge impact on the lives of thousands of girls and women. They'd helped change the law. It was an amazing and uplifting story. So it wasn't the story that floored me particularly, it was the photo accompanying the article.

It was of a seven-year-old girl, sat with her mother. She's not named. She has strawberry-blonde hair tied back in a bun, freckles on her nose and big brown eyes. She's wearing golden hooped earrings, a pretty red dress with a white collar and flowers on it, and a red and yellow bracelet. She looks like any other seven-year-old girl. In fact, she looks a bit like my daughter, who has a similar red dress from H&M, and a similar bracelet.

And then I read the caption which simply says, 'A seven-year-old girl receives a bag of sweets and pop from her mother after being circumcised in Iraqi Kurdistan, before the practice was outlawed.'

My feelings towards FGM, up until that point, had been of anger, frustration, outrage and upset, but because this little girl reminded me so much of my own daughter, it affected me in a different emotional way. It wasn't necessarily that I was MORE upset, I was just upset in a different way. It went right to the core of me. It's like the information was sent to another part of my brain. The look on the little girl's face is the same look my daughter gives me when I brush the knots out of her hair. All I've done is brush the knots out of her hair, but she has a very sensitive scalp, and it makes me feel terrible. This little girl has the same expression, but she's just been held down by her mother as another woman cut her genitals with no anaesthetic, for no other reason than 'cultural tradition.'

It made me think about my own childhood. To the seven-year-old me. The little girl in the photo is holding a plastic carrier bag full of pop and sweets, given to her by her mother, as a treat. When I was seven, dad would get us pop and sweets on a Friday night for tidying our rooms. She had pop and sweets for going through the most unimaginable cruelty. It made me think about the unbearable unfairness of it all, that geography was the only thing separating her experiences from mine and my daughters. And while I can't bear to look at this photograph, I also can't bring myself to throw the article away. Symbolically, that would feel to me like moving on, and I don't want to move on.

The picture is taken moments after the girl was cut. She's looking at her mother for some kind of reassurance and support; she's trying to make sense of what's just happened to her, but she can't, and she won't ever, because FGM doesn't make any sense.

Lots of images of FGM are just plain horrific and are extremely difficult to look at. This image isn't gruesome or graphic, but it captures, in one little girl's facial expression, what had, in real terms, just occurred; the pain; the physical and psychological trauma; a childhood innocence brutally taken away; the trust she shared with her mother broken down; the realisation that the world is actually shit and full of bastards. She's only seven, my own son's age, but her childhood, as she knew it, is over now, gone forever, just because some loser 5,000 years ago lost the plot and blurted out his magic cure for controlling women.

My reaction to this photo made me question everything, about myself and about the wider issue.

Have we become desensitised to what we consider 'Third World problems?' On the May bank holiday weekend, I stopped at a motorway service station on my way to the Machynlleth

Comedy Festival in Wales, where I was performing my most recent stand-up show, *An Ungrateful Woman*.

Above the hand dryers in the ladies' toilets were posters of African girls who were being sold as child brides. The girls were ten. They were being sold to men of fifty or sixty. It's obviously abhorrent and disgusting, but I watched woman after woman passively consume this information as they dried their hands. One of them tutted, but the majority didn't show any response.

The posters could've been about malaria or poverty or Ebola or HIV or for water aid, all things that don't directly affect us. The fate of the kidnapped Nigerian schoolgirls, who are still missing, doesn't affect us either. Where's that story gone? Why hasn't someone gone in to get them? If 200 white girls had been kidnapped from a school in Surrey, I'm pretty sure they'd have been rescued by now, and if they hadn't been, there would still be media interest in them.

If the poster in the ladies' toilet was of Maddie McCann, would more women have texted the number and given £2 to help? Or would they have just passively consumed her image too? I don't know.

An estimated sixty six thousand women are living with FGM in the UK. Twenty thousand girls under the age of fifteen are at risk here (cutters either come here and cut twenty or twenty-five girls at a time, or girls are sent away during the school holidays), and yet there have been no prosecutions. By not acting we are complicit in it. FGM is a violation of human rights, it's child abuse, but it's also a race issue. I'm pretty sure that if FGM was happening to white western girls there'd have been at least one UK prosecution by now. These girls are British citizens. It's our duty to protect them.

The photo of the little girl made me think about how we tackle issues affecting black, Asian and minority ethnic women. I think that if FGM, forced marriage and honour based crimes were happening to white European women they'd have been eradicated. There are brilliant activists in these communities but it needs wider support – it's not just an issue for black feminists and postcolonial feminists.

Practising communities see FGM as a tradition and I can see why people in certain communities want to hold on to their practices and cultural identity. In Iraqi Kurdistan, for example, the fall of Saddam Hussein led to a resurgence of the practice of FGM, which was seen as a mark of cultural independence for the Kurds. So while I can understand wanting to hang on to cultural traditions, and the concept of cultural relativism, I can't respect it when those customs involve the mutilation of a girl's genitals. They're not trying to hang on to some sort of hat, or strange wooden shoes, or an instrument. They're trying to preserve child abuse and torture. It's like being nostalgic for medieval forms of punishment, like being hanged, drawn and quartered.

It's not racist of me to say that FGM is wrong. It's racist to say it isn't wrong, because then I would be saying that it's okay for girls from certain countries to be cut, and it isn't okay for ANY GIRL TO BE CUT, whether it's a girl from Iraqi Kurdistan, a girl from Somalia, or a girl from Egypt.

But it's not just about becoming desensitised about things happening far away, it's also about something difficult to accept.

Did I react to that photo of the little girl in the way that I did because she was white? Does this make me a racist? Or did it just mean that I was affected by an image that I could relate to on a more personal level? Is humanity hardwired to empathise more with things we recognise? The reason we can't relate to images of non-white, non-Europeans' suffering, is because we don't think they are like us. On an intellectual level we don't think like this, but there are deeply ingrained responses to what we perceive as the other.

Since the start of 2015, more than 1,750 migrants have perished in the Mediterranean. The Foreign Office said it will not support future search and rescue operations because they encourage migration.

The Costa Concordia cruise-ship disaster resulted in the loss of thirty-two lives, many of whom were white Europeans. Will the Foreign Office support search and rescue operations for capsized cruise-ships carrying rich white holidaymakers? Or would that just encourage more people to go on cruises? The difficult truth is that there is a price list for human life, and some of us are deemed more valuable than others.

In their shameful decision to withdraw help, the British government dehumanised trafficked migrants, dealing with them almost as an abstract political issue, in order to justify their position. But they had to do this, because the alternative is to see them as individual human beings, just like us, each with their own story. And they can't afford to do this, because then it would be inconceivable to turn a blind eye and just let them all drown.

As a white westerner, there are things white westerners have to face in order for us to start dealing with issues effectively, however uncomfortable those truths might be. I've had to face it because of my reaction to a photograph of a girl who reminds me of my daughter. It reached a different part of me and I am shocked and ashamed to admit it.

I don't know if our lack of commitment on all these issues means we're all racist or not. But I do know that we are tolerating terrible abuses of black and minority ethnic women in a way that we absolutely wouldn't if they were happening to white western women, and that we're simply not doing enough.

Jaha Dukureh, Founder of Safe Hands for Girls, says 'It is all of our responsibility to make sure we end the suffering. By ending FGM we not only protect the future generation but we heal ourselves.'

The Girl Generation, a global campaign funded by the Department for International Development, which supports the Africa-led movement to end FGM in one generation, is exciting and encouraging, but still more has to be done. As a citizen of the world, I feel shame and guilt and responsible for every girl who undergoes female genital mutilation. The world needs to come together and sort this out once and for all.

I bumped into a friend of mine the other night, called Simon Munnery. Simon Munnery is arguably one of the finest comedians working in the world today. Anyway, he's just taken up morris dancing and we got talking. I reminded him that I had the Forest of Dean Morris Dancers at a party I once held, which he came to. It was lovely. Twelve middle-aged men danced around with little bells on their legs and waved white hankies about. One of them dressed up as a stag, which one of my friends found sexually arousing. It was all very embarrassing. She wouldn't leave him alone. I think it was his two-foot-high papier mâché stag's head that pushed her over the edge. She kept grabbing the poor man, saying, 'Ooh! Hello, Mr Staggy, what big antlers you have!' I was mortified. He was about eighty. She didn't know that, obviously, because he was wearing an enormous stag's head made out of paper and glue.

Anyway, waving white hankies around and dancing with bells on your legs hasn't been banned by the United Nations. Not yet. Not as far as I know. Although now that the 'dogmatic liberal elite' managed to get Jeremy Clarkson sacked for his sustained physical and verbal attack on an innocent BBC producer, it's only a matter of time before the BBC sack morris dancing as well.

The World Health Organization do not say the following on their website:

> Morris dancing is recognized
> internationally as a violation of the
> human rights of girls and women. It
> reflects deep-rooted inequality between
> the sexes, and constitutes an extreme
> form of discrimination against women.
> Morris dancing is nearly always carried
> out on minors and is a violation of the
> rights of children. It also violates a
> person's rights to health, security and
> physical integrity, the right to be free from
> torture and cruel, inhuman or degrading
> treatment, and the right to life when the
> dance routine results in death. Plus, the
> music is stupid.

Ban Ki-moon, the UN Secretary General, didn't say morris dancing was 'a serious health and human rights issue.'

and continue 'The effects include depression, insecurity, pain, infections, incontinence and deadly complication in pregnancy and childbirth. While some may say morris dancing is a tradition, it constitutes a human rights violation that must cease. If Ban Ki-moon had said that, I wouldn't have booked morris dancing as the main entertainment at my wedding, in breach of UN contraventions.

On 25 February 2014, Michael Gove, Secretary of State for Education, got involved with FGM as well. Good grief. Of all the men in the world who could be involved with FGM, from George Clooney and Michael Wood, the historian, to Robbie Williams and Zayn Malik, it had to be Michael Gove.

Gove agreed to sign an e-petition by the *Guardian* newspaper and Fahma Mohamed from the Bristol-based charity Integrate Bristol. The petition called on Gove to write to all schools with guidelines on how teachers could look out for signs for girls at risk of FGM. And he did. Which was good news for the anti-FGM campaign, but bad news for anyone suffering nightmares or flashbacks as a result of their experiences, because Michael Gove was going to be in them now as well.

Here's a few funny facts about Gove:

He loves Dairylea Dunkers and luxury coleslaw.

He's learning to play the ukulele because he loves Mumford & Sons so much.

There are as many photographs of Margaret Thatcher in his office as there are of his wife and children.

He loves Wagner so much that he came back from

holiday with a pair of lederhosen-style swimming trunks.

He eats too many Doritos.

So I wanted to talk about FGM in my new show. Many people still don't know what it is, and I don't think it can be eradicated until everyone does. I know that people don't know about it because they come up to me after shows and tell me or they write to me afterwards. Michael Gove's wife, the *Daily Mail* columnist Sarah Vine, doesn't think British girls, who live in British villages, should know about FGM and she didn't want her husband to sign the petition. She thinks that British girls who live in British villages aren't in any danger of having their British genitals mutilated, so they don't need to know about it.

As a mother of young children, I understand Vine's maternal instinct to protect and shield and preserve innocence. But she's wrong on this one. People need to know she was wrong about judging Ed Miliband on the basis of his kitchen as well. We've got to face up to FGM, however difficult that is, and stop judging main party leaders on the size of their kitchens, rather than on their policies.

I don't know if Michael Gove felt genuinely passionate about ending FGM or not. I think he probably did. Either that, or he just dislikes his wife so much that he contrived a situation whereby he was asked to sign an anti-FGM e-petition calling on schools and head teachers to be aware of the signs of girls at risk of FGM, which he knew would annoy the shit out of her because he's sick of her talking about him in her column all the time. Anyway, it doesn't matter why he did it. He signed up and I'm glad. He did a good thing. It's just a shame he made such a pig's cock of education.

I was introduced to Leyla Hussein by a great woman called Caroline Pridgeon, who was organising an anti-FGM charity fund-raiser. Leyla co-founded the Daughters of Eve with Nimco Ali and Sainab Abdi, and the Dahlia Project, and made the hard-hitting and powerful BAFTA-nominated documentary *The Cruel Cut*. Apart from Darius Danesh, the 2002 *Pop Idol* finalist, Leyla's the smartest, coolest person I've ever met. And I've met Peter Stringfellow, remember. Leyla is so intellectually, emotionally and spiritually evolved that when we meet up for a coffee, she makes me feel like an archaic *Homo sapien* from the Middle Palaeolithic. Or like someone from Gloucester. Which is exactly what I am.

I asked Leyla if a comedian, especially one from Gloucester, who had two webbed toes on her right foot, and hadn't yet mastered stone tools, had any right to talk about FGM in a stand-up set. And she said yes. I asked her if she thought it would be alienating to a comedy audience. And she said yes. I asked her if she thought survivors of FGM would be offended or angry if I tried to talk about it. And she said no. Survivors and activists don't care who talks about FGM, they just want people to talk about it. 'Aliens can talk about FGM if they want to,' she said.[30]

Great! I thought. Until I realised how good a joke about FGM would have to be and then I just felt a bit sick and regretted asking her and wished she'd said no, you can't write about FGM.

---

[30] She didn't say that.

Anyway, Leyla and I organised a benefit for the Manor Gardens Health Advocacy Service FGM Initiative unit where Leyla works as a counsellor and psychotherapist. We held it at the Bloomsbury Theatre in London with the comedians Daniel Kitson, Isy Suttie, Jo Brand and Shazia Mirza. Manor Gardens Health Advocacy Project does community-level FGM prevention work. At the heart of this work are their community facilitators who come from communities affected by FGM and are employed seasonally. Manor Gardens provides them with training and support to speak out against FGM and educate, support and empower their communities.

It was really important to me to have Leyla's blessing. I needed her to tell me that it was okay for me to talk about FGM. She made me think differently. She explained to me that everyone brings something different to the table. We can all apply the skills we have to an issue in order to inform and educate. I work in comedy, so that's where I come in.

In comedy, you don't 'own' subjects. Just because one comic talks about something, it doesn't then mean that no one else is allowed to. Leyla says the more voices the better, and the more diverse those voices are, even better, because you're reaching different demographics. The spread is wider. I always remember something she said when I first asked her about it: 'We struggle to get people along to FGM conferences and talks, so if you can get it into comedy clubs, then go for it!' Then she laughed at me, hysterically.

Loads of female comics have been talking about feminism for ages. I've seen explicitly feminist material from UK stand-ups Danielle Ward, Josie Long, Sara Pascoe, Sarah Kendall, Lucy Porter, Nadia Kamil, Katherine Ryan, Shappi Khorsandi and loads of others not to mention all the comics before us doing it! So it's not just me. I was aware that after I won the Edinburgh Comedy Award, if a female comic said the words 'vagina' or 'tit' or 'separatist feminism', journalists would often mention me, which must have been incredibly annoying for them. It's happening less so now, but I had no control over that. I didn't write the headlines and I didn't know the stories were being written. But I didn't 'bag' feminism. No one did. Also, Kate Smurthwaite's been talking about feminism for ten years, so if anyone 'owns' it – which they don't – it's her.

So none of us owns the subject, and we should be able to talk about whatever we like. If Tracey Emin decides to create a piece of explicitly feminist art, she should be able to do that, even if this piece of art included some of her used sanitary towels. I would just like to point out here that there seems to be one set of rules for eminent, award-winning artists of considerable repute, and quite another for feminist comedians, who would be absolutely torn to shreds by audiences and critics alike for even mentioning tampons, let alone throwing a load of used ones all over the place. Imagine the uproar if one landed in someone's drink.

Anyway, Josie Long, the eminent, award-winning stand-up comedian of some repute, has a *very* good menstruation routine, so stick that in your budget, George Osborne (Chancellor of the Exchequer as at April 2015), and reduce VAT on sanitary products from 5 per cent to 1 per cent or, better still, impose a zero tax rate and smoke it.

Hang on a second. Was that a period joke? Have I just done the very thing everyone accuses us all of doing all the time? Is that the only line people are going to pull out of this book now? Like Charlotte Runcie did with the taped farts? Oh well, at least I don't end the whole book on a period joke. Imagine if I did that!

I'm always hugely conscious of trying not to sound too worthy onstage, or to sound like I've worked anything out. I haven't cracked that yet. The Dutch comic Hans Teeuwen has. Hans Teeuwen wrote a very good pro-FGM routine. Teeuwen is from a very liberal background. He grew up in the politically correct Netherlands. We know his politics. He's an outspoken advocate of free speech and women's rights. It's funny that he pretends to believe that a woman's pleasure derives from giving her husband pleasure, and therefore that she doesn't really need a clitoris. It's a shocking position to take, but it's a brave and hilarious one and Teeuwen knows this. He knows how idiotic and ludicrous those ideas are, and what better way to communicate those misogynistic ideas than to pass them off as your own. Genius. Then again, I may have got Hans Teeuwen horribly wrong, and he might just be a complete asshole.[31]

So Leyla thinks that there is absolutely a place for FGM in comedy. In fact, she would argue that is completely necessary. Mocking FGM is a huge part of how she deals with it personally.

'FGM is about controlling women, pure and simple,' she says. It's saying, 'I am going to control what you do with your body, and how you use your body.' Her reaction is to laugh at that ideal and the people who hold those views. By laughing at FGM, you lower its status. If you mock something that is considered so important, and sacred, you take away its importance. You make it ridiculous.

Leyla and I made a short film together, called *What is FMG?*

---

[31] He is obviously anti-FGM.

We based it on Leyla's own experiences of being interviewed in the media, of people's innocent ignorance of FGM in the UK and of people's reluctance to criticise it out of cultural sensitivity, as she showed in her documentary *The Cruel Cut*. So it was all Leyla's idea. She suggested it one day as we were waiting to go into a Home Affairs Select Committee Hearing on FGM.

By the way, I know what you're thinking, and no, I didn't just befriend Leyla so that I could get into Home Affairs Select Committee Hearings on FGM. I wouldn't do that. I'm happy to go through the proper channels. It's just that Leyla was going and so got me in too. I really needed to see how it all worked for myself, and what the government was doing to try to stop this practice in the UK. If I wasn't planning on writing about FGM I would have gone anyway, but the more knowledge and first-hand experiences I had of what was being done to try to stop it, the better. We got front-row seats in the end, which was brilliant, so we had a really good view of Keith Vaz, the sarcastic chair of the select committee, in his actual chair's chair, being sarcastic to people and rolling his eyes as government officials and GPs spoke. One particular highlight was aimed at Edward Timpson MP, Parliamentary Under-Secretary for Children and Families, who told the select committee that 'more teachers read the email Michael Gove sent to schools with guidelines on FGM, than a lot of the other emails the department sends out'. This was in response to Keith Vaz's question on how successful Integrate Bristol and the *Guardian* newspaper's e-petition to send all head teachers guidelines on how they can spot the signs of girls at risk of FGM had been.

To which Vaz replied, in the most sarcastic voice he could

muster, 'Do you mean to tell me that teachers don't read emails from the Department for Education?'

Which I then turned into a piece of material that said:

> Why did they send teachers an email about
> something as important as FGM from
> Gove's own email account?! Of course
> they weren't going to open it! Even I
> know that? They should've sent it from a
> Thomson Holidays email address! With
> 'Claim your free cruise this summer' in the
> subject header.

Anyway, as we waited to go inside the hearing, Leyla said she'd watched some sketches of me on the internet that I'd done with Harry Hill. She said she liked the one of me as an ant inside a cardboard box surrounded by sugar, and suggested we made a film about FGM. Not dressed as ants, obviously. Her idea was that I could interview her in a funny, ignorant way about FGM, which would highlight all the ignorance surrounding it. Leyla had just watched Barak Obama's interview about ObamaCare on Zach Galifianakis's Between Two Ferns on the website Funny or Die, and she thought we could do something similar.

In order to pay for our short film, Leyla and I needed some quick cash, because we wanted to film it before our benefit that was coming up and show it there. The quickest way we were going to get some was for me to go on ITV1's *Celebrity Squares*. I would just like to reiterate here at this point all the sacrifices I have had to make and how much better I am than all those other completely unknown and ignored grass-roots campaigners and activists who put their lives at risk to try and eradicate FGM.

All the work these women do in educating communities and lobbying governments. In the UK alone, unsung heroes like Sainab Abdi, who co-founded Daughters of Eve with Leyla and Nimco Ali; Sarian Kamara of the Manor Gardens Health Advocacy Project; Jennifer Bourne, an FGM specialist nurse; Joy Clarke, an FGM specialist midwife; Janet Fyle of the Royal College of Midwifes, author of the RCM recommendations for tackling FGM; and Dana Jade, founder of Clit Rock. These inspiring, brave women are improving the lives of other women, and we must acknowledge their work, of course we must, but they didn't have to go on ITV1's *Celebrity Squares* did they? Therefore I am about a hundred times better than them and will reap the rewards in heaven, which I'm not going to because I am pro-choice.

Celebrity Squares isn't the sort of job I'd normally do. I don't have the right skill-set or personality for those types of show. I don't look right or sound right and I can't think of anything to say. It's nothing to do with being shit or being a woman, either, so don't get bogged down in all that bullshit. Plenty of my peers are excellent on them – Kath Ryan, Sara Pascoe, Jo Caulfield, Josie Long, Shappi Khorsandi, Holly Walsh, Lucy Porter, Sarah Millican, Sue Perkins, Susan Calman, Aisling Bea, Jo Brand, and Roisin Conaty for example, as well as all the others I haven't mentioned; but I'm not. I can't improvise with other comics in a competitive way either, or talk to the audience very well. I don't have those skills, but I have other ones. It doesn't matter. We all bring different things to the table.

And no, I didn't want to 'just ask my fictional husband for the money', because what kind of a feminist asks a man for money to fund her feminist film about FGM? I'd be thrown out of feminism by The Head of Women, Jimmy Somerville from Bronski Beat!

I've done other questionable things too. Eleven years ago I was single and living in a bedsit. A temp agency offered me two weeks' secretarial/admin work at the *Daily Mail* and I was broke so I took it. I ended up being there for three years because my new boss developed a debilitating neurological brain disease called PSP (Progressive Supranuclear Palsy) and I didn't feel like I could leave him to do his own filing.

I got my job on the *Daily Mail* gossip column by lying. After five years in London trying to be an actress and a comedian I still wasn't getting any work or paid gigs, so I signed on at a temp agency, invented some qualifications and took a job as a secretary on the *Daily Mail* Diary page. At the time, my act on the comedy circuit was to do impressions of how TV historians walk. It didn't normally go down very well. Not for seven minutes. There's a rule in comedy, always start with your strongest walk, and I remembering thinking, Shit, if they've not gone for David Starkey, they're not going to like Dan Cruickshank, who is even less well known than David Starkey.

I didn't even know what would make a good story. One Sunday I was walking past the River Café, a posh restaurant near Hammersmith, and there was some sort of do going on. I stopped to watch an older man who was dancing around. He was really drunk and dancing really badly. It was really funny to watch. It was funny because, on this occasion, it wasn't my dad. Anyway, then he stood on this plastic chair and did this weird dance thing. Then he fell off, and sent lots of other chairs flying. I laughed. Then I realised it was Alan Yentob, then Head of Entertainment at the BBC, but I still didn't think it was a story. I just thought Alan Yentob falling off a plastic chair was mildly amusing and then I went home and watched *Antiques Roadshow*. But the next day I casually mentioned it to a colleague of mine, and because she is so brilliant at her job, she turned it into a 400-word lead story. Alan Yentob falling off a plastic chair. Imagine that! They made him sound awful.

It was outrageous. The very least he should be able to do as Head of Entertainment at the BBC was dance as well as Fred Astaire. What the hell were the BBC playing at? It wouldn't be so bad if he was Head of Documentaries or something, but he was Head of Entertainment, and he couldn't even dance to a high standard. Dancing classes don't cost very much. He earnt £321,000 a year! We were paying for him to not even bother going to dance classes. And he had got a beard. We were paying for that beard to be trimmed and shaped. How does that make you feel? Taxpayer? You were paying for Alan Yentob to have his beard trimmed. Next time you see him on the telly, you can legitimately say that you paid for his beard to be shaped. It's absolutely outrageous! If Nostradamus said to me, when I was fourteen, that at thirty-three I'd be responsible for a story about a man innocently falling off a chair becoming a right-wing polemic against publicly funded broadcasting, I wouldn't have believed him. But his incredible prophecy would have been right.

We are not defined by our day jobs, but we are judged by them. Look at Hitler. He was an extremely talented artist and yet he is doomed to be remembered only for his day job. As a genocidal maniac. So I went on *Celebrity Squares*.

When I got to the recording studio Dame Edna Everage was in the green room. She'd just recorded the episode before mine. They got some pretty decent celebrities to do this series, I tell you. Jonathan Ross...some other people. Anyway, I didn't talk to Dame Edna Everage about FGM. She looked a bit preoccupied. I was sitting above Reece Shearsmith from *The League of Gentleman* and next to Andi Peters, from the Edd the Duck partnership, who kept falling off his chair. He said it was because the base wasn't wide enough. I'm sure Andi wouldn't mind me telling this story. The studio audience was aware of it, because he kept disappearing. So it's only like one of them putting it in a blog or something. It was probably all over Twitter after the recording anyway. I'm sure he'd be fine about it. He was very good on the show and funny and charismatic. Also, it's in a chapter about FGM. If Andi Peters complains about me telling an anecdote about him falling off a chair during a recording of ITV1's *Celebrity Squares* because the base of the chair wasn't wide enough, he's going to look pretty unreasonable. Perhaps he was discombobulated, being out without his duck.

Once we had the money for the film, we made it in an afternoon in the downstairs bar at the King's Head in Crouch End, a brilliant comedy club and London's longest-running, programmed by the legendary joke-archivist Peter Graham. A producer I knew called Colin Dench shot it on three cameras, like real telly. Leyla didn't know what I was going to ask her, but we agreed that whatever I said, she would try to remain completely neutral. I asked her what the film meant to her. She said, 'The film, for me, isn't about dismissing the pain of FGM. I was taking the piss out of a system designed to control me. Culture gave FGM status. By laughing about it, I was lowering its status. I was taking the importance of FGM away from it, in the same way that rappers reclaimed the N-word.

My response was to laugh at FGM. To take it less seriously. It has a status that it doesn't deserve. It says, "You will remain a virgin until you get married." Well, I tell you something, it didn't work.'

We shot the film and edited it. We made it quickly because we wanted to show it at our fund-raiser, at the Bloomsbury Theatre, but both Leyla and I wanted to show it to other survivors, just to make sure we hadn't horribly misjudged it.

She told me recently, 'I don't know a single person affected by FGM who was offended by our film. Survivors I have spoken to said it gave them the opportunity to laugh at it, which a lot of them hadn't had before. A lot of them found it cathartic.'

The film only works because it was Leyla's idea and Leyla was the star of it. I just feel privileged to have played a supporting role. Leyla has taught me so much about life and about comedy, and a lot in terms of how I approach my comedy. She doesn't think any subject should be off limits. You just need to be clear who or what the target is. The short film we made together, for example, to raise awareness for FGM, was about people's ignorance, not victims. It was an exaggerated take on her own experiences. Leyla's wisdom and generosity freed me up as a stand-up. But you're not going to please all of the people all of the time, so you just have to go with your instincts and hope for the best. Another thing I learnt is that we are all fallible. Everyone makes mistakes. But for me, failure is not trying and misjudging something, it's not trying at all.

Leyla says one of the most important elements in tackling FGM in this country is raising awareness for it. There is a lot of confusion surrounding FGM, and a lot of people in this country still don't know what it means. There's been a real momentum in tackling FGM in the last few years, from the government and the media, and it's down to tireless campaigners like Leyla and her fellow activists who keep the pressure on. The Home Affairs Select Committee report on FGM, outlining the case for a national action plan, which called the government's failure to tackle FGM in the UK an ongoing national scandal, was as a result of Leyla's e-petition. You can find their report on the Parliament UK website.

The media, culture and the arts can play such an important role in helping the anti-FGM campaign by keeping up the pressure and maintaining a constant media profile. Leyla gave me permission to laugh at FGM, its ideology and its perpetrators. All I had to do was to make sure my FGM routine wasn't shit. And I realised this was true of every single supposedly controversial subject out there.

CHAPTER ELEVEN

'Don't expect a blow job just because you've done the washing-up.'

I decided to write another show about feminism, with different hilarious examples of misogyny from last time, seeing as the last one ended up being so unexpectedly popular and lucrative.

So I thought I'd better capitalise on women's suffering while there was still some media interest in that subject. It was already beginning to wane. Luckily, I didn't need to bang on about the same sexists I'd harped on about in A *Bic for Her* in 2013. Even after a full Edinburgh show and one BBC Radio 4 series, there were still loads of sexists for me to choose from. I could be on my hundredth show and still not run out.

I thought everyone would hate A *Bic for Her* and then I could give up and be financially supported by my fictional husband. Unfortunately it went well, but not well enough to catapult me into TV, and so I've had to carry on working. It's been a disaster, neither one thing nor the other. I mean, as I said in chapter 1, what's the point in being a liberated free woman if I'm too busy and knackered to enjoy it? Just because

I believe in employment equality laws, it doesn't mean that I *personally* want to work.

I've only had about five nights off since August 2013! Feminism may have improved the quality of many women's lives, but it's completely ruined mine. I can't remember the last time I watched *The Real Housewives of Orange County*. Or clipped my own toenails. Or read a book. I haven't even read this one. I have absolutely no idea what it's about. Though I have written it myself, unlike most of the so-called 'writers' in my editor's portfolio.

I knew I had to come back straight away with a new show after winning the Foster's Award. Whether I left it six years or one year, the next show I did would be judged against it. Best to just crack on and get it out of the way. If I was going down, I'd rather go down fast and get it over with, and be spared another decade of uncertainty.

Things changed for me after I won the Foster's Edinburgh Comedy Award. Before then, I could do what I liked onstage. I wasn't accountable in the way I am now. I didn't feel any sense of responsibility to myself, my family, my cat, my audience or the opinions of my peers. I was just larking around without any sense of direction or plan.

I could hang three toy donkeys with parachutes attached to them from the ceiling if I wanted. I could wear an inflatable ballerina costume and slowly inflate myself. I could do a character of the Plague. I could eat an entire stick of celery in silence. But I can't do that now. Because I'm that woman who won that award and people have paid to see me. They haven't paid to see me doing any of those things. They've come to hear what the 'feminist' comedian has to say for herself, on behalf of all the women in the world. I've inadvertently become some people's idea of a night out. They've spent their weekly comedy-show ticket allowance on me; they've paid for babysitters; they might have travelled. When I toured in the autumn of 2014, women had come to see me from Iceland, to Shoreham-by-Sea. No one should have to do that. That's a big responsibility. Don't get me wrong, it's nice to be recognised by the industry and win awards, but they don't help you onstage. You can't say, 'Laugh, you wankers! What's wrong with you? Don't you know that some industry experts think I'm funny?!' then reveal your awards from behind some curtains. They don't mean anything to them, and that is entirely correct. I have a rule if I ever win anything: celebrate on the night, then forget about it.

People have high expectations of you once you've won an award. If you don't live up to the hype they don't blame the awards panel, or critics, or promoters, or the physical award. They don't jab their fingers into a big lump of plastic, shouting, 'You're wrong! You're wrong! You stupid lump of organic polymer,' they blame you and you only, and they let you know about it by sitting in the front row of your shows with their arms folded and rolling their eyes. And that was just my dad and my agent.

I feel like the underdog and that's a position I'm most comfortable in. I appreciate that after the last two years I've had, other people might not see me as an underdog. They see me as an overdog, if anything, but my own perception of myself doesn't change, depending on how well or not I'm doing.

For example, I shared a backstage green room with John Bishop (and about twenty other acts, not all at the same time) during the 2014 Edinburgh Fringe. We were both on at the Stand Comedy Club. There was some fruit in a bowl provided by the venue, which all the acts could help themselves to. It was nice of the Stand to provide fruit, although Edinburgh is in Scotland, where there isn't any real fresh fruit, so the fruit was waxed. Still … it had the appearance of fruit.

Anyway, John and I were chatting at the end of the festival, and I told him that I thought the venue got the fruit in for him, because he's John Bishop off the telly. Then he told me he thought they got the fruit in for me, because I'm Bridget Christie, who won the award! Of course we were both wrong. The Stand Comedy Club couldn't give a shit about awards or telly and so wouldn't have got either of us any fruit. It must have been for Simon Munnery, who is notorious for his fruit demands.

In 2013, when I wrote A Bic for Her, women's rights were really trendy, like the royal baby, Xbox One and twerking, so people were more open and tolerant to listening to women bleating on about them. I think this is partly why A Bic for Her did well. It was great accidental timing, a perfect storm that I inadvertently wandered into on my way to the toilets.

But that was over. By January 2014, we were done with it already, again. Caitlin Moran wrote a funny book about it and a stand-up had done a funny stand-up show about it and Karl Lagerfeld used feminism as a theme for one of his fashions shows. Everyone could go home now. During a post-Edinburgh press interview, in around September 2013, a journalist said to me, 'So, Bridget. You've done feminism now, what's next?' as if all that was done and dusted and we could all move on to other subjects.

I thought, Have I? What, all by myself? What about all the campaigners and activists, and the politicians, changing laws and implementing real, actual change? What about Barbara Castle, who introduced the Equal Pay Act 1970? Didn't she have something to do with it? Or Margaret Sanger, the American birth control activist and sex educator, who inspired

William Moulton Marston to create Wonder Woman? She popularised the term 'birth control' and opened the first birth control clinic in America – didn't she have any input? Was it all down to me? Crikey – I didn't expect to 'do' feminism just with some puerile jokes about gendered pens! I was only trying to make people laugh. Not solve anything. I can't even solve a Rubik's cube. Perhaps someone could let Ban Ki-moon know. He'll be so relieved. All this violence against women was really starting to get him down a bit.

Then he said, 'I see from your website you love waterproof jackets. Perhaps you could write a show about those next?' as if gender politics, and all that that entails, couldn't possibly generate enough material to sustain a *second* hour of comedy. I must admit, coming up with ideas had been a bit of a struggle. I really scraped the barrel for my second hour of comedy about feminism. There was no sexism getting around at all in 2014. Not a single bit of it. Not even the light-hearted, cartoon, milkman-type sexism you might see in a 1970s sitcom. Nothing at all. I read all the newspapers, watched the news every day, I went out of my own house ... nothing ... It was like living in an intergalactic matriarchal utopia, or in Finland.

I checked with domestic violence charities, and the End Violence Against Women coalition; I looked at the websites for Refuge and Karen Ingala Smith (whose campaign, Counting Dead Women, focuses on deaths caused by clear incidences of misogyny) – all the domestic violence had stopped. All rape had stopped. Everywhere. There wasn't a single rape in 2014. Not in India, or in a war zone, or in Weston-super-Mare, or on a university campus or in a marital bed. All of it stopped. Men just decided it was time to move on from all of that.

Mass sterilisation wasn't occurring in India; twelve-year-olds were no longer being forced into sexual slavery by ISIS; the Chelsea Football Club doctor, Eva Carneiro, didn't have Manchester United and Arsenal fans shout 'Show us where you piss from, you slag' at her as she treated an injured player; all twenty-eight countries around the world currently practising female genital mutilation had stopped cutting their girls; the kidnapped Nigerian schoolgirls were released by Boko Haram; honour killings had stopped. Nope. I didn't see or hear of a single example of sexism or misogyny or violence against women anywhere.

I also slowly worked my way through the media, social networking, broadcasting, the arts, finance, business, politics, the music industry, archaeology, advertising, the armed forces, sport, conflict, religion, the occult, aviation, science, cobbling, literature, medicine, fashion, Greek and Norse myths, Amnesty International's Women's Page, until finally I got to Charles Darwin's letters...sexist. This was an entry where he contemplated the advantages and disadvantages of having a wife:

Advantages	Disadvantages
Constant companion.	Terrible loss of time.
Object to be played with.	
Better than a dog anyhow.	
Someone to take care of the house.	
These things good for one's health.	

Wives of Britain! Stop taking up your husband's time with all your time-consuming companionship and housekeeping and build him a TARDIS so that he can time travel. Darwin's public statements on women contradicted his private actions.

He said publicly that there existed fundamental and enduring 'differences in the mental powers of the sexes', at the same time as being very supportive of women he knew. He became a mentor to the suffragette, biologist, astronomer and botanist Lydia Becker, and he encouraged women's scientific interests wherever possible, around the world. Perhaps he was just trying to keep in with the lads.

That's not very evolved, is it? Look, we know that men's brains are physically larger than women's, we've all seen them on *CSI* and *Last of the Mohicans*, but it doesn't necessarily follow that just because they are bigger in size, they are more intelligent. As my seven-year-old son pointed out to me while we were watching *Is Your Brain Male or Female?* with Dr Alice Roberts, 'Well, Mummy, that doesn't mean anything, does it? The extra space might just be taken up with rubbish. For example, the entire left-hand side of my brain is where I keep all my *Doctor Who* stuff.'

I also looked into farming, space travel, academia, geology, engineering, literature, children's books, ironmongery, stone-masonry, porn, astrology, history, IT, the world of gaming, the construction industry, mechanics, shipbuilding, mining, trainspotting, haulage, quantum physics, tailoring, the film industry, poaching, the criminal justice system, meteorology, the paranormal, terrorism, political activism, the comments section under any article about a successful woman, the comments section under any article about feminism, the comments section under any article about a female comedian, the comments section under any article about a feminist comedian, the comments section under any article about me...desperately trying to find just one example of sexism or misogyny that I could flesh out for my *second* hour on feminism.

But I drew a complete blank. I just about managed to cobble together seven minutes of material for the show. The other fifty-three minutes was about the marginalisation of straight, white, middle-class men. Luckily, there were always loads of them in.

When I 'took up feminism' in April 2012, as a marketing device, to boost my profile and win lots of awards, I had to become a full-time feminist, instead of the part-time one I'd previously been. It's absolutely exhausting. I'm like this all the time now. I'm never off these days. I'm like Rob Brydon on *The Trip*. There should be a spin-off to *The Trip*, with me and Rob Brydon, called *The Impressionist and the Feminist: A Battle of Wills*. Its listing in the *Radio Times* could be:

> An hour of Ronnie Corbett and Michael
> Caine impersonations interrupted by
> depressing statistics on gender violence.
> Starring Rob Brydon and a sarcastic woman
> from Gloucester. Watch Brydon's impression
> of 'small man in a box' as he struggles to eat
> a selection of patriarchal foods. This week's
> culinary treats are spare ribs, Cumberland
> sausages and Rocky Mountain oysters.

Doing Edinburgh is a daunting prospect at the best of times: the bad reviews, the poor turnouts, your own and your fellow comedians' deteriorating mental health and deranged behaviour, the haemorrhoids (I think I've already mentioned my own rectal grape community's annual Fringe outing).

Coming back straight away the following year after winning

the main award was intimidating. I wasn't nervous the year before, because I had nothing to lose, but now I wanted to hang on to my new audience. I prepared as much as I could for *An Ungrateful Woman*, but still, my insecurities gnawed away at me: an imagined critical backlash and the barely contained glee this would bring to my very closest friends. All fabrications of my own weak, Gloucester mind. 'Oh dear, what a shame. It took Christie ten years to find her voice, and a year to lose it' (*Guardian*). 'Oh, how embarrassing. We all thought she was great last year, but now she's shit again' (*Independent*). 'One-hit wonder Christie repeats herself with second show about sexism' (*Times*). 'Oh no. Not feminism AGAIN??!!! Same old, same old from one-trick pony Christie' (*Telegraph*).

The structure of *A Bic for Her* was much more straight-forward than *An Ungrateful Woman*. You can tell a lot about a comedian's show by what's written on the back of the comedian's hand. If there's nothing written on their hand, it's going to be a long hour. Either that, or they've just memorised it all and don't need prompts. So you can't read anything into that, actually.

The notes written on the back of my hand during *A Bic for Her* (I'm not drawing you a hand, you'll have to imagine it; I can only draw vile-looking men, I'm afraid) were:

> *Thatcher. Adam & Eve. Moss.*
> *Luther. Pens. Fake heckle. Refuge.*
> *Lads' mags. Feminist icons. Malala.*

For *An Ungrateful Woman*, my hand was covered in writing. There were routines within routines so I had to get the order right, or I'd miss out a crucial bit. In *A Bic for Her*, there was the odd call-back, but I didn't have to think too deeply about where things fell in the hour, except for the Malala routine, which I knew had to go right at the very end.

This is what was written on the back of my hand for *An Ungrateful Woman* (I'm not drawing you a hand, you'll have to imagine it; I can only draw vile-looking men, I'm afraid):

Jersey. Farage. Osborne. Brand.
British sexism. Manjoo. Taxi. Fart. Gisele.
Adverts. Mary Beard. Gisele. Yoghurt.
Celebrity Squares. Yoghurt. Michael Gove.
Gammon snowflakes. Yoghurt. Anti-rape pants.
Yoghurt. PSHE Association.

The first idea I had for *An Ungrateful Woman* came from a *Guardian* article I'd read, in November 2013, about a company based in New York, called AR Wear (anti-rape wear), who'd designed an 'anti-rape pant', built to stop rapists in their tracks. How they work is that a potential rapist (or convicted rapist or a rapist, or a rapist who has not been rehabilitated, or a rapist who has never been caught, or just any man really) would voluntarily put the $60-a-pair pants on first thing in the morning when he got up, before he'd had his breakfast and brushed his teeth, and then lock himself in at the thigh and the waist using a combination lock. Then he'd go about his day-to-day business, sweeping up the leaves and fixing leaks. Then, when he felt a rape coming on, he'd press a little red emergency button marked 'WARNING: RAPE IMMINENT', which would then send electroconvulsive shocks through the man's genitals, thereby putting him off. Not really. The anti-rape pants weren't marketed at rapists, obviously, but at rape victims, because it's the victim's responsibility to prevent herself from getting raped, rather than the rapist's not to rape. Everyone knows that.

So the pants were for potential victims with a disposable income to splash out on and wear. I don't want to start a class war here, and I'm not suggesting that the rape of a poor woman is any worse than the rape of a rich woman; I am obviously not saying that. All rapes are equally as abhorrent. All I'm saying is that I think it's unfair that some women can now wear expensive pants to stop a rape, while other women, who can't afford the pants, won't be able to. And I don't imagine AR Wear will be air-dropping millions of pairs of anti-rape pants down into war zones, for all the women and children being raped there. Also, only about 10 per cent of rapes are stranger rapes, so when do we wear the pants? Do we have to wear them *all the time*? What if we're not wearing them and something happens? Will a judge blame us for not being locked into our pants and therefore asking for it?

AR Wear managed to raise (from its crowd-funding appeal on Indiegogo) over $50,000 in just over a month, which means that lots of women thought that expensive, lockable, anti-rape pants were a good idea, which is really upsetting. I am not mocking the women who came up with this idea here, anything that might prevent or delay a rape is a good and worthy idea, and of course I'm not mocking women for wanting them. Women don't want to be raped. What would be much better, and cheaper and fairer is if men stopped raping. If that's not going to be possible, then maybe our judiciary systems can deal with sexual violence more effectively, rather than leaving it down to some expensive bespoke tailoring.

AR Wear kindly made a fun video demonstrating how the

pants work. The strapline for the video was 'For when things go wrong'. 'For when THINGS GO WRONG'?! Things haven't gone wrong, though, have they? A rape isn't a burnt lasagne, or some red wine on a white carpet or a flat tyre, or your cat vomiting in your shoe – a man decided to rape.

There is a culture that suggests that the woman is responsible for the crime simply by virtue of being a woman, which, of course, she never is. We have to stop this reverse-onus blame-the-victim thinking. 'Sorry you've been the victim of a serious sexual assault. Can I just ask, how womanly were you being? Were you wearing a short skirt? Were you flaunting your legs? I'm not saying it's your fault. I'm just saying that unfortunately there are rapists out there, and there are things you can do to try to be less like a woman.'

This doesn't happen with racially motivated attacks; nor should it. There isn't a culture that suggests a black person is responsible for the crime simply by virtue of being black, because, of course, they never are. 'Sorry you have been the victim of a racially motivated attack. Can I just ask, how black were you being? Were you wearing a Bob Marley T-shirt? Were you flaunting your blackness? Had you gone out without your anti-racist make-up on?'

Violence against women has been called 'the most pervasive yet least recognized human rights abuse in the world'. We need to stop trivialising it in our judiciary systems and in our media. These anti-rape pants are not 'simply recognising a threat and taking counter-measures to prevent it'; they are saying that it's the woman's responsibility not to get herself raped, rather than on the rapist not to rape. Also, what if I'm plastered and need a wee? Do I just have to piss myself?

So I had the routine, I just needed to find a place for it. I also wanted to talk about the column in the *Telegraph* defending British sexism. But the main issue I wanted to talk about in this show was female genital mutilation, and I described the experiences of working with Leyla that gave me a way into this in the last chapter.

Something quite easy to write jokes about is the way that women are portrayed in the media. Especially in advertising. Women in adverts are absolute divs, aren't they? My worst nightmare would be to go on a walking weekend with the woman from the Lenor advert. Even gnomes are better represented in adverts than women are. Gnomes are allowed to go fishing, drink beer, play the accordion. When was the last time you saw an advert for a cleaning product where the woman was necking back a pint of Bishops Finger, sitting on a toadstool, playing a musical instrument and smoking a pipe?

But most women in advertising conform to two very distinct stereotypes. We are either wanton and highly sexualised, or vacuous and passive. So we're either having an orgasm on a PVC window frame because we can't believe there's no draught coming through the double glazing, or – and this is the only other type – we're laughing at salads, and there's nothing in between. Those are our only choices: gagging for it or idiotic.

By the way, there is a Tumblr website called 'Women laughing alone with salads'. Some genius has collated loads of photos of women, all on their own, all laughing with salads. Some of the women are throwing their heads back in such utter joy you'd think they'd just seen that re-edited version of Nicki Minaj's bottom-fixated 'Anaconda' music video on the internet, dubbed entirely with farts, which made me laugh so much I got sick and thought my eyes and internal organs were going to come out. But they haven't, they're looking at salads.

I recommend having a look. The 'Weeping Angels Women Laughing Alone At Salads' is a particular highlight of mine. Look, don't get me wrong, I love a good salad, but clearly not enough.

Maybe I don't find salads hilarious because I'm a comedian. I'm analysing it too much. Looking for a subtext or a narrative. I'm trying to figure out why the salad has presented itself like that, with the lettuce on the outside and the olives in the middle. Is the position of the cucumber a satire of something? Are the tomatoes a metaphor?

So here's an example of a vacuous woman in advertising. There's an advert for Ambi Pur plug-in air freshener: a woman plugs an air freshener into a socket in the wall, sniffs the air like a truffle hog, and then dances around on her own for a bit, like she might do if she'd been dragged along to her friend's evangelical church service and had unexpectedly found Jesus, and Jesus *smelt great!* – while the rest of the family gets on with their own thing.

The woman's on-screen husband, who is sitting on the sofa reading the *Financial Times*, is completely oblivious to his wife's spiritual awakening. He's got no idea the room stinks of Fresh Cotton or that his wife's had a religious epiphany, because he's allowed to keep up on The World. Whereas her main area of interest is Smells.

All I'm saying is mix it up a bit. I read the newspapers, lots of my female friends read newspapers. Just switch the roles sometimes. More couples are splitting housework chores now, even if they are still split along gendered lines. All I'm saying is we could have the woman sat on the sofa reading the newspaper and have the bloke hyperventilating about lavender sometimes. Or better still, just make commercials more realistic. Why not just show an air freshener stuck to the side of a toilet and have a husband say to his wife, 'Darling, that lily of the valley air freshener really takes the edge off your shit. We'll have to buy that one again. The vanilla one just made it smell like vanilla-smelling shit. But this new one really does make a difference. What time are the cleaners coming? I hope they're late. They always think it's me.'

On the face of it, a Müller yoghurt advert, featuring a man inside a fridge, holding a yoghurt on a tray and offering it up to an aroused housewife who is home alone, sounds like a harmless bit of yoghurt-based marketing fun. I thought it was when I auditioned for that advert, but then the man farted in the bookshop and I realised that a Müller yoghurt advert, featuring a man inside a fridge, holding a yoghurt on a tray and offering it up to an aroused housewife who is home alone, was not only not a bit of yoghurt-based marketing fun, it was actually reinforcing stereotypes and perpetuating rape myths.

I auditioned for that advert, and it was no fun for anybody. I wrote a routine about it at the time.

I thought the idea of a man being inside my fridge, all scrunched up, and cold, was absolutely the funniest thing I'd ever heard. I was almost sick with laughing, and during the audition I had to go and stand in the corner with my back to them while I got myself together. What made it worse was that no one else in the room thought that it was anything out of the ordinary at all. They certainly didn't think it was funny. No one in the room was laughing at the idea of me opening a fridge door and finding a man in there. The casting director wasn't laughing, the actor auditioning with me (who was going to be the man in the fridge) didn't think it was funny, the people from Müller weren't laughing. The imaginary fridge wasn't laughing, the imaginary pot of yoghurt wasn't laughing. Even the camerawoman, who was eating a salad at the time, wasn't laughing. No one was laughing except me.

I thought that the routine the experience had inspired, about a silly yoghurt audition, could be rewritten now as a framing device for the anti-rape pant routine, and my routine about female genital mutilation, for the new 2014 show, An Ungrateful Woman. I recounted the experience from the moment I entered the audition room.

By the way, while we're on this sort of thing, my actor mate Dave, who I'd often see at castings for commercials, used to get annoyed with me going on about all this stuff all the time. He'd say things like: 'It's not just women who are objectified in adverts, you know. Men are required to be the meat as well sometimes, you know.' And I'd say, 'Yes, Dave, there is a Diet Coke advert featuring a good-looking, topless man, but he's not in a subordinate position. He's not emasculated or demeaned. He's not threatened, in a vulnerable position, vacuous, idiotic or passive, and he's not wanton or highly sexualised. He's not ejaculating into an oven while waiting for Cillit Bang to work its magic. It's different. A male actor wouldn't do that, anyway.'

So, my audition:

> They said, 'Hi, Bridget. So for this one,
> you're at home and you're peckish but not
> hungry, so if you could just convey that in
> your face.'

> Which I couldn't.

He went on: 'Thanks, Bridget. So, you
go to the fridge, open the fridge door and
there is a man in there, holding a tray
with a yoghurt on it. You are not to look
surprised, or threatened, or intimidated,
because we want it to look naturalistic.'

I said, 'Eh? I'm not to respond, at all, to a
man inside my fridge?'

'No.'

'Do I know him, then?'

'No, you don't. Why would you know
him?'

'So, he's a stranger, then?'

'Yes.'

'There is a strange man inside my
fridge, who I've never seen before, even
locally? But I'm not to look surprised, or
threatened, or intimidated, or worried.'

'That's right. Just be cool with it. It's no big
deal.'

'Hmmm. Okay. I think I would respond,
though. Is my husband at home, then?'

'No, he's not. Why would your husband—'

'He's not?! So, I'm home alone, then.
There is a strange man inside my fridge,
who I've never seen before, offering me
a yoghurt, and no one else is in, but you
don't want me to react in any way?'

'No.'

'Hmmm...Has there been any sign of a
break-in at all?'

'No, there hasn't...'

'So, how did he get in the fridge then?
How long has he been in there for? Is
he okay? What are his vitamin B levels
like...?'

'Look. Bridget,' he said. 'It's just a light-
hearted yoghurt commercial, it's only going
to be on for ten seconds, tops. You don't
need to know who the guy is, whether
your husband's at home, has he broken in.
It's not important. The viewers at home
won't be thinking about all that. They'll
just be thinking about the yummy yoghurt,
Bridget. Please, Bridget, we've a lot of
people to see today. It's very simple. You're
at home, you're peckish but not hungry,

remember, so you're glad he's not offering
you a massive lump of pork or anything,
he offers you the yoghurt, you take the
yoghurt, and swoon a bit, because he's a
very attractive man, then we're done here
today, thanks.'

I thought I could get Michael Gove and the FGM stuff in here, as an example of the last time I swooned at a man, as the audience would be preoccupied with yoghurt.

'I'm swooning at him now? Seems like an
odd reaction under the circumstances.
Also, I don't know what to do physically.
I'm not the swooning type. I don't think
I've ever swooned. The last time I came
anywhere near to swooning was when
the sacked Education Secretary Michael
Gove agreed to write to all schools with
guidelines on how teachers can spot the
signs of girls at risk of female genital
mutilation.'

But it wasn't a swoon as such, it was more like, Oh, no, not Gove. Why did it have to be Gove?! Why did Gove have to get involved with FGM? Oh, God. I suppose I'll have to give him that one, won't I? Yes, well done, Michael Gove. You did a good thing today. Well done. But it wasn't a swoon as such, it was more of a begrudging concession.

Then I went on to explain Fahma Mohamed and Integrate Bristol's e-petition, and I ended the FGM routine with my gammon snowflakes gag, which always got a big laugh and bought me a bit more time.

Anyway, back to the Müller advert routine. The message in the advert was that the woman fancied the bloke in the fridge, even though he was a stranger and she was in an incredibly vulnerable situation. I saw this as the yoghurt industry's re-inforcement of rape fantasy myths.

So I said to Müller, 'I just need to clarify something that's bothering me about this advert, then I'll go. I know you have a lot of people to see. I'm home alone, yes? Yes. There is a strange man in my fridge, who I've never seen before. Yes, that's right. He offers me a yoghurt, which I find passive-aggressive under the circumstances. I then take the yoghurt, which is technically consenting to the whole scenario and could be held against me in a court of law at a later date should something go horribly wrong here. Remember, Müller, I don't know who he is, no one else is in, he's in my fridge.

'Also, the lid is half off. That poses all sorts of questions, doesn't it? Is it past its sell-by date? Has he done something into the yoghurt? Has he spiked it? Does Rohypnol even dissolve in fermented milk? Or does it have to be a liquid? Sorry, Müller, but my point is this. I wouldn't accept an already-

opened yoghurt from my own mother. Let
alone a complete stranger, who has been
waiting in my fridge, for I don't know how
long, with the sole intention of feeding me a
yoghurt that he has already opened. I mean,
what's in it for him, Müller? Has he just
been waiting for me out of the goodness of
his heart? I'd be mad to eat it, Müller, mad!
I'm not even wearing my anti-rape pants,
Müller!'

Muller! That's not a joke, by the way, I
would not joke about something as serious
as rape, especially not in an audition for a
yoghurt advert. They are a genuine product.
The first thing I thought when I realised
these pants were not a joke was, Hang
on, surely if anyone's going to be wearing
anti-rape pants, it's the rapist isn't it? Not
potential victims?

I'd explain what the pants were and do my Anti-Rape
routine. Then I brought them back to the Muller advert
immediately following the Anti-Rape pants routine, like
this:

'Do I just have to piss myself? I'm sorry,
Muller,' I said, 'but this lid business is really
bothering me. Why is it half off? Is the
implication that because I am a woman I'm
too weak to get it off myself? The point I'm

trying to make, Müller, is this. I would not accept an already opened yoghurt from my own mother, let alone a man, a complete stranger, who's been waiting inside my fridge, for I don't know how long, with the sole intention of feeding me a yoghurt that he has already opened. I'd be insane to eat it, Müller! Insane! Then you're asking me to swoon because I find this 'intruder' sexually attractive. You are saying that I find this dangerous, vulnerable situation sexually arousing, because you're asking me to swoon when I see this strange man in my fridge.

'I am sorry to have to tell you this, Müller, but as it stands, this yoghurt advert is perpetuating rape myths. I know that sounds like quite a leap, but I'll explain it to you very quickly, then you can see the next actress.

'Women do not have rape fantasies in which they are the victim. A rape fantasy is exactly that. A fantasy. A woman, or a man, has come up with a scenario in which they are the victim, but they are in complete control, because it is a fantasy. They've had a chat with their sexual partner, nipped down the fancy dress shop and bought a fireman, Iron Man or Harry

Potter costume, or some yoghurt, and it's
all consensual. Your advert is easily fixed,
Müller. It's just a little tweak.

'You could have me waving my husband
goodbye, saying, "See you tonight, then,
love! Don't forget the yoghurts," and
winking. Then you should see him running
around the side of the house, coming
back in through the kitchen door, using
his own key, getting into position in the
back of the fridge, with his little tray and
yoghurt, while I pretend not to see him,
being all coy, trying not to be annoyed
because he's dragged all mud across the
floor from the garden, because we're in the
middle of a sexual fantasy. A nice touch,
Müller, would be to do a close-up of a
photo of us together on the fridge door,
of us on our wedding day or if we're not
married just having a great laugh together.
That way, viewers at home know that's my
sexual partner in there and this is just a
little yoghurt-based sexual fantasy we've
come up with between the two of us,
and I'm perfectly safe. I'll make a sort of
embarrassed face as if I've just been found
out.

'But at the moment, none of that is in
there. It's just a woman, home alone,

coming face to face with a potentially
spiked-yoghurt-wielding intruder. I'm
afraid you're just giving rape apologists
ammunition and I can't play any part in it,
even for a seven-thousand-pound buyout.

'And anyway, Müller, I think you'll find
most women's "rape fantasies" don't
involve already-opened yoghurts and men
in fridges. Mine certainly don't. My "rape
fantasies" involve more prosecutions and
longer sentences.'

* * *

I'd like to know who writes the adverts for these products. Is
it men, or women? We've had some great women writers. It's
just a shame they had to pretend to be men, like Mary Ann
Evans. She drew on a moustache, smoked a few Woodbines
and called herself George Eliot to ensure her work was taken
seriously. At the time, the general view was that female writers
were only capable of producing flimsy, light-hearted romantic
novels. Her disguise worked a treat until someone brought a
baby along to a book signing and her voice went up fifty-seven
octaves.

A lesser-known fact is that when Mary Shelley wrote
Frankenstein, she wore a hex bolt on a silver chain around her
neck, to silence her then-lover, Percy Bysshe Shelley, who
kept winding her up all the time. He thought her woman's
mind was too full of emotions and other ladies' things like

flowers and lace and feathers to be able to write horror. Lord Byron was there as well. They were all on holiday together and decided to have a competition to see who could write the best ghost story. *As you do.* Byron's was about a poltergeist that went around farting all the time; Shelley did one about a vampire bat that only came out at night; and Mary's was about creation, eugenics, the fragility of the human heart and the complexities of the human psyche. Oh yes, and glitter. Women's things, you know. Anyway, to shut the boys up, Mary told them she'd wear 'a potent symbol of the very essence of man' around her neck to help focus her mind on more manly things, like violence, construction and DIY. And that if she kept twisting it and looking at it she'd think more like a man and less like a lady. Like Thatcher. She was a lady, wasn't she?

This bolt, Mary Shelley said, used by manly men like carpenters and blacksmiths, would make her feel more like a man and less like a woman, less of what it's like to be a woman in a man's world. Of feeling oppressed, hopeless and trapped. Of despair and frustration. Of feeling powerless and isolated. Of how it feels to create life. Silly, frivolous women's things like that.

She wouldn't focus too much on regret either, because that counts as an emotion as well, and is very much women's domain. Along with depression, despair, confusion, emptiness and foreboding, and the guilt – did I mention the guilt of women at all? Always the guilt. When will it ever end?

She wouldn't touch on what it's like to bring someone into the world, only to be disgusted and repulsed by them. To cast them out into a cruel world, rejected and abandoned. Victor Frankenstein would not suffer post-natal depression, oh no. For that is a woman's thing, and is not interesting to men, who will mainly be reading this story while smoking, driving or shooting game.

She wouldn't devote too much time to her monster's emotions either. It doesn't matter what the monster thinks. It's a monster! It was only created for the man's gratification and ego, anyway. Who cares what it thinks?! It's lucky to be alive at all! It should be grateful! Doesn't it know how much the man has sacrificed for it?

She wouldn't write about how it feels to be trapped inside a body that was never really your own. A body that makes you feel vulnerable and exposed. A body that you have no rights or control over, especially if at some point in the future you live in the Republic of Ireland or the state of Kansas.

A body that, over time, you learn to hate, because it slightly deviates from the norm (okay, Frankenstein's monster takes an incredibly long detour from the norm but you know where I'm going with all of this). A broken body. A wrong body. A clumsy, grotesque body. If only it could afford to have a little nip here, a little tuck there, all would be okay. Or so the grotesque monster was led to believe by a capitalist society.

Her feeble lady's mind would not wander to the struggles of her own identity or of negotiating a society that neither valued, recognised nor understood her. A society that shunned her, even though she got on well with it and children liked her.

A society that couldn't work out whether it was disgusted and frightened by the mere thought of her, or by her potential. A blameless society. Her mind would not succumb to the sheer, crushing loneliness of how it feels to be a woman sometimes.

But she wouldn't be thinking about all these 'women's issues' for her story. She would try to focus on more tangible things that men could relate to, because it was 1816, and her story would mainly be read by men, what with girls not being allowed an education and all of that. There'd be plenty of brutality and violence and cruelty. Not much compassion or sympathy or fairness or silly light-hearted romantic things or things like that. Or abandonment or love. And she would publish it anonymously too, just to be on the safe side.

Then she got on with *Frankenstein*, and wrote arguably the best horror story ever written, at the age of twenty, with no formal education. And she was a *girl*. Did I mention that? I must just say also that Percy B. Shelley was incredibly supportive of Mary and encouraged her to write from the start. He even let her take his name when they were married, which helped her career no end. It must've been wonderful to have been constantly referred to as 'the wife of Percy Bysshe Shelley' (see chapter 1 on social gatherings).

Of course this is only *my* interpretation of *Frankenstein* after the man farted. I'd read and watched *Frankenstein* many times before the man farted in the bookshop and not seen any of these themes. See how he's ruined my life? I can't even enjoy classic horror now because of bloody feminism.

So the anti-rape pants and the FGM and the yoghurt advert made up the last twenty minutes of the 2014 show.

The first forty minutes were the lead-up to those. I wanted to make connections between the things we think are harmless, like cartoon sexism and gendered stereotypes, and the big issues, and how they are all connected and intertwined and all coming from the same place, how we go from a stupid advert about an air freshener to a death threat on Twitter in one easy step.

Gendered stereotypes endorse sexism. If we're only ever

seeing two types of women, i.e. highly sexualised or vacuous and idiotic, when a woman deviates from one of these two norms she's considered an anomaly, or a freak of nature, or poses some kind of threat to us, like a newly discovered giant wasp. She destabilises the status quo. Not the Status Quo. I don't even know if they're still going. And if they are, I am sure they are quite capable of destabilising themselves. I understand they used to run from side to side in their private jet to try to crash their own plane. And the group's 2013 light-hearted comedy caper movie *Bula Quo!*, set on the island of Fiji, has done little to enhance the group's reputation.

When Mary Beard, the classicist, appeared on *Question Time*, she confused lots of men. She wasn't an object of desire for them, but she wasn't passive or vacuous either. Mary Beard just didn't add up. She was simply a highly intelligent woman expressing her opinions. A bit like a man, really, but a woman version. They didn't know how to react, because they hadn't seen enough examples of women. They thought what type is this? It's not like my mother but I haven't got an erection either?! She's a bit like Uncle Clive but the wrong gender. Eurgh! Arghhh! Why hasn't it dyed its hair or bleached its teeth? How am I supposed to respond to this? What is it, though? Will it sting me? Are there more ones like this? Where do they live, in forests? Urgh! Argh! What shall I do? My brain's melting, oh no, and my willy's gone up inside my body. How do I get it back out? Shall I try to evolve? No, I won't do that, I'll go on Twitter, now a designated sexism conservation area, and say she's got cheese straws for teeth, eats too much cabbage, and speculate on the width of her birth canal.

The level of abuse Mary Beard received for not fitting

into one of the two norms was staggering and completely unnecessary. We just need to see more types of women. We're not all mothers or harlots, and some of us are both. Beard's crime was to go on television as a 58-year-old woman and voice her opinions without first dolling herself up. I mean, who does she think she is?! The Royal Academy of Arts Professor of Ancient Literature? An Officer of the Order of the British Empire for services to classical scholarship? Jesus. I don't even think she got her split ends sorted out. What an utter disgrace.

By the way, I talked about this in the second series of my BBC Radio 4 series. I was worried about offending Mary Beard, or saying something she didn't agree with, but then I got a text saying she tweeted about it, and was so delighted that I stopped concentrating on where I was going, got my foot stuck in a hole in the road and suffered a Type 3 sprain to my ankle and a broken finger. I ended up in A&E, and having my engagement and wedding rings sawn off. I expect she'd be really pleased about that, wouldn't she? Being a feminist and all.

So I wanted to try to demonstrate how even something that seems harmless and fun and light-hearted at first glance can have much more sinister undertones, like sour sweets, sea urchins and Nigel Farage from UKIP. I thought that as the audience were settling in nicely to the yoghurt advert, I could sneak in the other stuff: like Michael Gove's involvement with FGM, the UK's current position on it, some FGM facts and possibly my work with Leyla Hussein. The audience would be preoccupied with yoghurt, their minds would be anticipating the outcome of the yoghurt audition. A lot of them (*especially the women*) would probably be fantasising about the yoghurt. They wouldn't be expecting a routine about FGM at this point. Before they knew what was happening, I'd be back in the yoghurt audition again.

The yoghurt audition was my Trojan Horse. I know I've used that already, in chapter 2, about when I used to do an act about wood, which I suppose the wooden horse metaphor was more relevant to but I think it works here nearly as well because yoghurt was a Greek food, so don't worry about it.

Even though the FGM bit didn't last long, I wanted it to stay with people after they'd seen my show. I'd read the activist, campaigner and brilliant writer Maryam Sheikh Abdi's devastating poem 'The Cut' about her own experience of undergoing female genital mutilation earlier in the year and was so moved by it that I wanted my audience to read it. It's not an easy read, and I don't know if this was the right thing to do or not, but I figured that if it was the wrong thing, then at least some people went away knowing what 130 million girls in the world today have gone through, in some form or another. And if it was the right thing, then I'd done the right thing. All I can do is what feels right to me. Leyla, who knows Maryam, asked her permission for me, which she kindly gave, and so I handed it out at the end of the show as people were leaving, inside an envelope marked, 'This envelope contains a very powerful, graphic and upsetting poem about a woman's experience of undergoing FGM. Please don't read it as you're waiting for another comedy show to start. Enjoy your festival. Thanks. BC.'

I then went back to the Müller ad and thought I'd end the show there, with the line 'My rape fantasies involve more prosecutions and longer sentences', but then on 29 July I received an email from the Department for Education. I'd sent Michael Gove an email with links to our film and they replied, much to our surprise, saying they'd sent the film on to the PSHE Association (personal, social, health and economic education) for them to review and decide whether to make it available to teachers. I thought this was another opportunity for me to mention FGM again, just before the audience left, so that FGM would be the thing they took away with them, like I did with Malala the year before.

It was also really important to me that I didn't look self-righteous or worthy. I had to undercut this good news. I'm a clown. I wanted the audience to know that if even I could make a tiny difference, maybe they could as well, but I didn't want to look smug. I quickly wrote a new ending, as I was opening my run in a few days' time.

> Just before I go, I was going to end on a bit
> about how the government tackling FGM
> after twenty-nine years of doing nothing
> is just cynical spin, and that they've been
> shamed into action by the Home Affairs
> Committee – who've called successive
> governments' failure to prevent FGM in
> the UK as an 'ongoing national scandal'
> – and by high-profile media campaigns in
> the *Evening Standard*, *The Times* and the
> *Guardian*. Then four days ago I received
> the following email from the Department
> for Education.

Then I read the email, which basically said they'd enjoyed the film and had passed it on to the PSHE Association for them to decide whether to include it in the information they provide to teachers.[32]

> So where does that leave me? I was going
> to come back next year and slag off the
> government. But I can't now because I've
> been absorbed into their machine. I've got
> an email from them! They've endorsed my
> film. They've got me. What am I now? I'm
> nothing. I'm a comedian. A free agent.
> I'm supposed to be in opposition to the
> government, not in bed with them. I'm
> now compromised by association. And
> that's always how it works. I mean, it
> would be incredible to get our film into
> schools to raise awareness of FGM, but not
> at the expense of my onstage persona. If
> the PSHE decide to show it, and I want to
> do another show next year, I'll have to lie
> and say they wouldn't. There's only one
> thing worse than an angry feminist – and
> that's a smug one who thinks they're right
> about everything. Unbearable. That's the
> only problem with activism if you're a
> comedian, isn't it? Sometimes it works,
> and then you have nothing to complain
> about.

---

[32] As of May 2015, they are still reviewing it. But Leyla and I remain hopeful. I thought the TV commissioning process was bad enough. You try getting something off the ground with the PSHE Association.

The film is now being reviewed by the PSHE Association to decide whether they include it in the resources made available to teachers. Leyla told me it is being used by the Department of Health and the Met Police and in FGM training sessions and schools. She said that they show it at the end of sessions, as a way of 'not talking about it', just before everyone breaks for lunch, as it lifts the atmosphere. A GP came to my show and subsequently organised FGM training for all the GPs in her practice. A teacher came and has shown it to his pupils. Still, all of that counts for absolutely nothing, because I still haven't been asked to go on *Live at the Apollo*. Also, I had sex with everyone at the PSHE Association, the Department of Health, the Met Police, the GP in Scotland, the teacher and all the people running training sessions, in order to 'get on in this business', so I can't really take any credit for it.

The show did well. The general consensus, from critics and audiences alike, was that it was a step on from *A Bic for Her* rather than a step back, which was a huge relief. I'd got away with it, again. It sold out nearly nine weeks at the Soho Theatre and won Best Tour at the 2015 Chortle Awards.

Ah shit, I thought, I'm probably going to have to write another bloody show now.

CONCLUSION

'We're all doing our own little bit. And if we all do our own little bit, then together it's a big bit.'

So why am I still banging on about sexism?

Because unfortunately there is still quite a lot of sexism getting around. We're not in any danger of running out of it any time soon. DEFRA doesn't need to introduce sustainable sexism to keep UK supplies up. I haven't had to write sarcastic routines about mackerel, coley and pollock instead. Prominent British feminists are not being Twitter-trolled by trout.

I think that's enough of the fish analogies. I'm supposed to be wrapping it all up now. I'm just trying to say that Britain and the world doesn't need to find alternative methods of oppressing women. We don't need offshore sexism farms, or to start illegal wars in the Middle East to secure control over their patriarchy-rich fields. We don't need to do deals with China to build nuclear sexism plants, or frack Lancashire, or ask Germaine Greer to retrain truffle hogs to locate and extract all the forest-dwelling sexists.

I'm still banging on about it because there are treatment gaps in medicine, because researchers often focus more on

A BOOK FOR HER

men when they originally study treatments, meaning women are underrepresented in trials, and treatments are developed that are more suited to a male rather than a female body.

I'm still 'banging on' about it because in the UK, women are still excluded from vital positions of power, and I continue to find it darkly funny. From politics and business to the judiciary system and the police. In business, the arts and the media. Men outnumber women 4:1 in Westminster; women make up only 15 per cent of High Court judges; we are 5 per cent of newspaper editors. We are not involved in decisions which shape the society we live in. In terms of female representation in Parliament, the UK has dropped down to seventy-fourth place, according to the Global Gender Gap Report 2014. We're behind Sudan, China and Iraq. Look, I hate making decisions. I can't even decide how to end this book. But 9.1 million women didn't vote in the 2010 UK general election and I can completely understand why. Polling stations are unbelievably boring. When I went to vote in the local and European elections in May 2014, my daughter was told off for cycling around the hall. Is it any wonder most women don't bother when there's this sort of bureaucratic nonsense going on? Although, rather excitingly, Catherine Mayer, author and editor at large of *Time* magazine has just co-founded the Women's Equality Party, a new political organisation which will fight for gender equality so we'll see how that goes. Sandi Toksvig and Suzanne Moore are in and SO AM I! ARE YOU?

Random House isn't commissioning any more feminism from me. That's it. But feminism's not a fad, like *Angry Birds*. I mean, it does involve a lot of angry birds, being angry. That was a bad example, wasn't it? What I mean is, feminism's not just a passing trend, like Pop Tarts were in the eighties. I mean, it does involve lots of tarts, having a pop at the patriarchy. That was a bad example, wasn't it? What I'm trying to say is, feminism's not just something I can dip in and out of, whenever it suits me, like Catholicism, or hot tubs in Center Parcs, it's how I view the world. At least it is until I'm paid to view the world another way. And between you and me, I can't wait. I'm absolutely done with feminism now. And I'm sick of having sex with people all the time in order to be able to speak about it.

The problem is young girls don't want to be Angela Merkel, the German Chancellor, or Sally Davies, the Chief Medical Officer for England, or Mary Beard, Professor of Classics at the University of Cambridge. Well, some of them do, but not enough. They want to be Beyoncé with her ass-flavoured bubblegum or Kim Kardashian with her oil-flavoured ass. Legitimately powerful women don't fit in with the dominant media narrative, so they are not held up as our feminist icons. Newspapers and magazines have to shift copy and the internet needs hits, so editors choose our icons for us. What I want to know is, do I have to oil my bottom up to be on the cover of the Fawcett Society's monthly newsletter?!

I know perfectly well that throwing lads' mags into bins is a futile waste of time. It achieves absolutely nothing. I'm not making any difference to anything or anyone, but it was funny. Lads' mags are on the way out now anyway because of online porn. We can all watch whatever we like, whenever we want, for free. All I'm doing is making myself feel less irrelevant. I'm like the shit local mayor of a town built on a floodplain, giving everyone a free bath sponge to put under their front door. I'm pathetic.

Sometimes, you know, I think we'll miss the sexists when they're gone. If I'm in one of those old-fashioned sweet shops, I look at all the rows of sweets in jars on shelves and I think, Aw, we should have something like this. I don't mean we should display all the sexists in jars in sweet shops, but we could have something like the Paris Catacombs to keep them in, for future generations. Obviously we don't have catacombs in this country, but London has a fantastic sewage system we could utilise. I wouldn't mind doing the labelling. I've already made a start, actually.

> Bob. 46. Ran a second-hand bicycle
> shop in Hackney. He thought that fitting
> baskets on to bicycles was women's work
> and made his female assistant do it, while
> he concentrated on the manlier task of
> fixing punctures.

> Thailand's Prime Minister, General Prayut
> Chan-o-cha. When British tourist Hannah
> Witheridge was brutally murdered on the
> island of Koh Tao in September 2014, he
> implied that she was killed because she was
> wearing a bikini at the time. The itsy-bitsy
> polka-dot bikini the general is dressed in
> now, for all eternity, is from H&M's 2014
> spring/summer range.

Emily Wilding Davison was imprisoned nine times, and force-fed forty-nine times. She died after being accidentally trampled on by the king's horse at the Epsom Derby in 1913. She did this so that women could vote. Emmeline Pankhurst, the leader of the suffragette movement, was horrified by the screams of women being force-fed during hunger strikes. But I don't blame you for not voting. To be honest, I didn't bother either. *The Real Housewives of Orange County* was on and I've become a bit obsessed.

Women, in the West at least, have a level of freedom that even sixty years ago would have been unimaginable. We also have many more choices in terms of how to mutilate our faces and bodies in an attempt to beat time, so that's great. Lines will appear on our faces. Why don't we just not bother about that? Who wants to have a smooth old face?

I have lines now. I have two deep ones running down each side of my face, from my nose to my mouth . . . from laughing at *Spinal Tap* and *Laurel and Hardy* and from LAUGHING WITH MY CHILDREN ABOUT FARTS. Sometimes, if I'm bored, I'll run two Mini Babybels down my laughter lines and pretend that my face is Cooper's Hill in Gloucestershire, where they have the cheese roll.

Some of the best women we've got are older women. In 2012, towards the end of a brilliant performance in an old east London cinema, during which she spat onstage and called for revolution, the then-66-year-old punk pioneer Patti Smith started barking and growling like a dog. She didn't laugh, or break the fourth wall, but totally committed to the dog thing. If she was being intentionally funny, for her own amusement or ours, she didn't flag it up. I think Smith's unobvious, covert hilariousness is deliberate, designed specifically for the amusement of like-minded people, a sort of high-frequency dog whistle for fans. About halfway through the howling, I thought to myself, Wow. A 66-year-old woman's onstage, being political, spitting and making dog noises, and no one's the least bit embarrassed. Everyone just thinks she's really cool.

As a 41-year-old female stand-up, Patti Smith's performance had a profound effect on me. At the time, I hadn't really found my voice. I didn't feel confident expressing my opinions to rooms full of people and wondered if I was too old to continue. Yet here was an unembarrassed, fearless, uncompromising, funny woman in her mid sixties doing exactly that. For me, in terms of a professional role model, they don't come much better than this. So for any of you sexists out there still reading, which, as I've said many times before, you shouldn't be, you can also blame Patti Smith.

It feels arrogant to be writing a book about how I wrote stand-up comedy about feminism, and I find it embarrassing talking about my writing process in interviews, on television, radio or podcasts. It seems a bit self-aggrandising. However I needed an angle for the book, and the only other angle I had was the fact that I am a woman, and other feminists have already used that angle many times before. Also, people still ask me if I 'just make it up as I go along' and I wanted to explain to them, once and for all, that no, I don't just 'get up there and see what happens'. Except of course at new material nights, work in progress shows, corporate gigs, charity benefits, circuit gigs, tour shows, theatre runs and festivals. But all the other times I really think about what I'm going to say.

I'll be forty-four this August. My career took off, unexpectedly, when I was forty-two. I feel honoured and privileged to have a job that I enjoy and a job that has brought me into contact with some of the most amazing women on the planet. I've said before but I'll say it again, comedy doesn't need to be about anything, it just needs to be funny. But for me, at that point in my life, it did. I don't know what's next. Both BBC2 and BBC4 have decided that they can't develop any of my ideas for television and there won't be any more series of *Minds the Gap* on BBC Radio 4 either. I don't know how this book will go down. I will continue to do live work for as long as people want to keep coming to see me. Beyond that, there's no plan.

We're not going to have equality until we start valuing ourselves as co-habitees of earth. We need to view ourselves as joint owners, not tenants, dependent on the whims and moods of our volatile male landlords. Our names are on the deeds of this planet. We have a right to be here. Obviously humans don't own the earth. Dolphins do, I think. Or bees or something. Although I understand cockroaches and rats will inherit it. Even though George Osborne, the chancellor, refuses to explain the tax implications for this event. I wished I'd never thought of this analogy, I'll probably have the Green Party trolling me as well as feminists now! I was using the earth as a metaphor, that's all. Anyway, what I'm trying to say is that women currently account for 1 per cent of the world's wealth. 1 per cent!

When I feel that I'm not doing things properly, or that I'm not doing enough, or that someone else is doing something better, I always try to remind myself of a great quote from a female Olympic cyclist,[33] who said, 'When I'm racing, I don't look at who's behind me, or in front of me, or coming up beside me. I focus on my own personal time and if I don't win the race, but I beat my own time, I've won.'

It's important not to beat yourself up all the time about what you're not doing. That's what I think about campaigning. Just

---

[33] I can't for the life of me remember her name. I'd definitely have remembered if it was a man though. Ha!

do whatever you have time to do. I used to bin inappropriately displayed-at-toddler-height lads' mags whenever I went shopping because that's all I had time to do. Obviously, it's a good thing most human rights activists and campaigners don't have my attitude, otherwise nothing would get done. All I'm saying is that you don't have to lead marches or front campaigns, or dedicate your entire life to a cause. Your activism is the right activism for you. Don't measure yourself against what other people are doing.

It's much easier to be politically engaged these days, anyway. Modern technology has meant that we don't have to bother will all the legwork of protesting any more. We don't have to get dressed, or knock up a placard, or chain ourselves to railings. E-petitions have turned us all into armchair activists, and there's nothing wrong with that. We're all doing our own little bit. And if we all do our own little bit, then together it's a big bit. So there is a long way to go. We can celebrate all our advances and gains and yet still acknowledge how much there is to do. Here's a tiny example of how much we still have to do:

In 2003 Jeremy Clarkson drove a pick-up into a thirty-year-old horse chestnut tree, severely damaging it, in a car park in Somerset, to test the strength of a Toyota. The BBC was forced to apologise and pay damages to the local council.[34] Then in 2008 he made a joke during an episode of *Top Gear* about lorry drivers murdering prostitutes, which attracted more than a thousand complaints to the BBC. Then in 2010 he made jokes about Mexicans, which included them being branded 'lazy', 'feckless' and 'flatulent', sparked controversy

---

[34] Fucking lefty horse chestnut bastard. The tree was only there to support the UN's radical left-wing agenda, anyway. I don't know what all the fuss is about! There're other trees.

and prompted an apology from the BBC to the Mexican ambassador. Then in 2011, during a ninety-minute *Top Gear* India special, a car fitted with a toilet in the boot is described by Clarkson as 'perfect for India because everyone who comes here gets the trots'. Then in 2012 Clarkson is found to have breached BBC guidelines by comparing a Japanese car to people with growths on their faces. Then in 2014 Clarkson apologised to the Cornish after saying, during a debate on Scottish independence, 'It's Cornwall I've always wanted to be rid of. Bunch of pasty-munching ingrates.' Then, again in 2014, Clarkson was embroiled in controversy when it was claimed he used the N-word while reciting the nursery rhyme 'Eeny, Meeny, Miny, Moe' during filming. Then, again in 2014, *Top Gear* was ruled to have breached broadcasting rules after Clarkson used the word 'slope' to describe an Asian man. Then in March 2015 Clarkson verbally and physically abused his entirely innocent and blameless producer, Oisin Tymon, for not providing him with a hot meal. Clarkson called him an 'Irish, lazy cunt' and shouted at him for twenty minutes. He then physically attacked Tymon for around thirty seconds until a witness intervened. Then, far from showing any remorse for punching a completely innocent man repeatedly – who didn't retaliate, and who drove himself to A&E after the attack – which would be a normal human being's 'rock bottom' moment, Clarkson used the media attention surrounding this assault and his subsequent suspension to aim a political punch at Ed Miliband, who wasn't even in the hotel at the time, or eating a steak, by tweeting, 'Sorry Ed. It seems I knocked your "I'm a human" piece down the news agenda.' Over a million people signed an e-petition calling on the BBC, who paid Clarkson a seven figure salary, to reinstate him, before it was even clear what, if anything, he had actually done to his co-worker.

Menstruation is the periodic discharge of blood and tissue from the inner lining of the uterus through the vagina. Many women experience painful uterine cramps during menstruation. Between the approximate ages of twelve and fifty-two, a woman will have around 480 periods, or fewer if she has any pregnancies. Without the female reproductive system, of which the period is an integral part, the human race would cease to exist. Sanitary products designed to absorb this menstrual flow are considered a 'non-essential luxury item' by the UK government and therefore liable for VAT. Here is a list of things that Chancellor George Osborne considers more essential than sanitary products and are therefore tax exempt:

> flapjacks
> houseboat moorings
> exotic meat
> edible cake decorations
> aircraft repair and maintenance
> Jaffa cakes
> lentils and chickpeas
> sewer cleaning
> herbal tea

In 2011, an e-petition to end VAT on tampons gained *fifty-two signatures*. According to the 2011 census, there are 32,200,000 women in the UK. That means that 32,199,948 women weren't interested.

So just to reiterate that. An e-petition calling on the BBC to reinstate a man who attacked trees and men and made racist jokes and who was paid a seven-figure salary gained over a million signatures. An e-petition to end VAT on tampons gained fifty-two signatures.

As Leyla put it to me, 'Sometimes I think to myself, How am I going to eradicate female genital mutilation, when I'm taxed for having a period?'[35]

Oh, and by the way, I didn't get the yoghurt advert either. I know you've been wondering.

---

[35] Haha! Got you! I DID END ON A PERIOD JOKE. HAHAHAHAHA!

ACKNOWLEDGEMENTS

Firstly, I'd like to thank whoever invented words. Without them, this book wouldn't exist.

I'd like to thank my amazing editor, Francesca Pathak; all the brilliant female stand-ups I saw when I was starting out eleven years ago who inspired me, Janey Godley, Shappi Khorsandi, Sarah Kendall, Lucy Porter, Shazia Mirza, Jo Brand, Kitty Flanagan, Josie Long, Jo Caulfield, Nina Conti, Isy Suttie, Roisin Conaty, Shelagh Martin, Danielle Ward, Fiona O'Loughlin, Anna Kierle, Ayesha Hazarika, Helen Keen, Jo Enright, Gina Yashere, Jo Neary, Kerry Godliman, Francesca Martinez, Zoe Lyons, Ava Vidal and Charmian Hughes; my tour promoters, Mike McCarthy and Warren Lakin and Steve Lock at Soho Theatre; Tommy Shepherd at the Stand; Susan Provan, Tania Harrison, Jude Kelly and Nica Burns; my agent, Vivienne Clore; Amanda Emery, my publicist; Jane Berthoud and Caroline Raphael at BBC Radio 4; Alison Vernon Smith and Alexandra Smith, my producers on both series of *Minds the Gap*; James Hingley; Idil Sukan; Steve Ullathorne; all the writers and activists who have encouraged me, Laura Bates, Suzanne Moore, Lucy Anne Holmes, Caitlin Moran, Hadley

Freeman, Stella Creasy, Kat Banyard, Nimco Ali, Caroline Criado-Perez, Kira Cochrane, Lisa Clarke, Helen Pankhurst, Dawn Purvis and Lisa King; my babysitters, Renata R, Renata P, Jess and Collette; thanks to Dad and my brothers and sisters, Mike, Mary, Anna, Eileen, Sarah, Pete, Maggie and Jimmy; and Leyla Hussein and Maryam Sheikh Abdi.

A special and separate thanks goes to Leyla Hussein, Alexandra Smith, Alison Vernon Smith and Francesca Pathak for their guidance on the FGM chapter.

And thanks to the farting man. Whoever he is.

APPENDIX ONE:

Bridget Christie Interviews Leyla Hussein about FGM

Bridget Christie: Leyla Hussein, you're an FMG survivor, leading anti— FMG? Yes, FMG.

Leyla Hussein: It's FGM: female genital mutilation. It's FGM, female genital mutilation.

BC: GM?

LH: Yes.

BC: I've got MG here.

LH: No, it's FGM.

BC: Are you sure?

LH: Yes, it's female genital mutilation.

BC: I've heard a lot of people say FMG.

LH: Yes, I know a lot of people say it, but that's not correct.

BC: They're wrong?

LH: They're very wrong.

BC: Are you sure?

LH: It's FGM.

BC: I'm sure I heard Michael Gove say FMG, I'm sure you know.

LH: Yes.

BC: **I'm sorry about that, I'm going to have to change it all the way through.**

LH: It's female genital mutilation.

BC: **Not mutilated genitals?**

LH: No, it's female genital mutilation.

BC: **Right, we shouldn't get bogged down in this.**

LH: Yes, it's FGM, not FMG.

BC: **Okay, I'm sure you're right, I'll just— Okay, sorry, what is it again?**

LH: FGM.

BC: **Okay, FGM?**

LH: FGM, yes.

BC: **I'm really glad that you were available today. Out of all the people I asked, you're the only actual survivor, so I was really glad that you didn't have anything else to do.**

LH: There are other survivors out there who speak out, I'm not the only one.

BC: **Is it not just you?**

LH: No, no, no, I'm not the only one.

BC: **Oh, sorry, I didn't realise, because I really tried to get Bono. He's in France, in Cannes, collecting a big humanitarian award.**

LH: Bono, the U2 singer?

BC: **Bono – is it 'Bone-o' or 'Bonno'? People say different things.**

LH: Is that the person you're talking about?

BC: Yes, he does FGM, doesn't he?

LH: No, no, no, he's never been involved in this campaign. I mean, as a campaigner.

BC: Oh, is it AIDS he does?

LH: I think so, I think he does— God, yes, I think he's involved in other campaigns.

BC: I think he is AIDS and poverty, isn't he? Not FGM.

LH: No, not FGM, but obviously we would certainly welcome—

BC: Well, you should ask him.

LH: He's not involved in this campaign.

BC: He's not involved in this?

LH: No, he's definitely not.

BC: Have you asked him, though?

LH: No, maybe I should.

BC: Well, maybe he might—

LH: I've never asked him, no, he's never been involved, I would like to clarify that.

BC: So, not Bono, right. So, FGM's been illegal here since 1985.

LH: Yes.

BC: Over 66,000 women are believed to have already been cut, who are living here.

LH: Yes.

BC: There are 24,000 girls at risk now.

LH: Every year, yes.

BC: There's been no prosecutions.

LH: No.

BC: Do you think that part of the problem with tackling it here in the UK is that British people don't really know what it...they've sort of heard that it's kind of a tradition, but it's essentially sort of a foreign...because Britain is supposed to be one of the most tolerant countries in the world, tolerant, or racially tolerant, culturally...that people maybe think it's like an African tradition, like an...? Because we've got like morris dancing here, you might not have seen it if you don't go to—

LH: What's morris dancing?

BC: —villages and stuff. Well, it's normally about twelve middle-aged m— I had them at my wedding, actually, they were like the main entertainment for my wedding.

LH: Sorry, what was the relevance of the morris dancing and FGM?

BC: So, my point is that do you think that British people, because they think it's a tradition – female cutting – that it's something that they should be allowed to carry on? They tried to stop morris dancing, you know, the government...not the government, some people tried to stop it because it was dangerous. It's not *that* dangerous, they've just got some bells and hankies, but a lot of British people are like, 'No, no, no, it's a tradition, we've got to hang on to this.'

LH: No, I mean, I don't think we can compare female genital mutilation to dancing. I mean, that's just violence, full stop.

BC: They've got big...It's *not* the same thing, but they've also got these quite big, heavy sticks that they smash, and I think sometimes they go...so, they're dancing with the bells and everything, and the bells are making little noises – they're tied to their ankles.

LH: Yes, I don't think you can make that comparison to when women's genitals are being removed, just because they're girls. So, I think we need to be careful what language we use. It is violence, so we really can't—

BC: **No, I just meant that…they've obviously not comparable. I mean, I wouldn't have morris dancing at my wedding if Ban Ki-moon had banned it, you know? Do you think as well that maybe British people are scared to criticise it in case the Taliban blow them up or something? Do you think people have that? Because the Taliban are getting around, aren't they? There's quite a lot of British…**

LH: This has nothing to do with the Taliban or any extreme groups. I don't know why they ask about the— FGM has nothing to do with the Taliban. FGM's practised with all different communities, so it has nothing to do with the Taliban, I don't know why that came up.

BC: **The Taliban, is it not? So, it's not a religious practice?**

LH: No, it's not a religious practice, no, no, no, it's practised by people from different religious backgrounds, different class systems, you know?

BC: **So, different types of religious people?**

LH: Yes, it could be…yes.

BC: **It could be from, like, Scientology and Beliebers and all of those?**

LH: Scientology? No, I don't think it's practised in the Scientology religion.

BC: **Beliebers?**

LH: Beliebers? Who are the Beliebers?

BC: **They're ... You know Justin Belieber, the singer?**

LH: Justin Bieber?

BC: **Belieber, isn't it? Justin Belieber, he's that American singer.**

LH: Yes, I know who Justin Bieber is.

BC: **That's what they call his followers, Beliebers.**

LH: Beliebers? So, that's his fans, that's not a religion.

BC: **I think they think he's like Jesus or something, they sort of worship him, so I think he might've mentioned it or perhaps he doesn't know ... Do you think he knows that they're doing that?**

LH: No, I don't think he's mentioned it, not to my knowledge, I don't think he has.

BC: **Thank you so much for talking to me today. Hopefully we've raised a bit of FMG awareness.**

LH: It's FGM.

BC: **Sorry?**

LH: FGM. Female genital mutilation.

BC: **Yes, it is.**

LH: You have to say it in the right order.

BC: **You said that at the beginning.**

LH: It's important to say it right, yes.

BC: **I know, it's just easier to say FMG, I think that's why I keep saying it, sorry.**

LH: I would suggest you just stick to FGM, yes.

BC: So, hopefully we've cleared that up for people.

LH: I hope so, yes.

BC: Thanks so much for talking to me today.

LH: Thank you for having me here.

If you want to watch this interview, long and short versions of it can be found here: https://www.youtube.com/user/BridgetChristie.

APPENDIX TWO

A Vindication of the Rights of Woman, Mary Wollstonecraft
   (1791)
Letters on the Equality of the Sexes, Sarah Grimke (1837)
Woman, Harriet Martineau (1837)
Jane Eyre, Charlotte Brontë (1847)
The Tenant of Wildfell Hall, Anne Brontë (1848)
Little Women, Louisa May Alcott (1868)
On Woman's Right to Suffrage, Susan B. Anthony (1872)
Solitude of Self, Elizabeth Cady Stanton (1892)
Woman, Kate Austin (1901)
The Evolution of Sex, Dora Montefiore (1909)
The Age of Innocence, Edith Wharton (1920)
A Room of One's Own, Virginia Woolf (1929)
The Second Sex, Simone de Beauvoir (1949)
The Feminine Mystique, Betty Friedan (1963)
The Bell Jar, Sylvia Plath (1963)
Sexual Politics, Kate Millett (1968)
I Know Why the Caged Bird Sings, Maya Angelou (1969)
The Female Eunuch, Germaine Greer (1970)
The Dialectic of Sex: The Case for Feminist Revolution,
   Shulamith Firestone (1970)

Of Woman Born: Motherhood as Experience and Institution, Adrienne Rich (1976)

Fat is a Feminist Issue, Susie Orbach (1978)

Ain't I a Woman? Black Women and Feminism, bell hooks (1981)

The Color Purple, Alice Walker (1982)

The Handmaid's Tale, Margaret Atwood (1985)

Backlash: The Undeclared War Against American Women, Susan Faludi (1991)

The Beauty Myth, Naomi Wolf (1991)

Warrior Marks: Female Genital Mutilation and the Sexual Blinding of Women, Alice Walker and Pratibha Parmar (1993)

The Vagina Monologues, Eve Ensler (1996)

Female Chauvinist Pigs: Women and the Rise of Raunch Culture, Ariel Levy (2005)

She-Wolves, Dr Helen Castor (2011)

Living Dolls: The Return of Sexism, Natasha Walter (2011)

Superman is an Arab: On God, Marriage, Macho Men and Other Disastrous Inventions, Joumana Haddad (2012)

Do It Like a Woman . . . and change the world Caroline Criado-Perez (2015)

APPENDIX THREE:

'THE CUT'

I was only six years old
when they led me to the bush, to my slaughterhouse.
Too young to know what it all entailed,
I walked lazily towards the waiting women.

Deep within me was the desire to be cut,
as pain was my destiny:
it is the burden of femininity,
so I was told.
Still, I was scared to death . . .
but I was not to raise an alarm.

The women talked in low tones,
each trying to do her tasks the best.
There was the torso holder,
she had to be strong to hold you down.
Legs and hands each had their own woman,
who needed to know her task
lest you free yourself and flee for life.

The cutting began with the eldest girl

and on went the list.
Known to be timid, I was the last among the six.
I shivered and shook all over;
butterflies beat madly in my stomach.
I wanted to vomit, the waiting was long,
the expectation of pain too sharp,
but I had to wait my turn.
My heart pounded, my ears blocked;
the only sound I understood
was the wails from the girls,
for that was my destiny as well.

Finally it was my turn, and one of the women
winked at me:
Come here, girl, she said, smiling unkindly.
You won't be the first nor the last,
but you have only this once to prove you are brave!
She stripped me naked. I got goose pimples.
A cold wind blew, and it sent warning signs
all over me. I choked, and my head
went round in circles as I was led.

Obediently, I sat between the legs of the woman
who would hold my upper abdomen,
and each of the other four women grasped my
legs and hands.
I was stretched apart and each limb firmly held.
And under the shade of a tree...
The cutter began her work...
the pain...is so vivid to this day,
decades after it was done.

God, it was awful!

I cried and wailed until I could cry no more.
My voice grew hoarse, and the cries could not come out,
I wriggled as the excruciating pain ate into my
    tender flesh.
Hold her down! cried the cursed cutter,
and the biggest female jumbo sat on my chest.
I could not breathe, but there was nobody
to listen to me.
Then my cries died down, and everything was dark.
As I drifted, I could hear the women laughing,
joking at my cowardice.

It must have been hours later when I woke up
to the most horrendous reality.
The agonizing pain was unbearable!
It was eating into me, every inch of my girlish body was
    aching.
The women kept exchanging glances
and talked loudly of how I would go down in history,
to be such a coward, until I fainted in the process.
Allahu Akbar! they exclaimed as they criticized me.

I looked down at my self and got a slap across my face.
Don't look, you coward, came the cutter's words;
then she ordered the women to pour hot sand on
    my cut genitals.
My precious blood gushed out and foamed.
Open up, snarled the jumbo woman, as she poured the
    sand on me.

Nothing they did eased the pain.

Ha! How will you give birth? taunted the one with
   the smile.
I was shaking and biting my lower lip.
I kept moving front, back, and sideways as I writhed
   in pain.
This one will just shame me! cried the cutter.
Look how far she has moved, how will she heal?
My sister was embarrassed, but I could see pain in
   her eyes ...
maybe she was recalling her own ordeal.
She pulled me back quickly to the shed.

The blood oozed and flowed. Scavenger birds
were moving in circles and perching on nearby trees.
Ish ish, the women shooed the birds.
All this time the pain kept coming in waves,
each wave more pronounced than the one before it.

The women stood us up but warned us not to move
   our legs apart.
They scrubbed the bloody sand off our thighs and
   small buttocks,
then sat us back down.
A hole was dug,
malmal, the stick herb, was pounded;
The ropes for tying our legs were ready.
Charcoal was brought and put in the hole,
where there was dried donkey waste and many herbs –
   these were the cutter's paraphernalia.

The herbs were placed on the charcoal,
and we were ordered to sit on the hole.
As I sat with smoke rising around me,
I could hear the blood dropping on the charcoal,
and more smoke rose.
The pain was somehow dwindling but I felt weak
    and nauseated.
Maybe she is losing blood? my sister asked worriedly.
No, no. It will stop once I place the herbs, cried the cutter
    impatiently.

The *malmal* was pasted where my severed vaginal lips
    had been,
and then I was tied from my thighs to my toes
with very strong ropes from camel hide.
A long stick was brought and the women took turns
showing us how to walk, sit, and stand.
They told us not to bend or move apart our legs –
This will make you heal faster, they said,
but it was meant to seal up that place.

The drop of the first urine,
more burning than the aftermath of the razor,
passed slowly, bit by bit,
one drop after another,
while lying on my side.
There was no washing, no drying,
and the burning kept on for hours later.
But there was no stool…
at least, I don't remember.

For the next month this was my routine.
There was no feeding on anything with oil,
or anything with vegetables or meat.
Only milk and *ugali* formed my daily ration.
I was given only sips of water:
This avoids 'wetting' the wound and delaying healing,
    they said.

We would stay in the bush the whole day.
The journey from the bush back home began around
    four and ended sometimes at seven.
All this time we had to face the heat
and bare-footedly slide towards home...
with no water, of course.
We were not to bend if a thorn stuck us,
never to call for help loudly
as this would 'open' us up and the cutter
would be called again.
Everything was about scary dos and don'ts.

I stayed on with the other five
for the next four weeks. None of us bathed;
lice developed between the ropes and our skin,
biting and itching the whole day and night.
There was no way to remove them,
at least not until we healed.

The river was only a kilometer away.
Every morning the breeze carried the sweet scent of
    its waters to us,
making our thirst more real.

The day the cutter was called back
each of us shivered and prayed silently,
each hoping we had healed and there would be no
    cutting again.
Thank God we were all done
except one unlucky girl
who had to undergo it all again,
and took months to heal.

Our heads were shaved clean.
The ropes untied, lice dropped at last.
We were showered and oiled,
but most important was the drinking of water.
I drank until my stomach was full,
but the mouth and throat yearned for more.

It was over.
All over my thighs were marks from the ropes,
dotted with patches from the lice wounds.
Now I was to look after myself,
to ensure that everything remained intact
until the day I married.

Maryam Sheikh Abdi